The Lady is

THE LADY IS A SPY

The Tangled Lives of Stan Harding
& Marguerite Harrison

Melanie King

Ashgrove Publishing
London

For Ross

Contents

CONTENTS

Lubyanka, October 1920

She heard the men whispering and sniggering behind the partition as she endured the strip-search, efficiently conducted by two Russian women. The men were ripping her clothes apart, searching for anything hidden in the hems and seams. The contents of her bags, including English banknotes, lay strewn across the floor. Finally allowed to dress, she was led up three flights of stairs to a cell containing nothing more than a flea-infested straw mattress on a plank of wood. Scared and confused, she tried to collect her thoughts. There had to be some mistake.[1]

Lubyanka Prison, in the heart of Moscow, was a filthy labyrinth of dilapidated houses so sinister in appearance that Muscovites crossed to the other side of the square to avoid being too close to it. Her cell was in a building used before the Revolution as a cheap lodging house in which rooms could be rented by the day. Now, the windows were barred and stained to make them opaque and spyholes had been drilled in the doors. The room, she noted, was the shape of a coffin, with grubby wallpaper hanging in tatters. Previous prisoners had scratched calendars onto the wall and struck off the days as they passed. One wall was decorated with crosses daubed in blood. Had some former inmate, she wondered, been commemorating the deaths of comrades?

Food was brought to her: a small ration of bread full of straw and pebbles. Lunch consisted of an evil-smelling hot water swimming with fish eyes and fins, dished up from buckets borrowed from the prison hospital. Every three days, if she was lucky, a lump of sugar might arrive.

Worse than the food, though, was the lack of sleep. The soldier outside the door would frequently switch on her cell lights and peer, sometimes for minutes at a time, through the spyhole. Was she on suicide watch? No; they cared little about that. She noticed the hook on the wall and the strip of cloth that could be used as a noose.

She had been placed in solitary confinement. She had no pen, no paper, no books; no contact with the world outside. The only way to gauge the time was by the clanking of the huge copper kettle in the courtyard at 8 a.m., the singing of 'The Internationale' at noon, and the changing of the guard at midnight. Apart from these, measured time did not exist. The guards did not speak to her: it was as if they were afraid to communicate with someone whose crime – and whose fate – was so grave.

Other sounds sometimes reached her. She could hear off-duty soldiers dancing to the music of a balalaika. One night a worn-out gramophone in the guardroom played the same variety show over again and again, the screeching music and shrill laughter fraying her nerves and bringing her to the edge of insanity. Often she heard her neighbour in the next cell pacing endlessly up and down in his riding boots; at other times she heard prisoners praying for their sanity. Once, peering through the spy-hole, she saw two bodies dragged down the corridor; afterwards came the smell of burning straw – their mattresses. Typhus had come to Lubyanka from the fleas (she counted three varieties) that danced on her mattress and fed on her blood.

Worst of all were the unearthly screams of the prisoners dragged from their cells to be tortured or taken for execution. From the courtyard of the prison, at all hours of the night, came the tramp of feet and then the bark of rifles. The engine of a motor-car would be started just before the shots rang out – but her ears soon learned to distinguish the penetrating sound of the rifles. What was it for, this engine? To spare the nerves of the prisoners? The authorities, she guessed, would hardly waste petrol for such a trifle. No: it must have been to drown out the last defiant words of the condemned. After an execution, the prison would fall so silent that she could hear the ticking of the guardroom clock.

The purpose of her confinement was, she knew, to break her spirit – to destroy her both physically and mentally. But she would not surrender to them. She would not die without passing a message to the world. There is no thirst, she was discovering, like the thirst for justice. So she sat on the asphalt floor, meditating and practising the yoga she had learned in India. She thought of the River Ganges and the splendid light of the sun. She remembered her days searching for lost artworks on the upper reaches of the Yangtze in China. Most of all, she thought of Italy: of the Maremma coast, where she had lived in a tower overlooking the sea, and of the Villa Medici in Fiesole, with its hand-painted wallpaper and the scent of jasmine from the garden. It was curious to think that she had once been there, and that all of it still existed.

How had she come to be here? Stan Harding knew, of course: Marguerite. It was that American woman, Marguerite Harrison, who had betrayed her.

PART ONE

1878-1919

Chapter One

Born for Trouble

—⚬⚬⚬—

'I came into the world,' Marguerite Harrison wrote, 'on an October night in the midst of one of the most terrible storms on record in Maryland.' It was an appropriate début for a woman who was to lead such a tempestuous life.[1]

Marguerite Elton Baker was born on the 23rd of October 1878 in Catonsville, Maryland, to Bernard Nadal Baker and Elizabeth Livezey. Catonsville was a pleasant suburb of the city of Baltimore, its roads lined with large homes nestling comfortably in the middle of private parks and bordered on the west by the Patapsco River, the setting for Francis Scott Key's 'The Star-Spangled Banner'.

Well away from the smoke-filled squalor and disease-ridden city centre, it was a privileged and idyllic place in which to grow up and Marguerite and her younger sister, Elizabeth, born three years later, enjoyed a sumptuous childhood – a Gilded Age Elysium of imported clothes, nurses, governesses and summers in Europe.

Marguerite's grandfather, Charles Baker, had made a vast fortune in the production of glass. Proud of his worldly success, in 1880 he built a stately mansion in Catonsville that he christened Athol. It featured a mansard roof, a wrap-around verandah, luxurious carpets, stained glass windows and expensive bric-à-brac that no one was allowed to touch. Since Charles was a formidably religious man, Athol included a private Methodist chapel for the family's use. Ruling his seven sons and one daughter in the manner of, as Marguerite remembered, 'one of the patriarchs of old', all members of his household were expected to be present at morning prayers and Sunday afternoon Bible classes.

Charles' son Bernard, Marguerite's father, built on his father's commercial success to become one of the richest men in Baltimore. By his early twenties he had begun managing one of his father's various companies, which manufactured sulphuric acid and fertilisers, and then expanded operations to include coal transportation. In 1878, the year of Marguerite's birth, Bernard Baker began providing coaling services to ships in Baltimore Harbour and ten years later the company had expanded to include coal mines in Pennsylvania and a merchant-shipping firm, Atlantic Transport Line, that boasted offices in Pall Mall, London.

Bernard's wife Elizabeth Livezey came from humbler but still comfortable circumstances. The Livezeys were a local Quaker family whose forebears arrived in America with William Penn. Elizabeth at a young age had rejected the Quaker faith and concentrated her efforts on more worldly pursuits. Her ambition, according to Marguerite, had always been to be rich and socially prominent. To further these aspirations, she had begged parents to send her to Miss Maria Gibson's fashionable boarding school. She attended the school but, as her father toiled humbly in real estate, was not accepted by her higher-born peers.

Marriage to the wealthy Bernard Baker was certainly an achievement, but Elizabeth's social insecurities would lead to troubles with her eldest daughter, Marguerite, through whom she hoped to experience vicariously the life of a young social lioness. Marguerite later wrote that 'from my babyhood she trained me for the career she had mapped out for me.' This meant either marrying her off to an English Lord of the realm or a high-ranking diplomat. 'She had visions,' Marguerite later wrote, 'of my holding a salon in London or some foreign capital as a brilliant hostess and a figure of international importance.' Marguerite would indeed become a figure of international importance, though not of the sort fondly imagined by her mother.

Marguerite's mother was as controlling as her paternal grandfather, of whom, ironically, Elizabeth thoroughly disapproved. Instead of using religion as her weapon, however, Elizabeth's instrument of control was her illnesses and hysterical episodes. A cycle of neurotic outbursts, followed by the inevitable withdrawal from the family, the abandoning of any responsibilities and a period of complete rest, became a familiar feature in the Baker household. Marguerite learned to detach and distance herself from the effects of her mother's behaviour. She would later describe her young self as naturally impulsive – before she learned to 'repress outbursts of temper, to endure physical pain and to meet any and every domestic emergency with absolute calm and composure' – traits which would hold her in good stead during her adventurous life.

In contrast to her relationship with her mother, Marguerite was very close to her father – 'the only person in the world,' she wrote, 'for whom I felt any great affection', and claimed that she loved him 'with a passionate devotion that amounted to adoration'. From a young age she accompanied Bernard on overseas business trips and meetings. Such travels inevitably took their toll on her home life. No ponies, dogs, cats, rabbits, parrots and canaries that entered the Baker household ever remained for long. 'My mother made these migrations an excuse of getting rid of pets,' she was to recall. For companionship she took with her Eunice, a doll that, rather like herself, had her own trunk of clothes for every occasion.

International travel did, of course, have its benefits. Marguerite met many famous and influential people during her childhood, a veritable *Who's Who* of intellectual and political luminaries. They included Sir Robert Baden-Powell, founder of the Boy Scouts; the actress Ellen Terry; the financier J. Pierpont Morgan; Sir Henry Lucy, editor of *Punch*; the painter Lawrence Alma-Tadema; the naturalist Sir John Lubbock; Sir Henry Norman, the journalist famous for revealing the truth behind the Dreyfus Affair; and even Bram Stoker, author of *Dracula*. Marguerite took tea at Kensington Palace and was presented to Queen Victoria, whom she described as 'a little old lady in black wearing a hat like an inverted bowl and sitting in a Bath chair drawn by a small donkey, attended by a Scotsman in Highland costume'. Her family were friends with Winston Churchill's American mother and through her were invited to the Royal Enclosure at Ascot where Marguerite was introduced to the future Edward VII.

Young Marguerite had an innate facility for absorbing languages, learning French, German and Italian with ease. When abroad, she often acted as interpreter for her family. 'As a child and as a young girl,' she explained, 'I had been accustomed to change and variety. I was just as much at home on the other side of the Atlantic as in Baltimore.' But at twelve years of age this thrillingly peripatetic life suddenly ceased.

In 1891, her mother suffered a physical breakdown that required complete rest and freedom from domestic responsibilities. Marguerite was removed from Ingleside, her father's grand mansion in Catonsville, and sent to live with her maternal grandparents while her mother convalesced – for five years. Ironically, this hiatus may well have been the making of her. Her grandfather's house possessed a well-stocked library and, as he was a liberal freethinker, he encouraged Marguerite to read about and discuss subjects such as religious sectarianism, the single tax, the disenfranchisement of Negroes and other controversial topics.

Marguerite attended school for the first time while lodging with her grandparents. St Timothy's, in Stevenson just north of Baltimore, was run under the guidance of the Episcopal Church, its motto boasting 'Truth Without Fear'. Elizabeth agreed that it was an appropriate establishment for her bright twelve-year-old daughter to attend if only because it would enable Marguerite to enter elevated social circles when she came of age. However, her fellow students were not so welcoming, finding the well-travelled, multilingual Marguerite precocious and 'highbrow'. It soon became clear that she did not have the necessary social skills – modesty and the ability to hold her tongue – to mix with her own age group. 'I had acquired my knowledge of all of these things almost unconsciously and without effort, and encouraged by my mother, I had fallen into the habit of airing it on all occasions.'

Marguerite graduated from St Timothy's at the age of seventeen, but was too young for the débutante season. Craftily pointing this out to her mother, she persuaded Elizabeth to let her attend Radcliffe – a women's liberal arts institution in Cambridge, Massachusetts and sister college of Harvard – until she was old enough to enter upper-class Baltimore society. Radcliffe was to be Marguerite's first experience of freedom – which, in her mother's opinion, she immediately abused by falling seriously in love with the son of the landlady with whom she boarded. Elizabeth discovered love letters that the boy had sent to Marguerite during the Christmas break in 1895, and angrily removed her daughter from the college. Elizabeth then packed her wayward daughter off to Italy to collect her senses.

Marguerite returned to Baltimore in early 1897. Eighteen years old and 'trembling with excitement,' she attended every hunt ball and social occasion she could. 'I had lost my inferiority complex,' she later declared, 'and I was determined to devote my every ounce of energy and every feminine resource to making my first winter a success.' One man in particular caught her eye, Tom Bullitt Harrison.

The stepson of Joseph S. Ames, professor of physics at Johns Hopkins University, Tom was seven years older than Marguerite, good-looking, athletic and a lawyer by profession, though not particularly intellectual or ambitious. Marguerite had grown into an attractive young woman, slender of waist, with beautiful blue eyes and a shock of dark auburn hair. Despite Tom's lack of intellectual curiosity, she fell hopelessly in love with him, causing Elizabeth once again to despair at the romantic proclivities of her wayward daughter. Tom Harrison was not what she had in mind for the child of Bernard Baker. Tom had little money behind him, no title, nor did he have a distinguished career – and, to cap it all, his father had killed himself in 1885 after losing $5,000,000 (approximately $125 million today) while speculating on cotton. For Elizabeth, this would certainly not do. Once again, the errant daughter was temporarily exiled to Italy.

Bella Italia was perhaps not the wisest choice for a young, headstrong, romantic girl and, unsurprisingly, Marguerite acted – in her mother's opinion – thoroughly inappropriately. She flirted outrageously with the dashing Count of Turin, Vittorio Emanuele, nephew of the King of Italy. But it was with a totally unsuitable man that she admitted to falling in love. Reshid Said Bey, an intellectual Turkish embassy official on his way to Rome, captured her heart, not only with his dark, brooding looks but also with his sharp mind. Their friendship became so intense that he asked for her hand in marriage. Although she adored his intellect and their conversations on politics, Marguerite, still determined to marry Tom Harrison, turned the Count down. However, her mother remained unrelenting in her disapproval of the young attorney. Ugly domestic scenes followed. Elizabeth even threatened suicide should her daughter not give up Tom. 'I used to barricade my door against her,' wrote Marguerite, 'while she stood outside and beat on the panels and I cowered in bed.'

Tom was equally smitten with the strong-willed Marguerite and equally determined to marry her. Elizabeth was forced to reconsider her stance when Bernard intervened after hearing that their stubborn daughter had threatened to elope. Finally, the marriage was planned for June 1901. Elizabeth resigned herself to organising an extravagant event suitable for a Baker heiress. No less than forty custom-made gowns were commissioned, along with twenty-four hats and nineteen pairs of shoes with matching gloves and accessories. There were ten bridesmaids, ten groomsmen, two officiating clergymen and even a bishop in attendance.

The Harrisons' nuptial dwelling was not as opulent as her parents' home, though it was an impressive four-storey house, in North Charles Street in Baltimore. The domestically inexperienced Marguerite relied on the servants, Lizzie and Rebecca, although she also threw herself into her wifely duties: collecting recipes, keeping an eye on the household accounts and preserving fruit – the traditional annual activity of every good Maryland housewife. She even learnt how to sew, making curtains, cushions and lampshades. 'I read but little,' she later wrote, 'and no longer had any desire to travel.'

Nine months later, in March 1902, Thomas Bullitt Harrison II was born. Marguerite found the birth a 'terrible ordeal' that caused her to decide against having any further children.

Marguerite later remembered that at this time in her life she was content to be the homemaker. She got on extremely well with her mother-in-law, and Mrs Ames 'took the place in my heart that my own mother never could fill'. Of her husband she declared, he was 'gallant, chivalrous, high-minded, cultured and charming'.

The family might well have long continued in their comfortable domesticity and country club lifestyle but for Tom falling ill in 1914. He was diagnosed with a brain tumour and Marguerite was suddenly faced with having to earn a living so as not to rely on her family for money. She and a friend set up a decorating shop they named The Flower Studio. Although it was never to make a profit and closed within a year, it was her first experience of earning her own living – and she loved it.

Tom Harrison died the following year, at the age of forty-three, leaving Marguerite, now in her mid-thirties, a widow with an adolescent son. Only a few weeks before Tom's death, Marguerite's mother had died. 'We had been estranged for so many years,' Marguerite wrote, 'that I could not feel any deep sorrow at her passing.' Her feelings at Tom's death were quite the opposite. She was devastated and later confessed that she was determined never to feel so deeply for anyone – including her son Tommy – ever again.

As a young widow, Marguerite could have gone to live respectably at Ingleside in Catonsville with her widowed father. Although he had lost a substantial part of his large fortune when the shares he owned in a shipping company became worthless, Bernard Baker still had ample funds to live comfortably. Marguerite and Tommy would not have wanted for anything, but Marguerite refused to leave her home. On discovering that Tom had owed his wealthy sister, Kate Thompson, $70,000 from failed speculations, Marguerite was determined to pay the money back.*

Her first step was to open her home up as a boarding house – an action that certainly would have appalled her mother. Marguerite wanted a new job. Through her upper-class connections she met Van Lear Black, recently appointed Chairman of the Board of *The Baltimore Sun*. Black was 'handsome, athletic, and gregarious, but also soft-spoken and full of quiet humour.'[3] He gave Marguerite a letter of introduction to the managing editor of the paper, Frank Kent. When interviewed by Kent in the late summer of 1915, Marguerite admitted she was 'almost tongue-tied before the little man with keen, steely blue eyes' who had spent years as the newspaper's Bureau Chief in Washington. With such a letter of introduction, Kent had little choice but to hire Marguerite and duly appointed her to the post of Assistant Society Editor. When she admitted to the Society Editor, Mary McCarty, that she had never used a typewriter before, she was told to 'bluff it out and don't let anyone know it'.

A part of her job was to telephone her friends and other notable citizens to inquire about their activities. Although uncomfortable with this

---

* There is no record that the money was ever repaid, despite Marguerite inheriting $80,000 from her father on his death a few years later.[2]

task at first, she soon discovered that people were only too happy to share personal details of their social life for publication.

Marguerite also began writing stories for the news editor Clark Fitzpatrick and soon became the paper's music and drama critic, with her own weekly column, 'Overheard in the Wings'. She even persuaded Kent to send her to New York every couple of weeks to catch the latest shows and write up-to-the-minute reviews. Recalling her interview with the American actor Otis Skinner, renowned for his Shakespearean roles, she said he became so absorbed in their conversation that he began changing his costume for the next scene in front of her. Marguerite, finding it difficult to concentrate on taking notes at this point, recalled that she 'tried not to notice anything'. Realising the inappropriateness of appearing in his underpants before a woman he had only just met, Skinner sent her flowers by way of an apology.

Van Lear Black had facilitated Marguerite's gainful employment as a budding journalist, and now her brother-in-law, Albert Ritchie, secured a post for her in 1915 at the new State Board of Motion Picture Censors. With this position came an annual salary of $2,500, which, combined with her newspaper post, gave Marguerite a total of $4,000 a year – five times the average annual earnings.[4]

'Personally I do not believe in censorship of any kind,' Marguerite declared, claiming she took the job for two reasons only: money and art. 'An arbitrary control of public manners and morals by a small group of individuals savours too much of paternalism in government to suit me,' she added. She was appalled at how many on-screen scenes were forbidden: a kissing scene was to be fleeting, suicides had to be implied, and 'the struggles of the pure young girl to defend her virtue were cut to flashes, and her clothes must not be torn in the process'. In addition, fights must not be too brutal; an oxymoron which amused Marguerite as fighting was brutal. Another rule introduced by the state censors stated that 'no exhibition of defiance to constituted authority, if successful, was considered legitimate'.

Marguerite was now enjoying the kind of worldly stimulation that had been absent during the years of her marriage. Her husband had not provided the intellectual companionship she now knew that she could not do without and, at what would be a grave price for family harmony, her brother-in-law was supplying that companionship and more.

Marguerite had never been close to her younger sister Elizabeth, named after their mother. Marguerite, with her lively and aggressive nature, found her sister unwilling to join in any of her 'madcap adventures'.

She was later to remark unkindly of Elizabeth that she had 'no remembrance of any affection or any dislike for her, or even of what she looked like. She is a blurred outline in the dim recesses of memory'.

Shy she may have been, but Elizabeth had married well: in 1907 she wed a handsome attorney on the brink of a promising political career. Albert Cabell Ritchie was a graduate of Johns Hopkins and, by the age of 31, was the Assistant City Solicitor of Baltimore, in addition to his own law practice. In 1915, he was appointed Attorney General for the State of Maryland. However, a year later the marriage was over amid allegations of improprieties between Albert Ritchie and Marguerite. Elizabeth made no public accusations, claiming instead that Albert had deserted her to live with his mother. In any event, Elizabeth moved to Santa Fe, New Mexico, and never again spoke to either of them. Marguerite seemed to have had no compunction about sleeping with her sister's husband, and their relationship would continue.

* * *

On the 6th of April 1917 the United States of America, after remaining neutral for more than two and a half years, joined the Entente when Congress declared war on the Central powers – Germany, Austria-Hungary, Bulgaria and the Ottoman Empire. This was greeted, according to Marguerite, by 'bursts of cheers' from the newsroom of *The Baltimore Sun*. Eight days later, President Woodrow Wilson created the Committee on Public Information, chaired by George Creel. It would issue regulations to the media requesting voluntary support of the United States' entry into the war. In this way, Wilson could use the war to reaffirm American ideals and values and unify immigrant groups.

Marguerite's newspaper duties changed overnight. She wrote that 'Mr Kent suggested that I write a series of articles calculated to stimulate enlistment and patriotic activities.' Newspapers all over America complied with the government's request, and within weeks 73,000 men had enlisted. Marguerite found herself caught up in the tide of war sentiment. One of the first articles written in her new role covered the art and science of camouflage and described how Hollywood set painters and sculptors were working together on disguising military targets and vehicles. For another article she took on the role of a streetcar conductress to show other women that they could follow her example and help the war effort.

But her pièce de résistance was working as a skilled labourer in Bethlehem Steel Company's Sparrows Point Plant. Her articles ran for eight consecutive days from 9th to the 16th of May 1918. 'I have had the most wonderful, the most unforgettable experience of my whole life,' she wrote. 'For a week I have been a shipbuilder – the first woman to take part in the great program of the emergency Fleet Corporation.'[5] She even gave advice to women on how to dress in male jobs and coined the word 'womanalls' (as opposed to overalls), which she described as 'something like a child's rompers'.[6]

In this period of her journalistic career, Marguerite learned her trade as an investigative reporter and was even given, most unusually in that time, and especially for a woman, a by-line in *The Baltimore Sun*. In a 14-part series that she wrote during March 1918, she created a fictional character – a jobless war widow with a child – and in that persona applied for positions in factories, the government, public service, stores, businesses and even the theatre. Securing over twenty jobs paying between $2.50 and $25 a week, she argued that wages for unskilled female workers were too low to support a household. Her own salary at the newspaper had now been raised to $30 a week.

Even in these early days of her reporting career, Marguerite never shied away from tackling difficult and sensitive issues. And few subjects in America were more sensitive in 1918 than immigrants and their loyalties. Josephine Roache, a social worker, was hired by the Division of Work with the Foreign-born in Creel's Committee on Public Information to organise 'Loyalty Leagues' and rallies, to write pro-American and pro-war pamphlets, and to monitor the foreign-language newspapers. Marguerite, concerned about negative sentiments towards ethnic communities in Baltimore, wrote an eight-part series on the communities of Poles, Bohemians, Italians, Lithuanians, Serbs, Greeks, Scandinavians and even Germans, many of whom were clustered in their own neighbourhoods of the city, speaking their own languages and following indigenous customs. She highlighted the sacrifices they were making and their positive contributions to Baltimore and America. Appalled that foreign-language newspapers were being suppressed by Creel and his cronies – 'the foreign-language paper,' she wrote, 'should not foster nationalistic sentiment, but should be a vehicle for Americanisation, and this is best accomplished by reaching the people in their own language'[7]– she dedicated two articles to the German community and reminded readers that before the war they were the most respected and influential ethnic group in Baltimore.

On a lighter note, in August 1918, Marguerite explored reasons why there was a shortage of ice in the city and, putting on her womanalls again, worked for half a day at the American Ice Company. Never afraid to criticise, she concluded the shortage was caused by lazy and unmotivated male workers. If the men didn't want the work, she argued, then women could do the job just as well.

Marguerite claimed that during this period of her life she was working fourteen hours a day as an 'antidote to suffering', much of which was caused by the death of her husband. While she was searching for interesting news stories, her faithful domestics, Rebecca and Lizzie, were running the boarding house. The casualty in all this activity, however, was her son Tommy, whom she saw only for lunch on Sundays. And yet, despite missing her husband so deeply, Marguerite found time to have supper once a week with her friend and former brother-in-law, Albert Ritchie.

* * *

Marguerite was stunned to read, in the summer of 1918, newspaper stories that she could scarcely believe: 'German atrocities, the consumption of human flesh, and wholesale efforts to repopulate the country by official sanction of rape and extramarital relations'. These did not sit well with her memories of the 'gentle, kindly Germans' or her 'beloved Austrians'. Desperate to get to Europe to see the real situation for herself, Marguerite arranged for passage on a troopship. However, at the last minute she was denied official permission to travel. There was, she thought, only one other way to get to Europe at this time, and that was by entering the Intelligence Service. 'In plain English, I was willing to become a spy,' she declared, seeing nothing immoral about this course of action. Indeed, some female spies of the Great War – such as the Belgian, Gabrielle Petit, and the Frenchwoman, Louise de Bettignies – had become heroes in their own countries.

Even after America joined the war, President Wilson was never truly interested in the Intelligence services, unlike his Secretary of State, Robert Lansing, and Lansing's adviser Frank L. Polk. Both men realised that, with the country at war, the United States needed better intelligence, both domestically and abroad.

Before effective action could be taken, the turf war between the existing Secret Service, headed by William J. Flynn, and the Bureau of Investigation, whose director was A. Bruce Bielaski, needed to be resolved: the two men were willing to report to the State Department but not to each other. The solution was that Polk was appointed head of a unit called U-1, which became the clearing house or depository of information gathered from the various services. The two existing military offices collecting foreign intelligence, the Office of Naval Intelligence (ONI) and the Military Intelligence Department (MID), were swiftly expanded. The MID's staff increased dramatically from 3 to 1,441, and it became one of the four divisions of the War Department General Staff.* For a posting to Europe in an official intelligence capacity, Marguerite could have approached either the ONI or the MID; she decided on the former. Although the British and Germans were more than willing to use women as spies, American Naval Intelligence proved less eager. When she applied, she was told in no uncertain terms that 'the Secretary of the Navy is not in favour of employing women in that capacity'.[8]

Fortunately for Marguerite, her stepfather-in-law, Dr Ames, was friendly with Brigadier-General Churchill, Chief of the MID. 'If you use women in your foreign service,' Dr Ames wrote to Churchill, 'you could not find a better one.'[9] Churchill, a distant relative of Winston Churchill, sent a Colonel Martin to the Hotel Emerson in Baltimore to interview his friend's stepdaughter-in-law. When they met on the 28th of September 1918, Martin saw before him a woman 5ft 6 inches tall, weighing 120lbs, with blue eyes, extensive European travel behind her, a fluency in German, French and Italian, a smattering of Spanish, and a strong, cool and courageous spirit. He hired her on the spot. Churchill commissioned her as a captain, agreeing to pay her $250 a month with a further $250 for expenses. She was told to be ready to leave on the 1st of December.

Dr Ames, Marguerite wrote, 'did not find it in the least extraordinary that I should be willing to give up an assured living, the companionship of my little son and security, for a career that promised nothing but danger and uncertainty'. Indeed, both Ritchie and her editor, Frank Kent – the only other civilians who knew about her new career – also wholeheartedly supported her. Some years down the line, Marguerite was to appropriately entitle one of her volumes of autobiography: *Born for Trouble*.

---

* In 1917, Herbert O. Yardley (effectively a co-founder of modern American military Intelligence) was placed in charge of a new military intelligence and code and cipher unit called MI-8. It was to be responsible for translating foreign language messages in shorthand and uncovering messages in invisible ink.

Chapter Two

Agent 'B'

‒‒‒∞‒‒‒

'Armistice Signed, End of War!' read *The New York Times* front-page headline on Monday, the 11th of November 1918. Marguerite immediately suspected that peace would scupper her posting to Germany. But the following day she was summoned to Washington and told by Brigadier-General Churchill that she was now to report on economic and political matters there. The vast majority of German territory was not to be occupied by the victorious armies, and information was needed on German public morale, internal affairs, food supplies, revolutionary and pacifist activities, and the strength of the desire for an acceptance of the peace. Her reports would be seen by the State Department, Foreign Relations Committee of Congress and the military. 'I was to go into Germany with an absolutely open mind and report accurately and unprejudiced everything I saw and heard,' she wrote. 'This was exactly what I would have done if I had gone to Germany on my own.'

Marguerite was assigned the signature 'B' for transmission of messages and given a code name and cipher tables. She received her first salary cheque of $750 with instructions from Captain Dick Slaughter to report to the Military Attaché on arrival in Paris. He reminded her to talk to no one of her mission, and to 'act in all events and under all circumstances, as though you were simply a newspaper correspondent and nothing more'.[1]

Rebecca, Marguerite's maid, was left in charge of 16-year-old Tommy and the boarding house, and Marguerite set sail on the *Espagne* for Bordeaux on the 5th December. Frank Kent arranged her cover to go to France as a correspondent for *The Baltimore Sun*. The *Sun* had sponsored a series of films called *Miles of Smiles* featuring relatives of Maryland troops serving in France greeting their loved ones. Marguerite was to take these films and screen them to the troops in France. It was the perfect guise. None of the films survives, but Marguerite later remembered that the messages filmed were often amusing or pathetic, with offers of plum pudding and reports of beloved dogs giving birth.

On her arrival in Paris later in the month, Marguerite was briefed by Colonel Ralph Van Deman, previously head of the MID and now attached to the peace delegation. Paris in 1918 was very different from the pre-war city Marguerite knew and loved. She noted a distinct lack of young Parisian men; mostly boys and old men were in evidence, and large numbers of Allied officers crowded the cafés and restaurants. The streets were buzzing with Italians, Portuguese, Chinese, Japanese, Algerian, Senegalese and Russian soldiers, in addition to the American and British women from the Red Cross or Voluntary Aid Detachments (VADs).

Marguerite arranged screenings of the *Miles of Smiles* films to the American troops and was shocked at the conditions of their billets: 'I went to one stable occupied by seventy men,' she said. 'There was no firewood allowance and the only way to get warm was to go to bed. If you were wet, you simply had to wait until your clothes dried on you.' In order not to lower home morale, her reports were not published by *The Baltimore Sun* until the autumn of 1919, when the troops were safely back home.

After discharging her nominal duties in France, Marguerite was ready to begin her 'journalistic' trip to Berlin. Relying on her own resources, she made her way to Mainz, then under Allied control. From there, and without official travel papers, she sneaked onto a workers' train to Frankfurt, arriving in the city at 5.00 a.m. Heading for the Frankfurter Hof Hotel (where she had stayed before the war), she was told that to proceed further a pass from the local workers' council was required. Frankfurt was not under Allied control, but Marguerite acquired a travel pass and took the next train to Cassel in Northern France.

In Cassel, the well-connected Marguerite procured a rare military permit to travel on to Berlin from Major Gottlieb von Jagow, a former German foreign minister. Hitching a ride on a troop train, she arrived in Berlin's Anhalter Bahnhof late on a brisk January evening in 1919. There were no porters to be seen, and the station was deserted except for her fellow passengers and a few armed guards. Adjusting the long fur coat that was to become her trademark, Marguerite struggled to the station entrance with her luggage and typewriter.

The triangular platz in front of the station was empty and the tramlines silent. She sat down on her bags and waited. Before long, an old man appeared driving an ancient *droschke* (horse-drawn cab), pulled by a decrepit horse. Marguerite instructed the driver in her fluent German to take her to the Hotel Bristol, an elegant establishment where she had stayed pre-war. Described by the Baedeker guidebook as 'amongst the largest first-class hotels',[2] the Bristol was on the Unter den Linden, a wide, fashionable street in central Berlin that was home to numerous other first-class hotels, as well as the Prussian State Library, the Berlin

State Opera and St Hedwig's Cathedral. 'The Linden is to Berlin,' Baedeker exulted, 'what Bond Street and Piccadilly are to London.'[3]

The driver was appalled by the request from the woman in the fur coat. Berlin, two months after the Armistice, was in chaos as Communist, Socialist and Conservative forces battled in the streets to shape post-imperial Germany, and the Hotel Bristol was situated in an area open only to the military and presently at the heart of the fighting. She presented her pass to the driver, stating with an air of authority: 'I belong to the Military.'

The streets were deserted as they passed the elegant hotels lining the Potsdamer Platz, but all was not silent. Approaching the Brandenburg Gate, she heard 'the barking of rifles and the sharp put-put of machine guns in the distance.' Bullets bounced off the pavement and ricocheted from the walls of the ornate Beaux Arts-style buildings.

Once through the Gate, the cab soon reached the Hotel Bristol where the draperies were drawn and the wrought-iron doors bolted. The driver fled as soon as Marguerite and her luggage were out of his cab. She rang the doorbell and, after what seemed like an eternity, the door creaked open a crack and an anxious male face appeared. Once inside, she was surprised to find the atmosphere warm and cheerful, the lights blazing, the restaurant filled with diners, and an orchestra playing the barcarolle, 'Belle nuit, ô nuit d'amour', from 'The Tales of Hoffmann'. The diners were apparently insouciant to the fighting going on, quite literally, outside the door.

After checking in, Marguerite joined the diners for a meal from the well-stocked kitchen: oysters and venison were on the menu. Later, she retired to a room facing the inner courtyard to escape the sound of gunfire. Such were the flavours and sounds of the changed city she would come to know in the weeks that followed: bullets and vanilla bombes.

* * *

It may have been incredibly brave or amazingly stupid for an American woman to travel unaccompanied to Berlin during the beginning of 1919. No one could guarantee civil order and no one knew which political structure would prevail. The main combatants – the right-wing Freikorps and the left-wing Communists/Spartacists – were both an existential threat to the weak republican government formed after the Kaiser's abdication in November 1918.

Another recent arrival to Berlin, Captain Stewart Roddie, was on assignment for the British Mission with two fellow British officers. The

Entente Powers all had representation in the city and Roddie had been ordered to proceed to there from Cologne to report on the food situation and to discover whether Germans were taking the Armistice seriously. He noticed a distinct absence of dogs and cats in the city. 'All sausages long ago!' his guide informed him. Roddie had known the city well before the war, and was shocked by its decadence. Berlin, once the model of order and cleanliness, had become 'dirt, disorder, dancing and death!' The people were mad, the traffic chaotic, and 'all the dancing halls are crammed and when the bands stop playing one hears the shriek of a shell and the crack of rifle fire outside where the Spartacist and the Republican troops are shooting each other dead'.[4]

During the month before Marguerite's arrival, almost 5,000 Berliners had died from influenza. Every day saw demonstrations, strikes and exchanges of gunfire. Often there was no electricity or heating, and no transport due to the actions of striking workers.

Many thousands were now suffering grievously from the continuation of the Allied food blockades. The Germans had hoped that the signing of the Armistice would end these blockades, but the Allies were demanding that Germany hand over armaments, as well as numerous locomotives, freight wagons and lorries, before they would agree to distribute food.[5] One commentator described Berlin at this time as 'a city of tightened stomachs, of mounting, thundering hunger, where hidden rage was transformed into boundless money lust, and men's minds were concentrating more and more on questions of naked existence'.[6]

Marguerite had arrived amidst what would become known as the Spartacist uprising, a struggle that pitted the German Communist Party (KPD), with the left-wing Spartacus League, opposing the provisional republican Social Democratic government (SPD) led by Friedrich Ebert. Against the backdrop of a general strike of some half a million workers on January 7th, the Communists aimed to seize power and create a government akin to the Bolsheviks in Russia. They seized a number of buildings including train stations, newspaper offices and the Berlin police headquarters.

On January 9th, 1,200 Freikorps – a semi-independent organisation of battle-hardened ex-soldiers commanded by a politician named Gustav Noske – moved into the city at the behest of the Ebert government. Three hundred and fifty outnumbered Spartacists fought desperately against them. The Army and the Freikorps recaptured the Brandenburg Gate and central Berlin, and the strike was called off. Figures from Ebert's government suggest that 100 Spartacists were killed and 400 wounded, with 13 Freikorps killed and 20 wounded. Spartacists disputed these figures, stating that some 1,000 of their number were killed.[7]

On the 15th of January, two of the prominent leaders of the left-wing uprising, Karl Liebknecht and Rosa Luxemburg, were captured and taken for interrogation. Liebknecht was beaten unconscious with rifle butts and then shot. His body was discovered the following day in the Tiergarten, a public park behind the Hotel Bristol. Luxemburg was also beaten before being shot in the head and thrown into the Landwehr Canal in the Tiergarten. Her body broke through the ice and would not be found until the water thawed in May. Ebert's government had survived but Berlin's social and political order remained precarious.

* * *

After making contact with Colonel Bouvier, her American intelligence contact in the city, Marguerite soon was at work under her journalistic cover. Armed with letters of introduction from her well-connected contacts in America, she met with the American wife of General Hans von Below who had commanded German troops against the Americans at the Battle of Argonne Forest in the autumn of 1918. Von Below was, according to Marguerite, a 'typical Prussian, straight and broad-shouldered, with a bullet head, rugged features and bristling white moustaches'.

She thought that under the circumstances it might be awkward for the general to discuss the war, and indeed he received her 'haughtily and with an air of marked condescension', informing her that she was much mistaken if she thought the Americans had won the war. Through Frau von Below, she received invitations to meet other German officers and their wives, learning that many of them were bitterly anti-Semitic and blamed the Jews for the war. They despised the Social Democrats, regarded the republican government as a stop-gap, and believed the monarchy would eventually be re-established. The military were organising secret societies that admitted only people of pure Teutonic blood, and membership of these societies was running into the thousands.

The elections for the National Assembly were finally held on the 19th of January 1919. For the first time in German history, there was a universal right for all Germans over the age of 18 – including women – to vote. (In the United States, women were not given the vote until the following year.) Intrigued, Marguerite accompanied her chambermaid who was voting in Charlottenburg, an area in the west of the city. 'They were of all grades in the social scale,' Marguerite observed. 'Ladies in fur coats rubbed shoulders with their sisters in rabbit skin, working women with red faces and checked aprons elbowed breathless dowagers in broadcloth.'

However, Marguerite entertained few illusions about this display of sisterhood and noted that, despite getting the franchise, many women were still the staunchest supporters of German nationalism. In a later newspaper article, she wrote that she did not believe women to be naturally more moral or pacifist than men.

There was an 83% electoral turnout. Ebert's Social Democrats won 37.9% of votes, the Independent Socialists just 3.6%; the Communists boycotted the election. The remaining votes were spread amongst various independent parties. Gustav Noske, leader of the Freikorps and now Ebert's new Defence Minister, persuaded him to convene the Constituent Assembly at Weimar, 160 miles from Berlin, to avoid trouble from the Communists and Spartacists.

Weimar, a city known more for its famous past residents, such as Goethe and Johann Sebastian Bach, was so far untouched by the revolution. The first session of the National Assembly was held on February 6th. Marguerite managed to secure a special permit and travelled there, where she sat in the press gallery and heard the discussions of Woodrow Wilson's proposed Fourteen Points – the hoped-for basis for the terms of the German postwar settlement, which included a vision of a new Europe with free trade, open agreements, democracy and self-determination. Marguerite watched sceptically as the Germans bickered amongst themselves over the proposals.

When she returned from Weimar, Colonel Bouvier advised Marguerite to move for her safety to the Hotel Adlon, a few blocks from the Hotel Bristol in the Unter den Linden. In the shadow of the Brandenburg Gate, the Adlon was a favourite meeting place for the many foreign correspondents. Marguerite noted that its lobby was where 'schemers, intriguers and agents of the Foreign Office were always hanging around hoping to pick up information from the personnel of the Allied missions who were billeted there. Indeed, the Adlon was also the hotel where the three British captains, William Stewart Roddie, Claude Bell and Ernest Tennant, stayed when they arrived in Berlin a few days before Marguerite. Stewart Roddie noted that the French mission, the Hoover Relief Commission, and the American Chamber of Commerce were all there. 'They all thought we were spies, and had we told them what was the absolute fact, that we had nothing to conceal, no one would have believed us.'[8] Tennant reported that their closets and suitcases were searched whenever they left their rooms: 'All the thin bits of black cotton we stuck across the drawers and suitcases were snapped, even if we left our rooms for ten minutes.'[9]

The British and Americans were not the only foreigners in Berlin at this time. 'Berlin,' Marguerite remarked, 'was the meeting-place for all the international plotters and intriguers who had grievances, real or imaginary, against the Entente Powers.'

Marguerite had avoided the Adlon and the representatives of the Allied missions staying there as such might have compromised her mission to be seen to have any contact with them. However, there was now growing concern in Germany that President Wilson would not be able to get agreement with the Allies on the Fourteen Points, and everyday life might become dangerous for foreigners. Count Johann Heinrich von Bernstorff, the former German ambassador to America, told Marguerite that if Germany was not given a chance for economic recovery, then there would be Bolshevism throughout the country. Indeed, in Munich, Kurt Eisner, the Bavarian Prime Minister, had just been assassinated – ironically, on his way to make his resignation speech – and the Red Guard had taken over the city. Meanwhile in Berlin, the Communist Party of Germany was now led by a former Spartacist and associate of Lenin, Paul Levi.

Marguerite scoured the daily newspapers and, using her press credentials, established contacts within all the political parties, including the Communists and Monarchists. She attended the Oppressed Nationalities meetings, sponsored by German military officers. Here, Arabs complained of broken promises by Britain to create an Arab kingdom in the near East, and members of Sinn Fein discussed the terror in Ireland, while Indian nationalists denounced British Imperialism. There was also the gruesome Talaat Pasha, an ex-postman and deposed Grand Vizier, who was leader of the pro-German Union and Progress Party in Turkey. He took refuge in Berlin when the Allies occupied Constantinople (and would soon be cut down in the Hardenbergstrasse by an Armenian assassin). There were Russian imperialists and members of the Russian aristocracy, as well as agents of the Third International, the organisation devoted to overthrowing the 'international bourgeoisie'. Marguerite sought out opportunities to listen to Communist speakers and wrote of them that 'their ruthless advocacy of direct action and the class war appalled me', though she 'could not but admire their utter selflessness and devotion to their cause'.

Marguerite's talents as a high-society reporter also came to the fore. Making it her business to encounter as many people as possible, she attended the intellectual salons of Berlin and met writers, theatre people and musicians, mixing easily in Berlin society and gathering bits of information. She dined and mingled at the house of the Jewish publisher and art dealer Paul Cassirer, who had promoted artists such as Vincent van Gogh. In the meantime, she collected information for newspaper copy and left intelligence reports for Colonel Bouvier at the Hotel Adlon.

Entertainment was not hard to come by. The opera was crowded every night, and the 'stalls and boxes were sprinkled with plainly dressed burghers, elbowing great ladies in furs and satins,' Marguerite noted, while 'the Imperial box was usually filled with President Ebert's friends who had formerly occupied places in the peanut gallery'. Plays forbidden during the war now got an airing, and most restaurants had a cabaret show. Due to strikes and shortages, electricity was turned off in the dance halls by 11.30 p.m., although the festivities did not come to an end. Customers exited through the front door only to be readmitted through the back entrance to continue dancing by candlelight. Marguerite remained unimpressed. She claimed that 'love-making was brazen and the fun was coarse beyond description. It revealed to me a side of the German character I had never known, and I found it repulsive'.

Of the problems facing Berlin, the lack of food for some was the greatest disrupter of everyday life. Those with money could still eat extremely well. Because of her connections, Marguerite was invited into the homes of the rich, or to restaurants where on one occasion she was served 'a delicious soup, fish fried to a turn, Wiener Schnitzel, game, salad and ice cream with three types of wine and real coffee'. She noted that the cost for six of them was 800 marks, an exorbitant amount considering that the average Berliner spent 2 marks a day on food.[10] At the Hotel Bristol she ate 'delicious oysters, wild duck and venison', while in the Hotel Esplanade it was possible to eat its famous vanilla bombes with chocolate sauce. In another restaurant, Marguerite even came across real fillets of beef with two poached eggs. For the general population, eggs were only available on food rations once a fortnight. As for meat, just 200 grams of meat per person per week were allowed – when obtainable. Occasionally, Marguerite would eat at the cheaper cafés where she was served 'cakes made with potato substitutes for white flour, coated with icing made apparently with chalk and saccharine and flavoured with chemical fruit extract coloured in vivid aniline shades.' And at the still well-attended afternoon tea dances, she discovered a remarkable substitute for whipping cream.

But Marguerite estimated that 50% of the population of Berlin was close to starvation. Wanting to see how the poor could survive on the meagre food rations provided by the state, she asked her hotel chambermaid to find her a family with whom she might eat. The chambermaid suggested her sister, who lived in Moabit, a poor area of the city packed with factories, tenements and cheap, grubby shops. Locals called this area La Terre Maudite, the 'cursed ground', as it was where French prisoners had been incarcerated in the time of Frederick the Great. Marguerite climbed three floors to reach the run-down apartment. The door was opened by a small child, and then a woman appeared with a baby in her arms and a toddler clinging to her skirts. 'One look at the baby was enough,' Marguerite wrote. 'His little face was pinched and drawn, and he had that curiously old look that undernourished babies always have.' The baby, Marguerite discovered, rarely drank milk, and the rest of the family, too, were undernourished, subsisting mostly on potato soup, as meat was unaffordable. Stale bread was only sporadically available.

Such a situation was as far removed as could be imagined from Marguerite's own comfortable domestic life in America; it was also far removed from the Berlin she had hitherto known. At the Hotel Bristol with its hot baths and central heating, and socialising with the German upper classes, Marguerite experienced none of these shortages. Few of the people she met in the restaurants and salons 'seemed to have any sense of responsibility for the shocking conditions existing among the poor'. One woman told Marguerite that she missed Herbert Hoover's food packages, since American bacon was 'simply heavenly'! Her husband, when fighting on the Western Front, had been able to buy Hoover's food packages on the black market and send them back to her once a week.

Affluent Berliners, she knew, spent their money on furs, paintings, jewels and rare books while their clothes were made with patterns smuggled in from Paris. She visited Drecoll's, in the Budapesther Strasse, and noted 'the overdecorated salons in pinkish mauve with lace ruffles and ribbon bows in every available spot, suggesting nothing so much as an old-fashioned guest room pincushion, packed with mannequins and customers'. She saw expensive gowns with prices ranging from 1,000 to 3,000 marks. 'A sales lady was convincing a dowager that she would look slim as a girl of twenty in a chemise frock of red serge, a smart young matron was ordering a pierrette costume for a fancy dress ball, and a proud mamma was selecting a discreet décolleté for a very knowing-looking débutante.' There were also hats – albeit not as smart, the fashion-conscious Marguerite noted, as Parisian ones: German women, she believed, didn't know how to wear them at the correct right angle. There were shoes galore, which she found particularly surprising as, due to the supposed shortage of leather in Germany, Berliners were only allowed two pairs of shoes a year. In the cheaper shops, fashionable and expensive clothes were imitated – shirts and underwear were made of paper and slips of artificial silk, and shoes were made of paper, with wooden soles.

Marguerite was appalled by this new Germany, with its undernourished children on one side and its pampered princesses on another and her reports to Colonel Bouvier reflected her unease. 'I realised,' she later wrote, 'that if Germany was ever to become a normal and a sane member of the family of nations she must be treated as we would treat a person who has had a nervous breakdown, given a chance to come back and recover her balance.'

The long hours were beginning to take their toll on the forty-year-old American. Marguerite missed her son and despite her vertiginous social whirl, she had only a few friends in Germany – all of them male and mainly from the international press corps, which another American journalist called the 'news gang'.[11] These journalists would not have been too surprised to have found a woman in their midst. Another American, Henrietta Eleanor Goodnough, who wrote under the name of Peggy Hull, had been sponsored by the Newspaper Enterprise Association to report on the Great War, and there were over twenty other American women writing about the war in Europe. Corra Mae Harris wrote for *The Saturday Evening Post* and Frances Marion for the San Francisco *Examiner*, but by 1919 most of them had been sent to Russia to cover events there.

Since none of these women was in Berlin in early 1919, Harrison dined or went to the theatre with male foreign correspondents such as Karl von Wiegand of the *New York Sun* and Gordon Stiles from the *Chicago Daily News*. She longed, though, for female companionship. Another journalist, George Young of the *London Daily News*, made a suggestion. She should meet up with a British friend of his, Mrs Stan Harding. Unfortunately, Young informed Marguerite, Harding's health was not the best and she was financially hard up.

Marguerite had undoubtedly already heard of the mysterious and charismatic Stan Harding. 'Stan is everywhere,' wrote an awed Berliner, 'in the midst of it all.'[12] Everyone knew her, it seemed. Marguerite was understandably intrigued. Who was this woman calling herself by a man's name? And what had brought her to war-ravaged, revolutionary

Berlin? She immediately made arrangements for what would be a fateful rendezvous, calling on Stan that same afternoon at her boarding house.

Chapter Three

The Beauty and the Beast

The life of Constance Grace Lesslie Harding – known to everyone as Stan – was fated to be one of imprisonment and escape, triggered by a restless but passionate search for causes and ideals to believe in. She had much in common with Marguerite. They had both enjoyed cosmopolitan upbringings thanks to wealthy families, and each had a facility for languages, an ability to befriend the rich and famous, and the rebellious streak of someone unwilling or unable to settle into the roles for which others felt each had been destined. Both of them were, by the standards of the day, sexually liberated, unwilling to let the values and mores of society stand in the way of their love affairs, and both had a deep thirst for travel and adventure.

Stan Harding was born on the 12th of July 1884 in Toronto, where her English-born father, Edwin John Harding, in registering her birth, declared his profession as a 'gentleman', even though his Londoner father had been a tailor's trimming assistant. But Edwin Harding had married well after emigrating to Canada: his wife was a Lesslie, part of a prominent family of Scots who had left Dundee in the 1820s, fetched up in Upper Canada, opened a series of successful dry-good stores, and even minted their own currency, which was soon accepted as legal tender.* (The coins were introduced in 1823. On one side of the coins Lesslie & Sons was printed, on the other, the city of Toronto. Toronto did not exist until 1834, but the name was in discussion years before and John presumed, quite correctly, York would change its name to Toronto.) By the time Stan was born, the family lived in considerable splendour as proprietors of one of the most 'palatial and fashionable stores in Toronto'.[1]

Thanks to her family's wealth, Stan enjoyed, like Marguerite, a peripatetic childhood and education, mainly in Europe. The Harding family – Stan, her parents, and her only sibling, a brother named Harold – occupied a succession of grand hotels and apartments, with Switzerland featuring high on their itinerary. In Lausanne, Harold was sent to the Collège Gaillard while Stan, although mainly educated by private tutors, spent three months in a girls' school. As a result of these lengthy excursions, she became proficient in both French and German.

The family's success in the world of Mammon had been tempered by a devout spirituality. Both Edwin and his wife, Grace, were Plymouth Brethren, an austere, evangelical Christian sect. Until the age of thirteen, Stan had adhered strictly to the Brethren's philosophy. She even spoke Biblical English, with its old-fashioned array of thees, thous and giveths.[2] At thirteen, however, doubt crept in. Never one, even as a child, to remain silent on matters of faith and doubt, she summoned the courage to ask her brother his thoughts. Harold confessed his own lack of belief, and the pair embraced.[3] Her father had not been so understanding. He devised for her a punishment adapted from the Biblical description of the treatment of lepers: she was removed from school to prevent her contaminating other children and confined to her room. She survived this incarceration because – ever the rebel – after her father had retired to bed she was able to sneak downstairs and meet her brother in secret. However, desperate for her father's approval and unable to bear the strain, Stan soon begged Edwin for forgiveness, telling him she believed in God again. For seven days thereafter, she was forced to write the phrase 'The fool hath said in his heart: there is no God' a hundred times each day – words she would still remember more than fifty years later. The experience, she later claimed, was useful: it taught her how to keep a secret.

By the age of seventeen, however, Stan was looking for more permanent ways to escape her domineering father. The normal route for a well-bred Victorian lady to do so was through marriage, but she had no wish to replace a controlling father with a controlling husband – and so she began to save her pocket money whilst working out a plan of escape. She studied in England for two years at the Bristol School of Practical Art, and it was here that her eyes became open to the beauty of art (something frowned upon by the Plymouth Brethren, who did not even hang crosses in their meeting rooms), and its possibilities for her future career. She also became what she later called 'a good, all-round rebel'. She claimed that the 'drab squalor' of some of London's poorer neighbourhoods 'made me sick and angry', and gave her a vision of – and a profound sympathy with – the working class. 'I called myself a Socialist,' she wrote, 'though I had hardly an inkling of the problems involved.'

Stan's escape from religious strictures and societal conventions came in Florence, the city of art. In 1904, while staying in a luxurious hotel with her parents and brother, she gave them the slip, sneaking away with £10 of savings in her pocket and making her way to an unfurnished room that she had arranged to rent in Piazza Donatello. Stan said that she felt like 'a song-bird released from a cage', and promptly wrote to her brother asking him to join her.[4] Harold, however, turned down the offer: he was shortly off to China and was excited about the prospect of his new life in the Consular Service.

Although the escape granted her freedom at last, it must have caused Stan trauma. All her life she had been taught that society was wicked – and it was this wicked world that she was about to enter. The effect of growing up in a strict religious environment, and then abruptly leaving it, can profoundly affect a person's mental health.[5]

*   *   *

Florence in the first decade of the twentieth-century was full of expatriates and eccentrics. The English-speaking community was one of the largest with up to 30,000 members. Indeed, there were so many English that Florentines used the term 'Inglese' to refer to all foreigners. The Anglo-Florentines tended to wear flamboyant garments of a style and material – such as chiffon – quite distinct from those of the indigenous population. As Stan loved to walk everywhere, she doubtless soon recognised many of her compatriots by their clothes.

The doyenne of the expatriates was the writer and traveller Janet Ross, then in her seventies, who lived in a villa near Settignano where she had entertained writers like George Meredith and Arthur Symons. Also prominent were Mrs Ethel Ames-Lyde, a rotund lady who wore 'Victorian silks and laces and her iron-grey hair had black net folds falling from it',[6] and the formidable Lady Paget. The tall, slender German widow of the British Ambassador to Rome had been a maid of honour to Queen Victoria's eldest daughter, Princess Victoria, who found Paget 'affected and grand'.[7] She wore 'old lace concoctions on her head that made her look like the women in Gothic times'.[8] As well as dachshunds and vegetarianism, her interests included making medieval-style slippers of silk and velvet, stitching tapestries and studying theosophy.

The beautiful Lady Sybil Cutting, daughter of an Irish aristocrat, was the owner of the Villa Medici in Fiesole, in the hills above Florence. She hosted picnics and elaborate parties in a garden restored by another English expatriate, Cecil Pinsent. The ex-pat community was entertained by the two Reggies, a homosexual couple who had fled from London. Reggie Temple wore pale shirts complemented by lavender and mauve handkerchiefs and spent his days copying paintings in the Uffizi, while Reggie Turner delighted in mimicking the sayings of Oscar Wilde, telling friends it was as if the spirit of Oscar had taken possession of him.

One of the people to whom Stan became closest was an American ex-patriate, Mabel Dodge. Five years older than Stan, Dodge was later described as a 'freelance intellectual'.[9] She had been sent by her wealthy family to Europe in 1904, following the death of her first husband in a hunting accident and a scandalous affair with a gynaecologist in her home town of Buffalo. In 1905 she married her second husband, Edwin Dodge, a wealthy young Bostonian, and with him began restoring the Villa Curonia outside Florence in Arcetri. She filled it with both Renaissance artefacts and intellectual and artistic friends such as Gertrude and Leo Stein, the actress Eleonora Duse and the pianist Arthur Rubinstein. She compensated for her plain face and thin lips with extravagant turbans and exotic jewellery.

Another new friend of Stan's was the Lithuanian-born, Harvard-educated art historian, connoisseur and art dealer, Bernhard Berenson. Earning his living from writing and assisting rich Americans in the buying of Italian paintings, Berenson had married the widowed Mary Costelloe in 1900 and the couple made their home in the Villa I Tatti, a few miles north of Florence. Standing outside Florence on the road to Settignano, the house was famous for its approach through an avenue of cypress trees and for its beautifully manicured gardens. Over the years, I Tatti welcomed many famous visitors: the American writer Edith Wharton; Berenson's old friend and rival from Harvard, George Santayana; the British art dealer Joseph Duveen; Vernon Lee, a reclusive grey-haired English writer who wrote under the name of Violet Paget; and the Italian poet, novelist and dramatist Gabriele d'Annunzio.

Possibly the most exotic and exciting of the expatriates that Stan came to know was the English artist and avant-garde theatre director Edward Gordon Craig. The dashing, luxuriantly maned Craig had moved to Florence in 1907 after separating from his lover, Isadora Duncan. That year he designed a production of Henrik Ibsen's *Rosmersholm* at the Teatro della Pergola in Florence, and the following year he began publishing *The Mask*, a journal on the theatre.

Stan came to know not only Craig (who, mysteriously, called her KKK) but also his assistant – and later his lover – Dorothy Nevile Lees. There was a good deal of friction between the two women as they vied for Craig's affection. Dorothy seems to have taken an instant dislike to Stan, blaming her upbringing among the Plymouth Brethren for giving her a 'kind of a twist, so that she had to be eccentric and had to make mischief'. She claimed Stan was malicious, 'always trying to get in between and split up any friendships or good relationships in her environment. She slithered in and out like an adroit little snake, whispering poisonous things that alienated people from each other, completely false things.'[10]

No doubt there is an element of truth in what Dorothy claimed, but her own spite was motivated by sexual jealousy, since 'KKK' quickly became one of Craig's many lovers. He was so taken with Stan that he used her as the model for three black carvings – depicting Eve, Beauty and the Beast – made from soft pear wood. The three carvings are revealing about the trajectory of his feelings. He explained in his notebooks that KKK, the enchanting temptress and model of beauty, quickly became a nuisance, even turning up uninvited on the steps of his mother's house in Kent.[11]

Uncertain of Craig's wavering affections, Stan enlisted her friend James Strachey Barnes – who regarded Craig as a 'megalomaniac' – to teach him a lesson. 'He must be made to gnaw his heart for 48 hours in jealousy,' she explained.[12] Her plan was that Barnes was to take her out for dinner in Florence two nights consecutively. The first night passed without incident, but on the second Craig descended on their table in the crowded restaurant. He waved a large glove before casting it contemptuously at Barnes's feet and then seizing Stan by the wrist. She freed herself and fled to a horse-drawn cab. Before he chased after the cab, Craig seized the tablecloth and – as if an actor in one of his plays – hoisted it dramatically, sending an avalanche of china and cutlery to the floor. Barnes ran after them both as the crowd expectantly watched, cheering as Craig – continuing his swashbuckling role – threw himself into the moving cab and Barnes leapt onto the step.

Reaching her apartment, Stan wriggled free and escaped up the long flight of steps. The two men followed as the door slammed shut. Craig shrugged and 'swung disdainfully upon his heel' before marching back down the staircase, while Barnes laughed triumphantly. A few days later, Stan sent Barnes a thank-you note, but the plan had been too successful, and 'breakfast, luncheon, tea and dinner without Craig was no good at all'. Would Barnes be so good as to send Craig a note of reconciliation?

Such people, with their flamboyance, eccentricities and fierce intellects, were a world away from the prosaic world of Stan's childhood. As she made her way along the avenue of cypresses to the Villa I Tatti, or passed through the damask-hung salon of the Villa Curonia, listening to sounds of laughter and debate, she must have exulted in the freedom she had won for herself.

* * *

39

Young, attractive and rebellious, a 'Socialist' with artistic aspirations, Stan Harding made a striking new addition to the Anglo-Florentine community. Gordon Craig did not exaggerate in making his KKK a model of Beauty. According to the writer Jocelyn Hennessy, at this time she was 'a slim girl, with a lovely forehead, delicately chiselled features, eyebrows neatly pencilled by nature, contemplative blue-grey eyes that can twinkle with merriment, or flash fire when pity or indignation provoke her'.[13] She had, moreover, the 'straightest and most kissable nose; a sensitive mouth, lips made for speaking poetry; the whole balanced by a firm little chin, and auburn hair styled in an Eton crop'.[14] Though 'thin from an insufficient food supply' she was 'spotlessly clean in her scanty cotton frocks'.[15] Perhaps not of outstanding physical beauty, she was certainly handsome and enchanting with intelligent and lively eyes.

Stan adored Florence, with its medieval and Renaissance buildings with their red-tiled roofs and the churches and museums filled with blue-robed Madonnas and lean, agonised Christs. She also loved the Italian climate. Strachey Barnes called her 'an artist and a kind of salamander, worshipping the sun', and he noted that she was 'petite, demure, faded a little (or was it her dress?) from tramping in the summer sun'.[16]

Florence was to become her home for over ten years. Her routine was to rise at 6 a.m. and to stroll to a nearby café for a breakfast of coffee and croissants. At 8 a.m. she would head for the Accademia di Belle Arti in the Scuola Libera del Nudo for free art classes. Then it would be off to the Uffizi or Pitti galleries to copy paintings for the rest of the day: copies that were good enough for her to sell to tourists.

Not long after leaving her parents in Florence, Stan dropped the name Constance. 'In those far-distant days, if a woman painted, she was above all a woman painter: if she wrote for the press, she was a woman journalist. To avoid this accent on gender, I abridged my name to "Stan" which is the middle piece of Constance and which is now on my passport!'[17]

On a typical day, when the galleries closed at 5 p.m., Stan would take coffee with a fellow art student to discuss the day's painting. Lunch or dinner was eaten in an inexpensive trattoria, and consisted of bean soup and bread soaked in olive oil. She often took long walks on her own, even at night. The dangers of an attractive young woman undertaking such expeditions in Italy were averted thanks to a revolver that her father had taught her to use. According to a friend, she became known as *La Bocca Nera* – the black mouth – because of the gun barrel that greeted anyone who tried to approach her.

To supplement her slender income from the tourist trade, Stan began teaching English to German and French expatriates, enabling her to earn enough to move into a bigger apartment. Within walking distance of the Uffizi, the Ponte Vecchio and the Duomo, her new lodgings were situated in an old house adjoining the San Paolino monastery in the west of the city. They comprised two bedrooms, a kitchen, and a large studio with a glass roof. One expatriate who knew Stan at the time wrote that she was 'as poor as the proverbial ecclesiastical rodent'.[18] He also mentioned she was small and frail-looking and yet could outwalk a man. Someone had given her two police dogs. One day one of them got hit by a tram and was left writhing in pain. Unable to wait for a policeman to put the animal out of its misery, she strangled it with her own hands.[19]

Stan's new accommodation was a couple of minutes' walk from Karl Krayl, a German doctor who lived and practised medicine on Piazza degli Ottaviani. A 39-year-old surgeon from Stuttgart, Krayl was described by a friend as 'opinionated and loyal'.[20] His parents had wanted him to be a priest, and he even began theological studies before realising this was not his calling, turning instead to medicine. He had settled in Florence to treat the German, Austrian and Swiss immigrants who had established themselves there. Because more and more of his clients were English, Stan began giving him language lessons, whereupon he promptly fell in love with her. She in turn was attracted to his 'gentleness, humanity, and intelligence', but kept refusing his offers of marriage, as the images of her domineering father and her 'crushed mother' rose before her.[21] As a friend put it, she let Krayl 'give free rein to his love and courtship, but she was in no way keen to let someone else take control of her life'.

Florence in the early 1900s was an extremely tolerant place compared to other European cities, but even so, the unmarried Stan had to tread carefully to avoid being regarded as morally suspect. Marriage would certainly have given her more freedom to pursue her own path, and she finally agreed to marry the persistent Karl on the understanding that she would not be expected to carry out the duties of a doctor's wife, and that she would be permitted to continue her artistic career, to see her own friends, to earn her own living, and even to remain lodging in her own apartment. To her utter surprise, Karl agreed. 'He had the greatest respect for individual freedom and for another's point of view of any man I have ever met,' she said. 'He was tolerance itself.'[22]

On October 25th 1906, the pair married in a civil ceremony in the Palazzo Vecchio. There were only two witnesses: a German princess who was a patient of Karl's, and Charles Freegrove Winzer, a British artist friend of Stan's.

The 22-year-old Mrs Stan Harding-Krayl started her marriage as she planned to continue it, and on the very same day she set off for Rome to complete a commission to copy a Titian in the Borghese Gallery. Karl in the meantime performed an operation and then watched over the patient for two days until satisfied all was well, whereupon he joined his new wife in Rome for their honeymoon. After a couple of days, he returned to Florence alone.

The Harding-Krayls were happy, but the German Lutheran community in Florence was nonplussed by their civil marriage and unorthodox living arrangements. The couple lived separately, like man and mistress rather than man and wife, they rejected all marriage responsibilities, and concentrated on enjoying each other's company, their common artistic passions and other interests. They saw each other daily, regularly dining together at Lapo's cellar restaurant. Karl was looked after by a middle-aged housekeeper while Stan had her Italian servant, Emilia. Whether the marriage was ever consummated, or whether it was concluded for the sake of convenience, is unclear. Certainly Stan enjoyed the material benefits of being a doctor's wife. A friend pointed out that she could now take her long solo walks safe in the knowledge that a comfortable home and full table awaited her return. Karl for his part enjoyed saying to people who did not know that he was married, 'Ah, you must ask my wife about that. Why don't you look in on her? She lives just around the corner.'[23]

* * *

Two people who were to have a great impact on Stan's life arrived in Florence in 1907. The first was the German artist Käthe Kollwitz. At the age of 40, she had been awarded the Max Klinger Villa Romana Prize for 'The Outbreak', one of six etchings in her series called 'The Peasants' Revolt'. The award entitled her to spend a year working in Klinger's house in Florence.

The young Käthe had been influenced by both her maternal grandfather, Julius Rupp, who had been imprisoned for forming a community of freethinkers known as 'The Friends of the Light', and her father, Karl Schmidt. Schmidt had joined the German Social Democratic Workers' Party (SDP) following the slaughter of factory workers in 1848. He introduced his daughter to the inhumane conditions in which they worked, through poetry such as Thomas Hood's 'Song of the Shirt' and

Ferdinand Freiligrath's 'The Dead to the Living'. Her father's political views had significantly influenced her art.

Käthe studied art in Berlin and Munich and attended lectures by the workers' leader August Bebel. In 1891, her brother Konrad went to Berlin to write for the Socialist magazine *Vorwärts* (*Forward*), while she married his best friend, Karl Kollwitz, whom she had known since she was fourteen. Their first son, Hans, was born in 1892 and the following year, inspired by watching the play *The Weavers* by Gerhart Hauptmann, about the 1844 revolt of Silesian weavers, she began work on a series of works lithographs, 'Poverty', 'Death' and 'Conspiracy', and three etchings, 'March of the Weavers', 'Riot' and 'The End'. Thereafter, her work mainly portrayed the poverty and misery of the proletariat.

Whilst her husband and children remained in Berlin, Käthe met Beate Bonus-Jeep, an old friend from art school. The two women called each other by their surnames and took long walks together, reminiscing about the past. In the privacy of their rooms, Bonus-Jeep often posed nude for Käthe; on one occasion, while changing into a cooler dress, Jeep recorded finding 'Schmidt [Käthe] not reading the book, but quietly occupied with watching her'. Käthe claimed that 'although my leaning toward the male sex was dominant, I also felt frequently drawn toward my own sex – an inclination which I could not correctly interpret until much later on'.[24] She went on to explain that 'I believe that bisexuality is almost a necessary factor in artistic production; at any rate, the tinge of masculinity within me helped me in my work'.[25]

Käthe undoubtedly took the same sexual interest in Stan. Stan met Käthe through her husband, and as Käthe was also an artist, a keen hiker and a Socialist, they quickly became friends. According to Jeep, Stan was a 'character who seized her [Käthe's] imagination'. She brought Stan into her circle of friends 'to show her off as if she were an acquisition she had just made … Indeed, Käthe revelled in the sight of this bold and independent young person'. There was certainly much to admire about the fiercely independent Stan. When she suggested that the two of them walk cross-country to Rome – a distance of about 150 miles as the crow flies – Käthe was happy to oblige.

In early May 1907, the pair set off in the evening, to avoid the sun, wearing sturdy shoes, long dresses and rucksacks filled with maps, fruit, candles and matches. Stan also packed her revolver, which she was not shy of brandishing. 'I see that Stan's revolver is necessary,' Käthe wrote to Jeep. 'But I also see the sheer terror and the hurried flight of those who are shown it.' People in some of the villages through which they walked rarely saw strangers and were astonished to see two foreign hikers. They appear to have followed a coastal route, since they went by way of Populonia, a picturesque fortress town overlooking the Mediterranean. Stan and Käthe leant against the watchtower, admiring the beautiful colours bouncing off the sea. Käthe sent Jeep a postcard, explaining that she now looked like leather. 'I have lost at least ten pounds and I don't know who has lost more, Stan or I. Two nights ago we hiked straight through the night, and everything was there – full moon, lightning bugs, and singing locusts.'[26]

Making their way southward and inland through the Chianti countryside, they passed through Pitigliano. Perched on a steep rock rising more than 300 metres out of the sea, it was nicknamed 'Little Jerusalem' due to its large Jewish population. They finally arrived in Rome on June 13th where they were joined by their husbands. All four then went north to stay in a primitive stone cottage used by grape pickers and landscape painters in the fishing village of Fiascherino, on the sea near La Spezia, 30 miles north of Pisa. Stan amazed everyone by leaping from a cliff into the sea.

Soon afterwards, Käthe returned to Berlin. It would be more than a decade before the pair met again, this time in circumstances much less idyllic.

* * *

The second person to arrive in Florence who was to have a major impact on Stan's life was Stephen Haweis (pronounced 'Hoyse'). If the precise nature of Stan's relationship with Käthe Kollwitz – that is, whether or not they were lovers – can only be surmised, in the case of Haweis there was unquestionably a sexual relationship. Born in London and six years Stan's senior, Stephen had married the British artist Mina Loy in 1903. According to the American-born arts patron Mabel Dodge, one of the leading members of English society in Florence, 'Stephen was diminutive, black as a beetle, and very, very, inky.' And Stan – probably for the first time in her life – fell madly in love.[27]

In Stephen's childhood the Haweis family lived in Cheyne Walk, Chelsea, an address with a fine artistic pedigree: J.M.W. Turner, Dante Gabriel Rossetti and James McNeill Whistler had all lived in the street. His father, the Reverend Hugh Reginald Haweis, was rector of St James's Church, Marylebone, and a well-known scholar, author and musician. His mother Mary Elizabeth was the daughter of the artist Thomas Musgrave Joy and an artist herself. Their house was regularly filled with people discussing art, politics and religion; among them the first female barrister Cornelia Sorabji, and the Pre-Raphaelite painters William Holman Hunt, Edward Burne-Jones and Sir John Everett Millais.

Stephen had studied first at Cambridge University but, perhaps influenced by so many artistic luminaries, then decided to follow a career in art. He might also have been influenced by his wife, Mina, the Hampstead-born daughter of a Hungarian Jewish tailor. Escaping a claustrophobic family life with parents who wished nothing more than for her to make a good marriage, Mina had studied at a school for women painters in Munich and then at the Académie Colarossi in Paris. Moving to Paris with his new wife, Stephen used his family connections to meet famous artists such as J. S. Sargent, Augustus John, Eugène Carrière and Auguste Rodin. However, it was Mina who possessed the talent, and Stephen turned to photography instead.

In 1904, Mina's first child Oda was born, only to die of meningitis within the year, plunging the young woman into fits of grief and depression. It was this event that prompted the couple's move to Florence. Mina was pregnant again when the couple arrived in the city. They rented a villa in Arcetri on the city's outskirts. Stephen soon became bored by the isolation, however, and as Mina refused to accompany him, he began to seek out the English-speaking community, meeting Bernhard Berenson and in due course mixing with Stan and her friends. Mabel Dodge, who became a friend of both Mina's and Stephen's, declared that 'Ducie' (as Mina was known) was inches taller than her husband and that the pair were completely mismatched.

Mabel Dodge was aware, too, that Stephen had many affairs while married to Mina, who had become a Christian Scientist and mixed in different circles from her husband. Dodge bought some of Stephen's paintings, telling him he was a genius, although stating in her memoirs that she didn't really like him and couldn't bear to be alone with him. With his long, black hair cut in pageboy style (the style, incidentally, favoured by Stan) and in white linen clothing, 'he used to sit on the parapet after dinner and spread his short fingers nervously on the warm stone, and they looked exactly like a lizard'.[28]

Yet Stephen exuded a strange attraction for women. One of Stephen's conquests, Emily Sayre, who was visiting from India, fell so hopelessly in love with him that when she returned to India she committed suicide. An English lover, Amelia Defries, became so besotted that she begged Stephen to divorce Mina and marry her.

Stan likewise fell under Stephen's spell. Precisely when he began his affair with Stan, and how long it lasted, is unclear. Certainly Mina was aware of it, and was understandably embittered. She wrote in her 1919 poem 'Lion's Jaws' about 'Mrs. Krar Standing Hail – she is not quite a lady', a reference not only to the unladylike behaviour of stealing another woman's husband, but also to her adopted name and, possibly, to her lesbianism.[29] Stephen Haweis wrote several poems for Stan. In one, he speaks of 'Blind but to one another; love, / Those hours were comforting, even transforming' (see Appendix). Another poem, entitled 'For Stan H.K.', alludes to a traumatic event in their relationship – one that haunted Stephen:

> Child of our love whom we destroyed
> through fear, how well are you
> revenged upon me now! Yet you were
> never born, sorrow to know, and it
> is better for you not to be here.
>
> We did not make ourselves this
> tainted world: is every creature born to
> be preserved? And every blade made
> straight which had been curved
> Fair flags these are which never
> were unfinished [unfurled?]
>
> Child, you were part of Moloch's sacrifice,
> to pander to the mob of
> saints who sang praise for a
> virgin's illegitimate son, which
> their enthusiastic church bells
> sang the music for their
> seventh day ????? [last word illegible].[30]

The poem clearly refers to a child conceived together, one that was, apparently, aborted. Whatever the truth behind the poem, there is no doubt that Stan was devastated when her relationship with Stephen ended. According to Dodge, when he became bored with her, Stephen simply moved on to his next victim. Dodge, with whom Stan often stayed at Villa Curonia, described finding Stan one night in her white pyjamas staring out of the window, eyes wide and frightened, so she took her to her bed. She was 'cold and her hands were chilly and damp'. Stan reached over and said: "Oh love me. Maybe if you could love enough it would not hurt so."[31] Dodge, who later documented her lesbian fantasies in her autobiography, *Intimate Memories* (1933), replied that she could not.

Nor could Dr Krayl love her in the same way anymore. The German may have been tolerance itself, but even his tolerance had limits. According to Jeep, Stan's infidelities came close to driving him mad and he began exhibiting strange behaviour, such as accosting friends in the street to feel their pulses. Eventually, he turned against his errant wife 'in an openly inimical manner' and their strained marriage was approaching the breaking point.

Chapter Four

Mrs Harding, I Presume?

In the summer of 1911, Stan Harding travelled to China. The ostensible reason for her voyage was to visit with her brother, Harold. She was also fleeing Florence, with its claustrophobic expatriate community, her unhappy love affair with Stephen Haweis, her (probable) abortion, and her disintegrating marriage. But she was, as usual, also looking for adventure. In 1911, with China convulsed by civil war, Stan spied an opportunity. As Bonus-Jeep put it, 'There was chaos and a revolution. How many old works of art would be damaged or would disappear? If only one could buy some of them and add them to one's fortune!' So it was, according to Jeep, that Stan, rather quixotically, set off in search of endangered Chinese artefacts.

Arriving in Hong Kong Harbour during the monsoon, Stan sat on deck lashed to a rail as the ship lurched heavily. Harold, recently married to the daughter of an English missionary, was based in Yichang in Hubei province on the northern bank of the Yangtze River. Although he spoke and understood Mandarin extremely well, Harold had a penchant for speaking the coarsest version. Throughout his career, he gained a reputation for being 'rude, hot-headed, undisciplined and insubordinate'; later he became a Buddhist, a vegetarian and, in the opinion of one observer, an 'eccentric crank'.[1] He hosted dinner parties at which his guests were forced to race cockroaches across the table. When an alarm clock sounded at 10 o'clock, he promptly retired to bed, leaving his guests – no doubt to their relief – to their own devices. In hot weather he removed his trousers in his office and received callers without putting them on again.[2]

Stan, it seems, saw nothing of this strange behaviour, but, soon tiring of the 'office-bound, golf-linked, black-tied round of a British Consul', ventured off alone on a sketching tour of the Upper Yangtze.[3] The voyage shows both her independence and her foolhardiness. Her first trip was as a passenger on a cargo junk with a crew of 125, where, 'sketchbook in hand and curled up in the hollow of a coil of bamboo hawser, she watched the primitive navigation and listened to ancient songs'.[4] She then bought her own local Hongchuan boat (red boat) in order to travel further upriver, presumably in search of imperilled artworks.

The Yangtze-Kiang (Great River) emerges from the Tibetan peaks at 17,000 ft, slashes through gorges for 120 miles before continuing for almost 4,000 miles. In parts it can be extremely dangerous. When Stan and her crew of three approached the Nuikan rapids, she left the boat to sketch. Suddenly her sketching was interrupted when the boat became engulfed by a bubbling rapid, capsizing with her crew and possessions – including some of the artistic treasures she had liberated. The boat spun twice around 'like a top' and overturned. Stan stood on the riverbank, paintbrush in hand, stunned by the sudden violence.[5] She was alone, without money, and miles from any help. Fortunately, the accident had been observed, and another Hongchuan bobbed valiantly through the rapids. A tall, slim, white man in Western clothes leapt ashore, removed his Panama hat, and said: 'Mrs Harding, I presume?'[6] It was Albert W. Pontius, the US Consul in Chungking, who was on holiday recuperating after an illness. Harold had asked him to keep an eye out for his sister and, when Pontius heard she was upstream, he agreed to pay his crew a bonus if they could catch up with her.

After this unfortunate incident, Stan returned to Yichang, only to find that Harold had been sent 600 miles away to Foochow on the Min River in Fukien province, a coastal city midway between Hong Kong and Shanghai.

Contrary to Jeep's assertion, Stan claimed that until she arrived back in Yichang and found the British consulate dismantled, she was unaware of the chaos and revolution in China. As she was travelling by boat down the Yangtze River she was to pass through Hankow, which was one of the three sister cities at the centre of the revolution. The civil war began in earnest on the 10th of October in Wuchang in Hubei province, and within a few weeks fifteen other provinces followed suit. The revolution was motivated by the Qing's government's inability to prevent foreign intervention and anger at the corruption of the ethnic minority, the Manchus, who occupied the seat of government. After years of discontent, the majority of Han Chinese rebelled in an outburst of violence. In a letter to Mabel Dodge, Stan explained that Hankow was in a 'haze of smoke'. She was so excited she persuaded a couple of crew on the boat to take her to see the fighting. 'We kept about fifty yards behind the firing line' as they watched the rebels drive the loyalists back.[7] Approximately 5,000 people were killed in the ensuing battle.

When she arrived in Foochow, the wealthier classes had already fled and the city was half-empty. She watched from the consulate window as streams of poorer refugees left the city, some carried in sedan chairs, others dragging their possessions in a variety of carts. Despite the chaos around her, Stan felt awkward and superfluous living with her newly wedded brother and his wife, so against his advice, she rented a house in the native quarter. She took with her a teacher of Mandarin and two young boy servants.

On the 11th of November 1911, the Manchu surrendered in Foochow and Stan witnessed the consequent slaughter, looting and mayhem. She heard that many Manchu women were swallowing fatal amounts of opium or leaping down wells to avoid being raped by the revolutionaries. However, as a white woman she was relatively safe and continued to walk and sketch daily. When the rains came she had to be carried in a sedan chair, the coolies wading in water up to their knees. Her house became damp and cold, with mushrooms sprouting under her bed and table.

To while away the long, monotonous hours, she read voraciously and discovered the Taoist philosopher Chuang Tzu. By the spring of 1912, to relieve her boredom, she decided to rent a houseboat and take a trip up the River Min. Stan was to make many more sketching tours and, not deterred by her earlier experience, even returned to the Yangtze gorges. On her river journeys she shocked some American missionaries by travelling with her *Meyu Kudzedi* (not-wearing-pants) boat crew. She justified travelling this way by explaining that if they did wear pants they would probably get pneumonia in their wet clothes, as they were continually in and out of the water.

* * *

Stan left China in early 1913. When in later years she was asked if she had ever been happy, she replied: 'Yes, at times ecstatically, but there have also been other days when life was like a thin soup with a hair in it.'[8] Her time there, she admitted, was the happiest of her life – a strange admission in the light of some of the horrific events she had witnessed in Foochow.

Stan was 28 when she began her journey back to Florence. She took a four-month detour via India, spending most of that time in Madura, near the country's southern tip. It was there that she discovered one of the great loves of her life: Devadasi Attam, a school of ritual temple dancing derived from Hindu mythology and involving girls who devoted their lives to the gods. However, since the Muslims had conquered South India in the 16th century, this form of dance had been in decline, and the temple girls became synonymous with prostitutes. Although

Devadasi Attam was revived in the early 19th century, the Christian missionaries, shocked by images of temple prostitution, were determined to have it banned. Stan, however, saw only beauty and drama in this exquisite dance form and persuaded Averdaiappa Pillai, of the temple Nattuyvan, to take her on as a pupil.

When she arrived back in Florence in 1913, Stan was dressed in white clothing 'made by Chinese hands' and, according to Bonus-Jeep, 'looked ravishing'. Karl had played the part of a dutiful husband during her long absence, even sending a pair of sandals to China when she requested them. But when Stan returned to the troubled marital home she discovered that her husband had not prepared her studio and sleeping quarters for her; they were inches deep in dust and 'the mess she had left there on her departure'. A furious Stan complained about her husband to an unsympathetic Bonus-Jeep. In Berlin, Käthe Kollwitz, learning of the state of affairs, lamented how Stan's 'selfishness and coldness' had ground down the relationship and destroyed Dr Krayl, and felt that 'Now a radical separation seems to me to be the best solution'.

Stan noticed that Mabel Dodge had continued to collect exotic friends, including an Indian mystic, Swami Paramananda, whom she sponsored to visit her in Florence to teach the Vedanta philosophy of self-realisation. Another was John Reed, the American Socialist journalist. In 1913, the 26-year-old, Harvard-educated Reed – 'handsome outside and beautiful inside', according to a friend[9] – was beginning to make a name for himself as a journalistic firebrand. His central passion in life, as a right-wing commentator would acerbically (and somewhat unfairly) remark, was 'an inordinate desire to be arrested'.[10]

Reed had met Dodge in the United States in the spring of 1913 when they attended a rally supporting striking silk workers in Paterson, New Jersey. Mabel swept him off to Europe that summer, consummated their affair in Paris, then brought him to Florence. It was perhaps inevitable that Stan, too, would be attracted to the young American writer. As Dodge recalled in her memoirs: 'Stan Krayl padded up to the villa and told him about the Maremma – the long stretches of beach – the sea – and only birds for company.' Dodge's friend Mary Foote told her later that Stan ran off with Reed right under her eyes. Dodge replied that 'if this is so, it was so painful to me that I have completely forgotten it'.[11]

Reed was probably attracted by Stan's enthusiasm for Italian art and architecture – passions not shared by Mabel, who detested his delight in what she called 'the things men have done' and jealously resented 'seeing his eyes dilate with some other magic than my own'.[12] It was fortunate for Stan that Mabel – unable to bear the thought of Reed enjoying an opera or a fresco – was unaware of her lover's dalliance.

But it was to Mabel Dodge, and not Stan, that Reed was ultimately devoted. In his poem 'Florence', Reed saw the city 'choked with the crowding-up, struggling souls of the dead', and appealed to her: 'O let us shake off this smothering silly death, let us go away, / My dearest Mabel! What are we living things doing here?'[13]

* * *

Florence was soon to be drained of many 'living things'. The onset of war in the summer of 1914 foreshadowed the end the charmed life of garden parties, summer balls and romantic flirtations. Some Italian members of the Florentine avant-garde had been eagerly anticipating the onset of conflict. The journalist Giovanni Papini exulted in 1913: 'The future needs blood. It needs human victims, butchery. Internal war, and foreign war, revolution and conquest: that is history'.[14] But the Italian people and their politicians remained more cautious and ambivalent. Though a member of the Triple Alliance, Italy declared its neutrality in August, but by the following May, in the belief that an Entente victory would bring favourable territorial gains, she declared war on Austria-Hungary, and then the following year on Germany.

By the outbreak of the Great War, Mabel Dodge and John Reed had already left Florence for New York, and Stephen Haweis (after meditating with Swami Paramananda and indulging in further love affairs) for Fiji, Tahiti and Australia. Somewhere along the way, he cabled Mina to ask for a divorce. In 1916, after an affair with the Italian Futurist poet Filippo Marinetti, Mina moved to New York and soon afterwards, in Mexico, married a boxer and poet named Arthur Cravan. Karl, too, was gone. Humiliated by Stan's behaviour, he was back in Germany before the onset of the war, and was serving with the German Medical Corps.

Other members of the Florentine community likewise departed. Gordon Craig left Florence for Rome and then Rapallo. Berenson at first gave up his active social life, sequestering himself in I Tatti and writing a book on Venetian art in America. Accused by the authorities of being a German spy, he dropped the Teutonic 'h' from his forename in order to allay suspicion, becoming Bernard rather than Bernhard.[15]

Life was no easier for Stan, who had a German passport, a German surname, and a German husband. According to Käthe Kollwitz, she was 'so suspect that she was threatened with internment'. Her situation eased somewhat when she became acquainted with two figures of influence in

Florence. The first was Herbert Trench, an Irish-born, Oxford-educated poet and former artistic director of the Haymarket Theatre in London. For the past few years he had lived near Florence in Settignano, in the Villa Viviani, the ancient house where, a quarter-century earlier, Mark Twain had completed *Tom Sawyer Abroad* and started *Pudd'nhead Wilson*. During the war, Trench continued writing poetry – including 'Ode from Italy in Time of War' – and served as vice-chairman of the Istituto Britannico, a newly founded organisation, funded by the British government, that sought to promote good relations between Britain and Italy.

The second person of influence was Algar Labouchere Thorold, an Old Etonian journalist and writer who had served on the staff of *Truth*, written for the *Edinburgh Review*, and edited books on mysticism and religious philosophy. After joining the Foreign Office during the war he was sent to Italy as the head of Britain's Propaganda Mission. The Great War was the first war in history in which governments realised the efficacy of propaganda, described by one German at the time as 'more powerful than the navy, more dangerous than the army'.[16] Journalists, writers and artists were all called upon to participate in the propaganda effort against the Germans.

Stan's acquaintance with both Trench and Thorold raises the question of whether or not she was employed or used unofficially by either the Propaganda Mission or the Istituto Britannico during the first years of the war. It certainly would have made sense for the government to utilise the artistic and literary talents of someone who knew Florence well, and spoke Italian fluently. If so, it would not be the last time that the British government interested itself in what Stan had to offer.

Whatever her relations with British Intelligence or the Propaganda Mission might have been, Stan had plans that did not involve either spying or Italy. In a somewhat quixotic career move, she was thinking of returning to India and began making plans to leave Florence in 1917 to continue her study of Devadasi Attam. However, she found that her German passport did not allow her to travel to India, and therefore she would need to regain her British citizenship. To do this she would have to go to the Passport Office of the British Embassy in Rome.

Stan duly went to Rome and while visiting the British Embassy, she later admitted, 'a certain proposition' was made to her.[17] British Intelligence was extremely active in Italy during the war, in particular through the British Military Mission, part of Vernon Kell's MI5. The British ambassador to Italy, Sir Rennell Rodd, feared that Italy, like Russia, would witness a revolution and withdraw from the war.[18] MI5 therefore set up a Rome station, headed by Sir Samuel Hoare, to run a network of a hundred agents dedicated to ensuring that the Italian government stayed the course in the war (one of them was an ex-Socialist journalist named Benito Mussolini, who published pro-war propaganda and sent his men into the streets to beat peace protesters into submission).[19]

The 'proposition' made to Stan undoubtedly arose from Hoare's team of agents, many of whose names, as she would later reveal, were known to her. She was asked if, once in Germany, she would be willing to 'put my information at the disposal of the Foreign Office'.[20] She later claimed adamantly that nothing came of this arrangement, and that she did not serve as a British agent in Berlin. But this association with the British Military Mission in Rome would return to haunt her.

Towards the end of the war, Stan received a letter from Karl via friends in Switzerland, asking her for a divorce because he wished to remarry. He suggested that the divorce could be achieved through the offices of the Swiss consul. Stan agreed to the divorce, but thought it would take too much time if conducted through the Swiss. Anxious to return to India as soon as possible, she conceived another plan.

* * *

'Now I have something proper to write to you,' Käthe Kollwitz wrote from Berlin to her friend Bonus-Jeep in the autumn of 1918. 'Where do I start? Straight with the scoop: Stan is here! The doorbell rang. I opened. Although she was standing against the light, and, although I had not seen her for eleven years, I recognised her immediately. She came in without a word and we fell upon each other's neck, and then she was inside, laughing and crying.'

Stan Harding had entered Berlin at the end of September 1918, almost two months before the Armistice was signed. She came by way of Berne in Switzerland, where a friend of her brother's, an Englishman whom she had met at the Swiss Consulate in Peking, asked her to work in Germany for British Intelligence. Afraid of compromising her divorce, she turned down the request. Other members of the consulate tried to persuade her not to pursue her travels into Germany: it was clear that Germany was losing the war, and famine and devastation loomed. They also explained that German citizens were allowed to enter the country; once in, however, they were not allowed to leave. Although Germany's Supreme Army Command had called for an armistice in September, it was possible that war would continue indefinitely, in which case she would be trapped inside an enemy nation.

Stan was not to be deterred. She followed up an introduction to Frederic Sefton Delmer,* a talented linguist who had left Australia in 1900 to take up a post as English professor at the University of Königsberg in East Prussia.* He eventually moved on to teach at the University of Berlin, publishing on English literature in the German language. During the war he was interned at the British Ruhleben prisoner-of-war camp on the outskirts of Berlin, where he was fondly remembered for founding the camp's Literary and Debating Society. Repatriated to England in 1917, he returned to Europe as correspondent for *The Daily News*. He tried to dissuade Stan from entering Germany but, realising she was determined, offered helpful advice.

Arriving in Berlin, Stan immediately ran into difficulties. She was suspected of being an Italian spy and, according to Käthe whom she looked up soon after arriving in the city, was 'seriously questioned' by the German authorities. Käthe was impressed by the friend whom she had not seen in eleven years. 'She is no longer the old Stan who used to live on 30 centesimi per day, she has become a lady but it suits her well.' She was also awed by Stan's abilities to insinuate herself into the corridors of power: 'People even compete now to smooth her way into all sorts of places.'

The war years had not been quite so kind for Käthe. Both her sons had joined the Army at the beginning of the war, and one was killed soon after. As a result, she was a confirmed pacifist, adamant that the war must end: 'Enough of death,' she wrote, 'not one more man must fall.'[21] She remained a Socialist and maintained connections with the Socialist Democratic Party via both her husband and her brother, the latter of whom had once been acquainted with Friedrich Engels. Käthe was also friends with the Socialist artists, Hans Baluschek and Martin Brandenburg. It may have been through Käthe that Stan heard about plans for a plot to overthrow Kaiser Wilhelm II. In any case, she was invited to attend a secret meeting to discuss the subject. 'Stan is everywhere,' wrote Käthe, 'in the midst of it all …'

November 1918 was a crucial month for Stan. The Kaiser abdicated on the 9th, and the Armistice was announced two days later. Shortly afterwards, she learned that her father had died in Bristol. Then she literally bumped into Frederic Sefton Delmer in the street in Berlin. He was one of the first journalists to arrive in the city after the Armistice was declared, and began paying her for newsworthy information.

* Not to be confused with his son of the same name who also was a journalist.

Whether due to a sluggish German bureaucracy – understandably in a chaotic state at the end of the war – or because of the exciting prospect of earning a living as a journalist, Stan did not immediately pursue her divorce. Käthe believed it was a 'sense of adventure' that kept her in the turbulent city. So she remained in Berlin, taking a room in a boarding house and witnessing the violent upheavals following the Armistice. Käthe continued to be enthralled by her friend's daring exploits in the war-torn streets: 'She isn't shy of any exertion,' she wrote to Jeep, 'of machine-gun fire, not even of the cold.' She added: 'It's a miracle she didn't die during the Spartacus [League] week.'

And it was into this penurious and uncertain life that, one day in the early spring of 1919, strode the confident and beautiful Marguerite Harrison.

Chapter Five

The Convergence of the Twain

At the age of 34, Stan Harding was well-educated, slender, elegant, intense, artistic – and prone to exaggeration. She also possessed a list of contacts and admirers that rivalled Marguerite's own.

When Marguerite first met Stan in the spring of 1919, Stan was living in a boarding house bedroom that Marguerite described as 'poorly furnished, under-heated and dreary beyond description.' If the accommodation did not impress, its occupant did. Marguerite's immediate impression was of 'a frail-looking woman, with delicate features, hair close-clipped like a man's and the most engaging smile'. Marguerite, as many others had, immediately took to her, and was concerned about Stan's strained circumstances.

Stan, by her own account to Marguerite, had journeyed to Berlin to secure a divorce and had been a correspondent for a London newspaper, before being dropped for obscure reasons. She said that she was trying to be retained by another newspaper and was waiting to hear the outcome. The Englishwoman was in dire need of nourishing food, and so the American began to take her out for meals. Eventually, as Marguerite would write in one of her autobiographies, she invited Stan, with the idea of saving expenses, to share her room at the Hotel Adlon.

It was understandable that these two talented women had struck up a friendship. In the aftermath of the war, it was unusual for ladies to travel unaccompanied, especially to a dangerous city such as Berlin. Opportunities for female companionship were limited as there were very few women from the Entente Powers in Germany at this time, except those married to Germans. Marguerite discovered that most of these were expatriate Americans, sympathetic to Germany and prone to blaming the Allies for provoking the war.

Was the motivation behind Marguerite's invitation to share a hotel room merely, as she later claimed, an economic one? With her generosity, Marguerite clearly made a favourable impression on Stan, who was drawn, as her experiences with Käthe Kollwitz and Mabel Dodge reveal, to independent, capable women. The coolly intelligent Marguerite was certainly captivated by the force of Stan's energy. Conversely, Stan might have been sexually attracted to Marguerite, who evidently had gained Stan's trust very quickly. According to Marguerite, Stan shared many confidences with her, such as her voyage up the Yangtze River, when she had, as she somewhat lavishly claimed, 'collected a vast amount of information about local conditions for the British government'. According to Marguerite, Stan also boasted that she had joined the British Intelligence Service in 1918 and had travelled to Germany via Switzerland to gather military information.

Marguerite was inclined not to dismiss outright this latter story. As Stan was still married to a German, her papers enabled her to easily enter that country in wartime. Also, Stan was often seen in the company of British officers. Indeed, she later insisted that Marguerite accompany her to meet General John Spencer Ewart, head of the British Military Mission, to recount a story Marguerite had overheard about Lord Kitchener's death. The story concerned a 'very pretty' German woman whom Marguerite had encountered at the Hotel Adlon. The woman, the wife of an English naval officer, had a small apartment where she entertained Allied officers with her gramophone and a seemingly endless supply of sparkling wine. Suspecting the German of trying to glean information from her well-lubricated visitors, Marguerite's American Intelligence contact, Colonel Bouvier, instructed her to befriend the wife – which she was able to do by catering to the woman's love of chocolate and American coffee.

Marguerite was charged with making sure that the conversation at these parties did not 'drift into dangerous channels, and, if possible, to prevent her guests who usually took more Sekt than was good for them from making indiscreet remarks'. She became a fixture at the soirées, surreptitiously emptying her own glasses of Sekt into a potted plant and staying on the alert for loose talk.

The story that Marguerite repeated to General Spencer Ewart concerned an event in London during the war. By her own admission the German woman had, over dinner in a restaurant, learned from an indiscreet friend of her husband, another British naval officer, information about the presumed destination of Lord Kitchener's armoured cruiser, HMS *Hampshire*. Later that evening she stopped in to visit some Anglo-Germans, one of whom, after hearing the information, pressed a one-hundred-pound bank draft into her palm and said, 'Thank you – you have done us a great service.'

Kitchener had died on June 5th 1916, when HMS *Hampshire* struck a mine and sank in the North Sea. Marguerite claimed not to know whether the woman's story was true, but the underlying true cause of

Kitchener's death – 'one of the great unresolved mysteries of the World War,' as Marguerite pointed out – was something that Stan evidently wished the British officials to hear from Marguerite's lips.

Nevertheless, Marguerite was curious as to the real reason why her new friend had come to Berlin. Was it primarily to procure a divorce? Was Stan really a spy? Did she agree to share Marguerite's hotel room for reasons of economy, or was there a different motivation? If Marguerite sensed that Stan was attracted to her, she may well have been willing – in the age-old way of spies – to dangle her charms to gain information. Whatever the truth, their meeting and subsequent friendship would extend well beyond Berlin and cause serious repercussions in both of their lives.

* * *

Marguerite had been in Berlin for two months when, on the 3rd of March 1919, she received information warning that the Council of Workmen's and Soldiers' was organising a general transport strike, with the aim of bringing down the government. Martial law was declared and the streets of Berlin filled with the troops of Gustav Noske's Freikorps. On the 5th, the sailors of the People's Naval Division joined with the Spartacists. All manner of vehicles appeared to transport demonstrators to Alexanderplatz in the heart of the city. At first, groups merely huddled in corners, listening to speakers. Then the atmosphere changed dramatically as Marguerite, watching from a shop doorway, saw the Freikorps open fire on the crowds.

The latest uprising had begun and the streets around Alexanderplatz were engulfed in fighting as the Freikorps manoeuvered to cordon the area off. Marguerite recounted that she 'felt as if the world had stopped'.

It took four days of fighting for the government to control of Alexanderplatz and the insurgents withdrew to Lichtenberg, an area near the Frankfurter Allee in southeast Berlin. By now, the Council wanted to call off the strike, but the Communists refused. Harry Kessler noted in his diary that executions continued around Lichtenberg. And yet, 'apart from a glimpse of numerous steel-helmeted patrols and a few barbed-wire entanglements, none of this leaves any mark on the West [of the city]', he wrote, 'but the brutalities and the shootings defile the moral atmosphere.'[1]

Jumping a queue of some five hundred people, Marguerite managed to acquire a press card from the *Kommandantur*, the headquarters of the volunteer troops, that allowed her to enter the cordoned-off areas of the city. Setting out to Alexanderplatz with her guide, she was soon witnessing the heavy fighting first-hand. In addition to the casualties of the combatants, Marguerite observed that: 'The women had the peculiar waxy pallor that comes from insufficient nourishment and low vitality. The children were pitiful'.

As the fighting worsened, Marguerite's guide urged her to leave. Walking down Landsberger Strasse through the aftermath of a battle, she saw a woman, deathly white, leaning against a lamp-post. Gently encouraged to talk, the bewildered woman explained to Marguerite that her husband was fighting with the Spartacists and had not been heard of for three days; she had left her baby of four months in the house as he was crying all the time, desperate for milk. As they spoke, Spartacists began running past so Marguerite and her guide retreated, walking the six miles back to Alexanderplatz, arriving only minutes before curfew. To their surprise, the underground railway, operated by the military, was working and they were able to gain the relative safety of West Berlin.

By the end of March 12th the main battles were over. A few days later Count Kessler wrote of being haunted by witnessing the execution of 24 sailors in the courtyard of a house in Französische Strasse, only a couple of blocks from Unter den Linden. It appeared, he wrote, to have been 'sheer gruesome murder: the sailors simply came to collect money from the paymaster's office'.[2] On the 16th of March, Kessler witnessed another gruesome event in the vicinity of the Hotel Eden. A lieutenant shot a soldier who did not have his identity papers on him and who gave an impertinent answer. The man's comrades, 'whether from grief or fury, wept'.[3] Marguerite, too, witnessed horrific sights, such as 'two young boys whose eyes had been gouged out by Volunteer troops as they lay helpless on the ground'.

Elsewhere in Berlin, however, the public continued to shop and drink in cafés, while at least twenty theatres remained open. Fancy dress balls, horse racing, boxing at the Berlin Ice Palace and athletics, swimming, rowing and boating competitions: all continued to be enjoyed in the city. In the surreal world around Unter den Linden, the only difference was that beer was served in the intervals of theatre and opera performances, along with black bread sandwiches wrapped in newspaper. Despite the fighting in the streets, the music halls remained crowded and every restaurant offered a cabaret, as it had during the first Spartacist uprising two months previously.

Of the continual strikes that broke out during six months that Marguerite was to spend in Berlin, in only one of them did the working and middle classes join together in retaliation. In Königsberg that April, trams, trains, electricity and water supplies were cut, so shops, cafés and restaurants were boarded up. Food was unavailable, pharmacies closed, hospitals refused to admit or care for patients, and physicians and nurses took a holiday. Marguerite wrote that she wore her fur coat in the hotel because she was so cold, and she dined by candlelight. As with any modern city, collapse would soon come in the absence of basic services. However, this dispute was settled within 48 hours and Berlin returned to its barely managed chaos.

* * *

Germany was ever alert to news of the negotiations being conducted at the Paris Peace Conference that had begun on the 18th of January 1919. Diplomats representing more than 30 countries were in attendance; Bolshevik Russia and Germany had not been invited. In February 1919, Wilson had persuaded delegates to the Conference to endorse the foundation of a League of Nations as an integral part of the Peace Treaty. However, he was less successful in gaining a consensus allowing Bolshevik Russia to attend the conference. Prime Ministers Georges Clemenceau of France and Vittorio Orlando of Italy were adamantly opposed; David Lloyd George was in favour, although the British Secretary of State for War, Winston Churchill, told Lloyd George that 'one might as well legalise sodomy as recognise the Bolsheviks.'[4] Churchill, in the meantime, was waging his own war with the Communists on Russian soil through backing the White Armies in the then raging civil war there.

As details of the Treaty of Versailles (Treaty of Peace between the Allied and Associated Powers and Germany) began to leak from Paris in the early months of 1919 there was uncertainty and rising dismay in Germany. At the time of the Armistice, the country had embraced Wilson's Fourteen Points (issued in January 1918) which, *inter alia*, called for policies of self-determination, free trade and transparent treaties between nations. But now rumours circulated that Germany (and her allies) were to pay a harsh price for losing the war.

Berliners were now becoming increasingly angry toward the Allies, and the Americans in particular. Professor Friedrich Archenhold, an astronomer and director of Berlin's Treptow Observatory, regularly took coffee with Marguerite at the Hotel Adlon. One day in April he informed her that he would be unable to talk to her again, as he was involved in urging loyal Germans not to speak to Americans unless President Wilson upheld his Fourteen Points at the Paris Peace Conference. Wilsonian idealism had become a benchmark and any shortcoming in fulfilling its aims were seen by the Germans as an American failure. When Marguerite passed Archenhold in the hotel corridor a few days later he 'laid his finger on his lips with a cryptic gesture' and passed by. Most Germans did not take such a stance, but when Marguerite attended a concert by the Berlin Philharmonic Orchestra, conducted by Richard Strauss, she approached him after the concert and Strauss told her that he didn't care to discuss matters with any American. 'Our future is our own. America has boycotted German artists during the war, but it takes two to play the same game. I hope that you will never hear a note of my compositions again in your accursed country.'[5]

In April, the MID instructed Marguerite to visit the Second Polish Republic and report on the political situation and sentiments of the people. On Armistice Day, Jósef Piłsudski had declared Poland's independence, and the Poles disarmed any Germans on their territory and claimed the province of Posen (part of Germany), Cracow (part of Austria) and sections of Russian Poland. The Poles also wanted to include Upper Silesia and its coal mines, along with land bordering the Vistula River, to give them access to the Baltic. If this was agreed, Germany would be split into two, separating East from West Prussia; if not, Poland would remain a vulnerable inland country.

Marguerite travelled to Danzig (present-day Gdańsk) which, although historically part of Poland, had been part of the Kingdom of Prussia (and subsequently of the German Empire) since 1815. Around 5% of the population was Polish Catholic, the remainder German Protestants. Poles had been prohibited under Bismarck from buying land, which meant the Polish Corridor – the land that would give them access to the sea – was inhabited by German landlords. Danzig might have been overwhelmingly populated by Germans, but Marguerite found other towns in the region in which it was difficult to distinguish Polish Catholics from Protestant Germans – a demographic, she rightly concluded, that would prove problematic in the tricky road towards self-determination.

In Danzig, Marguerite met General Otto von Below, brother of Hans and husband of her American friend in Berlin. Von Below was in command of the Freikorps that formed part of the OstGrenze Schutz volunteer force, with units stretching from Danzig to the southern borders of Upper Silesia. The force had been organised by diehard imperialists, Generals Max Hoffmann and Wilhelm Groener, who were openly contemptuous of the Weimar government and who acted as if the war had not ended. Later, these generals would seriously consider rejecting the

Treaty of Versailles and seceding the eastern provinces from the rest of Germany.

Marguerite returned to Berlin with an abundance of information for the MID. Colonel Bouvier ordered her to report immediately in person to the American Chief of Intelligence in Europe, General Dennis Edward Nolan, in Trier, a German city on the Moselle River near the Luxembourg border. As well as gathering information from American agents all over Europe to feed back to the American peace delegation, Nolan served on the subcommittee that had drafted the terms for German disarmament.

Before setting off to Trier, Marguerite returned briefly to the Hotel Adlon. There, Stan told Marguerite that she would remain in Germany to obtain a divorce in order to regain her British passport. She then planned to return to London, take up interior decoration, and write a book about China which she would illustrate with her paintings. 'I admired her courage and her sportsmanship, her keen mind and her independence of thought,' Marguerite explained, 'although I did not share her apparent sympathy for the extreme leftist radicals of Germany.'

Before leaving the hotel, Marguerite tore up some carbon paper relating to notes she had made for Colonel Bouvier and threw them into the waste-paper basket. The notes, she later wrote, 'would not have been intelligible to the average person … but anyone familiar with Intelligence work might have seen that they were part of an official report'. This carelessness is perplexing given that she, like Ernest Tennant, must have known that her room in the Adlon was under constant surveillance and any intelligence information so carelessly discarded would have fallen into the hands of spies almost immediately. However, according to Marguerite, the carbon papers were probably discovered by Stan, who pieced them together and then realised that her American room-mate was a spy.

When Marguerite returned to the Hotel Adlon 36 hours later, Stan was there to greet her 'with an announcement that took my breath away'. The frail-looking English woman suggested that she work for Marguerite, and requested payment for any information she provided. Somewhat at a loss, Marguerite then spoke to Colonel Bouvier, whose advice was that the Englishwoman must be kept on-board, if only to prevent her from making trouble. Despite this arrangement, Stan would always maintain that she did not know at this time that Marguerite was working as a secret agent and believed her to be merely a journalist attached to *The Baltimore Sun*. She also would claim that the only payment she received from Marguerite was for information destined for *The Baltimore Sun*.

* * *

A few weeks after Marguerite's report to General Nolan in Trier she was sent on a mission to Lithuania. In the fourteenth century, Lithuania had been the largest country in Europe, its borders extending into Belarus, Ukraine, Poland and Russia. By 1918, Lithuania, like Poland, had been incorporated into the Russian and Prussian empires. Subsequent to the Armistice, she had declared herself, in February 1918, an independent nation.

On arrival in the capital, Kovno, in May, Marguerite stayed in the Hotel Metropole. Despite the hotel's pre-war first-class reputation, the conditions were basic and far worse than she had endured back in Berlin. There were no sheets, no towels, no plumbing, no heating and bedbugs galore.

Her contact there was Madame de Turcinovicz, an American married to a Lithuanian. She was the Minister for Charities in the new Lithuanian Cabinet and Marguerite had met her earlier in Berlin when she had come the to enlist the aid of Lieutenant-Colonel Edward W. Ryan of the American Red Cross Commission. Despite Lithuania's independence, the German military was still very much in evidence in the country, so Marguerite had been sent by the MID to gather intelligence on German intentions.

On the 7th of May, the final draft of the Peace Treaty, comprising 200 pages containing some 440 articles, was received by the German delegation. When its contents leaked out, German soldiers showed their discontent by demonstrating at the Allied missions in Kovno. Marguerite reported that many foreigners staying in the hotel were afraid of venturing outside. Not she: Marguerite decided to attend a meeting in the municipal theatre, posing as the wife of a German officer. Her report detailed the anger and anti-Semitism that she witnessed amongst Germans.

When Marguerite returned to Berlin, foreigners from the Entente nations, as in Kovno, were being insulted on the streets, so machine guns were placed outside the Adlon for the protection of the Entente guests. A few days later, on the 9th of May, Berlin was again in turmoil as the trial of the murderers of the Spartacist leaders Karl Liebknecht and Rosa Luxemburg began. Marguerite was unable to get the special pass required to attend the trial, but with her usual guile, and a supply of American cigarettes to bribe the guards, she gained her way into the spectators' gallery, where she witnessed the accused, Lieutenant Kurt Vogel and Captain Lieutenant Heinz von Pflugk-Hartung, wearing uniforms covered in medals and giving the impression they were attending a wedding party rather than a murder trial. Pflugk-Hartung was acquitted, while Vogel was sentenced to two years and four months' imprisonment. He was never to see a cell, as he was allowed to escape, fleeing to Holland on false identity papers. Concurrently, Marguerite began to investigate a prominent nationalistic movement, the League of German Men and Women for the Defence of the Personal Liberty and Rights of Wilhelm II. Founded in 1918, it had rapidly gained a membership of approximately a million and was of interest to the MID. Marguerite joined the League under an assumed name and reported her findings back to the MID.

* * *

There was uncertainty, fear and anger leading up to the signing of the Treaty of Versailles. The Allies had declared in June that hostilities would resume if the Germans refused to sign. By agreeing to the terms, Germany would, essentially, bear total responsibility for the war, cede home territory, relinquish her colonies, disarm, and pay heavy reparations to the Entente Powers. The government baulked, but, facing a threatened invasion within 48 hours, finally signed on June 28th, 1919. Marguerite and other foreign correspondents (and spies) in Germany were no doubt relieved as they might have faced increased hostility within a perilous political structure. For Marguerite, now physically and mentally exhausted after seven months of intense activity for the MID in addition to her journalistic duties for *The Baltimore Sun*, there was one final mission to undertake before she was to return to the United States.

The American cartoonist, Robert Minor, had been arrested and imprisoned in a military prison in Coblenz, accused of spreading Communist propaganda among American and British troops still stationed in Europe. Since Marguerite had met Minor in Weimar in February, she was tasked to pose as a Socialist and to visit him in prison so as to gather evidence against him. Despite having previously stated that she would not 'pose as either a Socialist or reactionary and thus get information under false pretences', and claiming that she had 'contempt for such tactics'; Marguerite now agreed to do so.

The 34-year-old Minor had until recently been the highest paid cartoonist in America, first as chief editorial cartoonist on the St. Louis *Post-Dispatch* and then on the New York *Evening World*. He had been converted to Socialism in 1903 by a doctor who treated him for his increasing deafness. In 1907, Minor joined the Socialist Party of America, supporting women's suffrage and first opposing the war in Europe and then America's participation. A contributor of radical cartoons to *The Masses*, he then journey to Russia in 1918 on behalf of the *New York Call* and subsequently covered the Spartacist Uprising in Berlin.

When Marguerite visited him in prison, Minor protested his innocence of spreading propaganda, but did admit to being a Communist. Marguerite was able to winkle out of him not only the name of the leaflet printer in Düsseldorf, but also that of his female accomplice, Meta Fillip. Armed with this information she immediately took a train to Düsseldorf and paid a visit to Minor's colleagues, posing as a fellow Socialist. Marguerite had gathered enough information to secure Minor's conviction. Nevertheless, after a month he was released and soon returned to the United States. According to the *New York Times*, his father, Robert B. Minor, a federal judge in San Antonio, had pulled a few strings on his son's behalf.[6] His cause was also helped by the 'muckraking' journalist Lincoln Steffens.

Whatever the true story behind his release, Marguerite later claimed that at the time she thought it all a storm in a teacup and that many of the American and British troops who read the leaflets were just war-weary and disillusioned. Arresting leaflet distributors, she believed, merely helped the Communists gain more recruits. Nonetheless, she had been given a real taste of the spying game, expertly assuming an undercover persona, and such experience would later prove valuable in much more dangerous circumstances.

* * *

In July 1919, Marguerite arrived back in Baltimore for a well-earned and much-needed rest. At about the same time, Stan Harding was unsuccessfully attempting to renew her British citizenship at the Netherlands Consulate in Berlin. She claimed that her *decree absolute* from Karl Krayl had been granted in September 1909, but this was not accepted as the *decree* had been a verbal agreement and Stan lacked supporting documentation.

She then travelled to Stuttgart where she obtained the relevant papers and spent three 'enjoyable' days with Karl. Describing herself as an 'Independent Gentlewoman', she returned to England to visit her mother, now in poor health and living in a nursing home in Bristol. Her re-application, which would prove successful, was submitted in October 1919.

Neither Marguerite in Baltimore nor Stan in London would have had any reason to suspect that their paths would soon cross again.

Chapter Six

Agent 'B' Redux

When Marguerite Harrison returned to Baltimore, via London, in July 1919, she found the United States a changed country from the one she had left eight months earlier. Events in Europe had been traumatic, but America was now experiencing its own turmoil, fuelled by passionate anti-Bolshevism.

After America entered the war in 1917, a truce had been declared between employers and the workforce, with old grievances temporarily put on hold. Once the war was over, inflation raged, the cost of living soared, and anarchists launched attacks. In December 1918, bombs exploded at the homes of prominent Philadelphians, including that of Acting Superintendent of Police William B. Mills, who was quick to point the finger of blame at the Bolsheviks. In January, Victor Berger of the Socialist Party of America was sentenced to twenty years' imprisonment for his airing of anti-war sentiments. Behind his indictment was the growing fear that the 'Reds' were everywhere.

When Marguerite's ship docked in New York, the strikes were continuing. Seamen along the Atlantic and Gulf coasts struck for better pay and conditions, machinists walked out in Chicago, and other actions were in full swing in Boston and St Louis. In Washington, D.C., and Chicago, racial unrest fuelled the fire, as African-Americans battled for jobs and housing. Police and Federal troops were called in to crush the riots. Predictably, the newspapers blamed racial unrest on the Bolsheviks. In August, railwaymen from New York to Los Angeles went on strike; even actors struck for better conditions, fed up with lack of pay during rehearsals lasting up to three months, and having to buy their own costumes.

Against this ambience, with its resonances of the unrest she had witnessed first-hand in Germany, Marguerite found it difficult to return to her old life as music and drama critic for *The Baltimore Sun*. Her thoughts began to turn to events in Russia: 'As I thought over all these things I told myself that I could perhaps perform a great service to my country by going to Russia and attempting to secure information that would help our government to formulate some definite policy with regard to the Bolsheviks.'

Soon, she was in contact with Brigadier-General Churchill. He at first intended to post her to Mexico, but Colonel Davis wanted her back in Europe, based in Berlin, with access to Europe's capitals. 'She can take care of the outside of the spider's web,' Davis was to tell Churchill.[1] And so it was agreed that Marguerite was to be re-employed as an undercover intelligence agent. On the 24th of October she received $650 as salary and expenses for November, reassigned the personal code signature 'B', and handed a cipher table.

Only Frank Kent, the editor of *The Baltimore Sun*, and her stepfather-in-law, Joseph Ames, were told of her plans. Tommy would be placed in a boarding school in Switzerland, which she looked on as an opportunity for him to perfect his languages, and where she would be able to visit him more easily – although she was, perhaps unsurprisingly, finding it difficult to bond with her son. She was given press credentials from the *New York Evening Post,* from Associated Press and, of course, *The Baltimore Sun.*

Before her departures, and perhaps with her ultimate mission in mind, Marguerite visited Ludwig Martens, the Bolshevik government representative in New York, to present him with her press credentials and to request the relevant permit to enter Russia. Martens told her emphatically that the Soviet government was not allowing the bourgeois press into Russia. This meant she could not legitimately enter Russia from Estonia, Finland or the Soviet courier service via Murmansk, nor could she apply to Maxim Litvinov's bureau in Copenhagen. There was only one option left: to enter Russia via Poland, Lithuania, or Latvia – all of whom were presently at war with Russia. 'I was deliberately taking a desperate risk,' she later wrote, 'and I had no one but myself to blame for the consequences.'

Immediately prior to her departure, a memo marked 'secret' was sent from the MID to the American Military Attaché in Paris containing a cypher table and instructions on how 'B' would communicate. 'In case you should receive a message from her bearing only the word 'well', you will immediately forward this to this office, and this will signify that she has lost her code book.'[2]

In November 1919, Marguerite and Tommy boarded a ship bound for Europe – the first leg of what would prove to be a fateful journey for Marguerite into the unknown cauldron of the new Bolshevik state.

PART TWO

1920

Chapter Seven

An Unkindness of Ravens

———∞∞∞———

Three months after leaving Europe, Marguerite arrived back in England. Conditions there were grim: the Defence of the Realm Act (DORA) was still in force, limiting the hours when food and drink could be served, bread was coarse and both meat and butter scarce. Coal was rationed to two shovelfuls a day and Marguerite complained that the houses were permanently cold. London was flooded by the return of military personnel and accommodation hard to find, but she was fortunate in being able to lodge in a flat in Westminster belonging to friends of her father's.

Before starting her mission, Marguerite spent a few days in Plymouth with Nancy Astor, Waldorf Astor's American wife. She had recently been elected as a Conservative Member of Parliament and was the first woman to serve in the House as an MP. Then, after talking at length to Robert Collins, the London-based European manager of Associated Press in Moscow, Marguerite travelled with Tommy to Switzerland, where he was enrolled at the Auckenthaler School. Whilst there, Marguerite interviewed the exiled Prince Christian of Hesse who had resigned from the German Navy in 1917 in opposition to Germany's U-boat strategy of attacking civilian ships, and she also saw the exiled King Constantine of Greece who had been forced to abdicate in 1915.

On the 26th of November 1919, Brigadier-General Churchill in Washington cabled the American Embassy in Switzerland with the message: 'Do not let Mrs Harrison enter territory under Bolshevist control until further orders.'[1] Of this, Marguerite was unaware as she already taken a train to Warsaw. The message was forwarded to the US military attaché in Warsaw and, as a result, Marguerite would be stuck in Poland for two months, during which time she took Russian-language lessons.

This was Marguerite's second stint in Poland, following her earlier visit in the year to Danzig at the behest of the MID. She described in detail a nation reincarnated after its loss of independence 150 years before when it was absorbed into the Russian Empire. Although Poland was now free from Russian domination, the cost of living had soared and the poor, she reported, were dying from starvation. She also noted that the Russian inscriptions had already been chiselled off the buildings which, although run-down, were brightened by red and white Polish flags.

Marguerite took a room at the once-famous Hotel Bristol in the heart of Warsaw. It comprised eight floors, once furnished in Gdańsk Baroque, Louis XV, Chippendale and Louis-Philippe styles. All possible amenities had been available: a restaurant, banquet room, ballroom, hairdresser, barber, shops, a florist and a photographer. However, she was to experience none of the luxury of bygone days, for the brass and copper trappings had been melted down for munitions by the invading Germans, leaving a bare and desolate building. Her room was small, shabby and unheated.

During her sojourn in Poland, Marguerite interviewed the first Prime Minister of independent Poland, Ignacy Jan Paderewski, who had recently resigned. Paderewski, a composer and concert pianist of international fame, had taken up his post in January 1919. He had tried unsuccessfully to obtain financial assistance from France, Britain and the United States and as a result was blamed by his embittered countrymen.

Marguerite also wrote a number of articles on Poland for the *New York Evening Post*, but these were suppressed by the MID who found them far too honest and potentially harmful to American morale. She continued supplying the military attaché with information gleaned in the course of her role as a journalist, reporting deaths of children from malnutrition, nightly queues outside bakeries, and a lack of basics such as meat, potatoes, coal and milk. Thousands of Poles were unemployed and families sublet their rooms to save money, with as many as five groups living in a single room. And she witnessed the difficulty the new government had experienced in getting people to work together, for in these early days there was rarely agreement between the parties and factions within the Polish government.

Christmas was shared with her cousin Emily Graves, who had arrived in Poland with the Grey Samaritans,* sponsored by the Young Women's Christian Association (YWCA). New Year was spent in Białystok, 100 miles from Warsaw, where the American Red Cross ran a large orphanage and helped in the care of Russian prisoners of war. The camp that Marguerite visited was filled with half-starved Russians, the buildings

* The Polish Grey Samaritans were bilingual Polish-American women trained by the Young Women's Christian Association as nurses and social workers. At the height of their activities they were to feed more than a million Polish children a day.

were in a state of collapse, the sick were herded in with the healthy, causing more infection, while dead bodies were not removed until there were enough to fill a cart. Marguerite reported that out of 5,000 inmates incarcerated at the beginning of 1919, only 1,500 had survived. 'It was several hours,' she said, 'before I recovered my equanimity sufficiently to don my one party frock for New Year's dinner.'

Her party frock saw good service in Poland, and at a ball held by the Red Cross in Warsaw to raise funds for the Kościuszko Squadron, she danced with a 26-year-old American pilot by the name of Merian C. Cooper. During the Great War, Cooper had been shot down four times and, in late-September 1918, he barely survived a crash with serious burns and was imprisoned by the Germans. When Marguerite met him, he had served as head of the U.S. Food Administration in Galicia and Lwów before joining the Kościuszko Squadron. Formed in late-1919, the Squadron comprised a band of volunteer Polish, American, British and French pilots fighting against the Bolsheviks in what would come to be known as the Polish-Soviet War. Cooper would soon be taking to the skies above Russia.

* * *

In January 1920, Marguerite was finally given permission by Brigadier-General Churchill to enter Russia. As her Russian was still rudimentary, she hired Dr Anna Karlin, a Russian who had emigrated to Chicago after the 1905 revolution, to act as her interpreter. At the beginning of the 1917 revolution, Karlin had returned via Siberia to Russia, where she worked for a year as a doctor for the Bolsheviks in Galicia. She was arrested when the Poles occupied the territory. Because of her American citizenship she was eventually released, but was banned from entry back into the United States. Marguerite described her as 'a funny little soul, fat and dumpy, with a ruddy complexion, blue eyes that seemed to express perpetual astonishment and a head covered with reddish curls'.

On a cold January morning the two women set off for Minsk (Belarus), then part of the Second Polish Republic. 'I wore a fur-lined coat that came to my heels, a fur cap and fur-lined gloves,' Marguerite recalled. Karlin wore a skirt, sweater and sheepskin coat and hat. They took very few possessions, fully aware that they would have to carry everything themselves. Nonetheless, Marguerite admitted that she did throw one simple, dinner dress into her case, as well as an Army bedding roll, blanket, and pillow.

Marguerite's plan was to enter Russia via Beresina, a no man's land between Russia and Poland through which contraband flowed. To no avail,
she called on General Jelikovski who was in charge of Minsk, but had
better luck with General Stanisław Szeptycki, commander of the 4th
Army on the Polish north-east Front, based in Vilna (Vilnius), the capital of Lithuania. After a journey that normally took three hours lasted
twenty-two due to the dilapidated state of the railways, General Szeptycki issued a pass. Then, returning to Minsk, Marguerite collected Anna
Karlin and they set off to rendezvous with a Polish Intelligence
officer in a dugout on the Beresina front. He had been charged with
escorting the women by sleigh through the three miles of no man's land
to enter Russia. The officer did his best to persuade them to return
home, insisting that they would be shot within 24 hours, but the short,
dumpy Russian and the elegant American were adamant. With Bolshevik Russia in her sights, the thought of turning back was the last thing
on Marguerite's mind.

They entered Russia on the 8th of February. It would take the women
more than two weeks to reach Moscow, travelling via Krupki where
Commandant Shevilov, a former actor, welcomed them. He sent them
on to Vitebsk where the commissar arranged for his wife, desperate to
visit the city, to unofficially escort the women to Moscow. They spent
36 hours in a boxcar that was 'stiflingly hot and the window hermetically
sealed'. The rest of the train was made up of cars packed with 'people
even sitting on the roofs, on bumpers, and there were fights at every station between persons trying to get on and off'. Marguerite was amazed
at the friendliness of the Red soldiers and Russian people. At stops along
the way, they were shown around villages, visited schools and hospitals,
and offered food and hospitality. Marguerite was feeling optimistic
about the reception she would receive in Moscow.

Alexandrovsky (now named Belorussky) railway station in Moscow
would have been an impressive sight to anyone arriving there. Opened
in 1870 but vastly expanded four decades later, it was a sprawling architectural confection of domes, archways and turrets, all made from con-
crete and steel. On arrival, and realising that without official papers they
would be unable to secure accommodation, Marguerite asked Karlin to
telephone the Foreign Office and announce their arrival.

'In about half an hour I saw a small, thin, dark, nervous-looking man
with a pronounced stoop that made him appear almost like a hunchback,
enter the waiting room, glancing about as if he were looking for some-
body,' Marguerite recalled. It was Mikail Rosenberg from the Western

Section of the Commissariat of Foreign Affairs. She did not take to him, finding him 'physically unprepossessing, typically Jewish in appearance, with vile manners'.

Rosenberg made it clear he was not happy that they had arrived without permission and persistently quizzed them on how they had entered Russia and travelled to Moscow. He demanded that they hand over their passports, and Marguerite her press credentials, informing her that reporters from the Associated Press and the *New York Evening Post* had been refused permission to enter Russia. Their arrival was something of an embarrassment for him and sulkily he drove them to a government guest house before discussing the problem with his superior, Georgy Vasilievich Chicherin.

As they were driven through the streets to their lodgings, they passed buildings decorated with red flags, banners and evergreen garlands celebrating the second anniversary of the founding of the Red Army. The propaganda posters of the Third International, depicting the capitalists of the world sitting on their money bags and lording it over the workers, amused Marguerite and she recorded that a buzz was in the air. She was feeling optimistic. 'The only sinister impression I received was from the flocks of ravens that hovered over the city, sitting in the bare branches of the trees in the parks and on the eaves of all the public buildings.' A group of ravens is known as an unkindness – and an unkindness of ravens was indeed a suitable metaphor for the Moscow of 1920.

Marguerite and Karlin arrived at the Haritonevsky Guest House, previously the home of a German merchant. The house possessed a huge garden, and, although it had been attacked in 1915 during the anti-German riots, and ransacked again during the November revolution, it was still luxurious enough. The two women were shown to a large room with velvet curtains, an oriental rug, easy chairs, a brass bed and an enormous couch on which Karlin would sleep. The guest house employed four maids, bedlinen was changed every two weeks, but work such as cleaning the floors was carried out by prisoners. The main deprivation Marguerite was to experience was the lack of heating, with hot water for baths being available only once a week. Lunch was served at 2 p.m. in an oak-lined dining room, the 'thin meat soup, thickened with cereal or noodles made of rye flour, mashed potatoes or kasha, tea, black bread and sugar,' laid out on tables with white linen and silver cutlery.

Dinner was served at 9 p.m. and hosted by the 'manager' of the guest house, Ivan Axionov, a former member of the Tsarist secret police now employed by the Cheka. Axionov, a poet and admirer of Elizabethan literature who had translated the works of Ben Jonson, was small, blond-haired with a middle parting, and possessed, Marguerite recalled, shifty blue eyes and a 'soft purring voice which gave me the creeps'. They were joined at dinner by several unidentified Russians, a Korean, a Norwegian who had become a naturalised Russian citizen, and Michael Farbman from the Chicago *Daily News*.

The next night Mikail Rosenberg took Marguerite to the Foreign Office, situated in a wing of the former Hotel Metropole, on the square facing the Grand Opera House (renamed the Bolshoi). It was here that the People's Commissar of the Foreign Office, Georgy Chicherin, would decide what was to be done about Marguerite's unauthorised entry into the country. He only worked at night and she saw him at 2 a.m. Because of his important position, Marguerite expected to find a tall, self-confident, rather masterful-looking person, but instead saw 'a thin, delicate-looking man of about forty-eight, with sandy hair, decidedly thin around the temples, and a small pointed beard and moustache'. He wore a woollen muffler and his tired, pale green eyes peered over at her.

Chicherin spoke excellent German from the days when he was general agent for the Siemens Electric Company in Berlin, and his English was as good as that of any Englishman. Marguerite recalled how he sat 'in front of a huge table desk buried under an avalanche of documents and papers'. Remarkably, he was willing to permit Marguerite to stay in Moscow as a journalist for two weeks.

* * *

The press corps was given the former sitting room of a deluxe suite at the Hotel Metropole for use as an office. It boasted a marble-top table, an ornate Florentine mirror, gilded pseudo-Louis XV furniture covered with green brocade, and a boudoir lamp with a yellow silk shade. Hardly the usual workplace for a group of newspaper reporters, it was nevertheless where they hung around chatting and writing their despatches until two or three in the morning. Marguerite felt quite safe walking home to her guest house at night, unlike during the day when the streets were full of feral children. She witnessed a great deal of immorality and depravity, but never elaborated further.

It was at the Foreign Office/Metropole that Marguerite was to meet the handsome Armenian Lev Karakhan, Georgy Chicherin's second in command; Joe Feinberg, a Jewish Socialist agitator from London;[2] Julius Rozinsky, a Communist from London's East End, and other international correspondents approved by Chicherin, including the American

Griffin Barry of the London *Daily Herald*; his editor George Lansbury; John Clayton from the *Chicago Herald*; and Ambrose Lambert, representing the *Daily Express* and the *Chicago Tribune*. All despatches by the journalists were checked and corrected by both Rosenberg and Chicherin before transmission.

Given Marguerite's knack for languages, her Russian improved by the day. In reading the news in Russian from the Russian Socialist Telegraph Agency (ROSTA), a propaganda tool of the Communist Party, she could get her news bulletins out ahead of almost everyone else. Rather surprisingly, she persuaded Chicherin to allow her to go to Lubyanka where ROSTA was based to read the bulletins. Marguerite soon came to the conclusion that American government's belief that the Bolsheviks would not retain power was misguided: they were there to stay. She grasped that the Allies' support for the counter-revolutionaries only strengthened the Bolsheviks, as did Japanese occupation of Eastern Siberia and Polish claims to parts of Russia. More importantly, the majority of Russians were clearly, in her mind, simply not ready for a popular government.

* * *

During her first two weeks in Moscow, Marguerite was given free rein to explore the city alone. This privilege did not seem to strike her as unusual, although most foreigners were banned from entering Russia. An American who met her in Moscow a short while later was taken aback by her alacrity, energy and determination. He claimed that she 'went to Russia with a purpose – to get a story – she had no scruples about it [and] did anything to ingratiate herself… Anyway, she showed remarkable ability'.[3]

As in Berlin a year earlier, Marguerite concerned herself with the economic situation and its impact on the working people. She visited schools, hospitals, Soviet stores and public dining rooms. She saw no evidence of 'The Terror' and concluded that the economic ruin of the country was due to the World War, the civil war and the Entente blockade.

Within a stone's throw from the Foreign Office on the Okhotny Ryad was the Soukharévka market. Anything one needed, legal or illegal, could be procured there. She saw aristocrats and ex-Imperial functionaries mingle with peasants as they attempted to sell their monogrammed linens, ball gowns, porcelain, bronzes, and paintings. Wares tended to be grouped together in different sections of the market – shoes, clothes, household, tools, furniture, rugs, soap and cigarettes – and, if a raid was imminent, vendors would miraculously pack up and disappear in a matter of minutes. Selling gold and money was illegal, so it was prudent to keep an eye out for the police who seemingly could appear out of nowhere.

Marguerite was soon a regular visitor to the market, supplementing her diet with eggs, milk, cream cheese, honey, fruits and vegetables bought at colossal prices with gold she had smuggled into the country strapped to her waist. Indeed, she noted that she was not the only smuggler. Many people were so desperate to sell their belongings to supplement limited food and fuel rations that they would make deals with Estonians and Letts, the only people at this time legally permitted to take property out of the country, to smuggle rugs, paintings, jewels, and bibelots in return for a cut of the profits when sold in Reval or Riga.

* * *

Marguerite was delighted when the Foreign Office granted her permission to stay for another month. She set about interviewing key political figures in the Bolshevik regime, speaking to Leonid Krasin, the Commissar of Ways and Communications, Karl Radek, a Polish Jew involved in the 1919 Spartacist revolts in Berlin and to Nikolai Semashko, the Commissar of Public Health, who created illustrated pamphlets on sanitation for the general public. She also met Anatoly Lunacharsky, the Commissar of Education who was bringing the classics and drama to the proletariat. The proletariat, however, was not quite ready for his brand of culture. A very sophisticated man, Lunacharsky was a polyglot and lived at the Kremlin in an apartment that he called a 'Palace of Little Pleasures'. He proudly declared himself 'an intellectual among Bolsheviks and a Bolshevik among intellectuals',[4] and organised drama clubs for workers and sent the Moscow ballet to give performances in rural areas. Many peasants were so shocked by seeing dancers in tights that they walked out in protest before the performance ended.

Undoubtedly the most powerful person Marguerite interviewed during this time was Felix Dzerzhinsky, the Polish-born head of the All-Russian Extraordinary Commission for Combating Counter-Revolution and Espionage, otherwise known (by its Russian acronym) as the Cheka. A devout Catholic who turned to Marxism while studying at the University of Vilnius, Dzerzhinsky had spent much of his adult life in either Tsarist prisons or Siberian labour camps. Soon after the Bolsheviks seized power, Lenin appointed him to head the organisation, which he quickly turned into, in the words of one historian, 'the most awesome political police empire the world had ever seen'.[5] Dzerzhinsky and the Cheka were, as Karl Radek explained, the great 'disinfector' of the revolution.[6] To an American observer in 1920, he was a 'foul, blood-drenched scoundrel' and 'a man without a heart or a conscience, a veritable bird of prey, whose appetite for blood is insatiable'.[7]

For Lenin, democracy, freedom, justice and civil liberties were relative concepts only to be won through harsh dictatorship and denial of freedom to the former ruling classes and their allies. These included all other political parties such as the Left and Right Socialist Revolutionaries, the Anarchists and the Mensheviks.

The Cheka was a vital factor in achieving Lenin's aims. It had been preceded by the Tsar's secret police, the Okhrana, which in its turn had been removed by Kerensky's Provisional Government after the Russian Revolution of February 1917. It took Lenin just six weeks after the October Revolution to install his own police force. By early 1918, the Cheka's powers were extended from search and arrest to summary trial and execution of sentence, including the death penalty, which Lenin reinstated in June 1918. 'How can one make a revolution without firing squads?' he had demanded in anger when the death penalty was repealed immediately after the October Revolution.[8]

For the first year as head of the Cheka, Dzerzhinsky worked, ate, and slept in his office, putting in 16- to 18-hour days, 7 days a week. He inevitably suffered physically and mentally, and the tuberculosis contracted during his eleven years in prison constantly troubled him. By the summer of 1918 he headed a huge organisation whose tentacles spread across Russia. He was based at the Cheka HQ (Cheka Collegium), better known as Lubyanka 2, situated in Lubyanka Square.

Dzerzhinsky shunned all personal pleasures and comforts, working away like a monk shut away in his cell, possessed by revolutionary rather than religious zeal. Indeed, despite his gruesome reputation abroad, he was known as 'the saint of the Revolution'.[9] He was an intense, serious man, known to keep his feelings tightly under control. The only time Dzerzhinsky publicly allowed his inner thoughts to surface was on New Year's Eve 1918 when, hopelessly drunk and weeping, he repeatedly asked Lenin and Politburo member, Lev Kamenev, to shoot him on the spot: 'I have spilt so much blood that I no longer have any right to live. You must shoot me now.'[10]

Dzerzhinsky's plea was no doubt heartfelt and his guilt well warranted. The Cheka was appallingly brutal. Torture was officially forbidden by the Soviet Government; however, beating and mock executions were commonly used to elicit confessions. Local Chekas employed different techniques. The Kharkov Cheka scalped and hand-flayed, whilst the Voronezh Cheka threw victims naked into nail-studded barrels and rolled them around. Foreheads were branded with six-pointed stars, priests were crowned with barbed wire, whilst others were buried alive, stoned or crucified. Some had their bones sawn through or were alternately immersed in tanks of boiling or freezing water. Sometimes water was poured over naked bodies in freezing temperatures so that they became human icicles. Routinely, women were raped before execution. In one rare incident, a Chekist was examined by a doctor during the winter of 1920 and pronounced insane because he interrogated prisoners immersed in icy river water. However, most Chekists were left alone to do what they liked to prisoners under their jurisdiction. Some executions were performed in prison cells with a bullet to the back of the head, while others were staged in the prison courtyards, with motor vehicle engines running to block out the noise.

Chekists did not have a special uniform, but many took to wearing black leather jackets and carrying revolvers in holsters, making them instantly recognisable. They needed no particular qualifications and were awarded privileges such as exemption from military conscription and excellent food rations. In a nation of starving people, the latter would have been especially appealing, but Victor Serge, a Belgian anarchist turned Communist who fled to Russia in 1919, observed that Chekists were attracted to the profession for other reasons. He noted that the Petrograd Chekists he encountered had particular characteristics: 'The only temperaments that devoted themselves willingly and tenaciously to this task of "internal defence" were those characterised by suspicion, embitterment, harshness and sadism. Long-standing inferiority complexes and memories of humiliation and suffering in the Tsar's jails rendered them intractable, and since professional degeneration has rapid effects, the Chekas inevitably consisted of perverted men tending to see conspiracy everywhere.'[11]

Since June 1918, the Cheka had been playing a key role in punishment and executions alongside the Revolutionary Tribunals – which it would bypass if thought necessary. At these trials there were no witnesses, judicial laws or procedures, no counsel for the defence, and they were conducted in secret. Those who escaped execution would be sentenced to spend time in one of three types of prison: a conventional prison presided over by the Commissariat of Justice; a forced labour camp, often in Siberia, run by the Commissariat for Internal Affairs in conjunction with the Chekas; or a concentration camp for class enemies. None of these options was preferable, though the chances of returning to one's old life from Siberia, even if one survived the conditions, were slim.

* * *

Despite not witnessing any first-hand evidence of 'The Terror' that began and subsequently swept through Russia after the attempted as-sassination of Lenin in August 1918, Marguerite was aware that its in-stigator and coordinator was Dzerzhinsky. She arrived to interview him at his office in Lubyanka and was escorted to a room lined with books from floor to ceiling, with the instruction to wait until called. Eventually, a bookcase opened revealing a secret passage that led to Dzerzhinsky's office. Waiting at the end of the passage sat a small, blond, frail-looking man with a sharp nose, pointed beard and chiselled lips, who was clearly suffering from some sort of respiratory illness. At first she mistook the insignificant-looking man for a secretary – but then realised with a start that she was in the presence of 'the most feared man in all Russia'. Two years earlier he had written an article in a Moscow newspaper stating his aims. 'We stand for organised terror,' he declared, 'terror being ab-solutely indispensable in current revolutionary conditions. We terrorise the enemies of the Soviet government in order to stifle crime at its in-ception. Terror serves as a ready deterrent.'[12]

It was to be a short interview during which Dzerzhinsky did most of the talking. He explained by way of justification that the majority of executions carried out by the Cheka were not for political but rather eco-nomic reasons. Lenin, after all, had claimed to be 'looting the looters', and encouraged local Chekas to wage 'a war to the death against the rich, the idlers, and the parasites'.[13] One of the main activities of the Cheka was indeed to police the economy – to prevent speculation, forgery and thefts from storehouses. Banditry was regarded as one of the most serious offences, with hundreds of alleged offenders executed in Moscow alone.

But of the thousands of arrests made each week, often on trivial charges, Dzerzhinsky had little to say, and he showed none of the con-trition that had caused him to weep in front of Lenin. 'I had heard enough to realise that it was just as well to appear ignorant of these mat-ters,' she wrote, 'so I merely listened to what he had to say and made no comments.' Marguerite thought Dzerzhinsky a modern Maximilien Robespierre; and she soon would come under his power and that of the Cheka.

Chapter Eight

With a Gleam in Her Eye

While Marguerite was establishing connections and forming a network in Moscow, Stan Harding was in England, still entertaining the ideas of a career in interior design or in the study of classical dance in India. But she had not begun preparations for a return journey to the sub-continent, no doubt in part because of a lack of funds. She also had not heard from Marguerite since their parting of the ways – quite possibly with bad feeling – at the Hotel Adlon in Berlin. However, like Marguerite, Stan found the experience of routine life a difficult adjustment from one imbued with politics and revolution.

Opening her morning newspaper in London on the 13th of March 1920, Stan read that Germany was on the verge of another revolution. In Berlin, Captain Waldemar Pabst of the Guards Cavalry Division had been arrested on the orders of Gustav Noske, Defence Minister of the Weimar Republic, following the discovery of incriminating material at his house. All immediate plans to return to India or a career in design were put on hold. Stan immediately contacted *The Daily News* to persuade the editor to send her to Berlin to join the paper's correspondent there, John Chrysostom Segrue.

Just a few days earlier, Segrue had reported that the Junkers were becoming increasingly vocal and anti-republican. Fuel was added to the fire when the Prussian Prince Joachim Albrecht was arrested for provoking an assault on a French military officer at the Hotel Adlon. The Frenchman's offence had been to refuse to stand while the orchestra played 'Deutschland, Deutschland über alles', one of a number of patriotic songs the prince had ordered.

Yet, Germans were also desperate for life to return to normal; indeed, Segrue had reported in *The Daily News* that etiquette schools were springing up all over the city to educate those who had been elevated to a higher social class by the war.[1] However, discontent had continued to simmer. Following the Treaty of Versailles, which had come into effect two months earlier, the Weimar Republic had been ordered to reduce its remaining army of 400,000 troops to 100,000 and to disband the Freikorps. This demand meant that German involvement in the Baltic and in Poland would come to an abrupt end. Many members of the

Freikorps, unhappy with the terms, merely regrouped in police or sports clubs, shooting
associations and, bizarrely, detective agencies. One Freikorps commander in particular, General Freiherr von Lüttwitz, refused to obey Noske's order to disband the Ehrhardt Brigade. This Brigade, commanded by a naval captain, Hermann Ehrhardt, and stationed at Döberitz, fifteen miles outside Berlin, was notorious for its ruthlessness, having fought the Poles on the Eastern Front and the Bolsheviks in the Baltic. In response to the order, Lüttwitz sent an ultimatum to President Ebert demanding that demobilisation be halted and that the old imperial colours of red, white, and black be restored. Ebert refused.

Lüttwitz's gathered his troops and marched through the Brandenburg Gate. Joined by Dr Wolfgang Kapp, co-founder of the extreme-right wartime Fatherland Party, they advanced directly to the Chancellery on Wilhelmstrasse and proclaimed that the Reich government had of that moment ceased to exist. Dr Kapp, announced Lüttwitz, was to be the new Reich Chancellor. The Chief of General Staff, Colonel-General Hans von Seeckt, refused to support Ebert's order to send his regular troops to confront the Freikorps, whereupon Ebert and his government fled first to Dresden and then on to Stuttgart.

The Weimar government was not alone in the worrying about the Ehrhardt Brigade's coup d'état. One of Lüttwitz's demands was the forcible suppression of all strikes, and as the Brigade marched they sang: 'Worker, worker, what's to become of you, when the Brigade is ready to fight? The Ehrhardt Brigade smashes all to bits, so woe, woe, woe to you, you worker son-of-a bitch!'[2] As a result of these threats, Ebert was able to persuade the Majority Socialists, the Independent Socialists and the trade unions to work together and to call a general strike to protest the actions of the Freikorps. The Communists refrained from joining the strike, which they claimed was an argument between two imperialist factions.

As a consequence of the strike there was no water, transport or power in Berlin. Chaos once again engulfed Germany. London's *Daily Herald* correspondent, Morgan Philips Price, reported on March 18th that Kapp's new government was 'caught like a rat in a trap', with so many sections of society against it. He noted, however, that it was not going to give up without a struggle, and that it had considerable support among the uneducated classes and peasantry. 'Anti-Semitic propaganda is a method by which it is trying to make itself popular among the dark and ignorant elements of the population.'[3] Price added that living near him was a 'notorious Jew-baiter who has been engaged for some time past in manufacturing rubber batons for use in pogroms'.[4]

After four days, the putsch collapsed and the Freikorps marched out of Berlin, shooting a few bystanders en route. Dr Kapp fled to Sweden, Lüttwitz to Hungary, and Ehrhardt to Bavaria, where the city of Munich in particular had attracted all sorts of right-wing extremists – including the young Adolf Hitler.

Stan had managed to persuade the editor of *The Daily News* in London of her suitability for the assignment. She arrived in a dangerous and unstable Berlin three days later on the 16th of March, just as the Kapp putsch was disintegrating. The Socialists had refused to call off the strike, which had spread nationwide, until the government agreed to an eight-point programme of reforms: these were to include the socialisation of industry, the right to be involved in the reconstruction of the government, and the removal of Defence Minister Gustav Noske and Chancellor Gustav Bauer.

Stan Harding's first article for *The Daily News* appeared on March 23rd under her by-line, a rare honour, especially for a female journalist. She had interviewed troops encamped at the Berlin Zoological Garden, where they were preparing to fight the 50,000-strong workers' army that had seized control in the Ruhr Valley, and noted the men had painted swastikas on their helmets – the ancient 'sunwheel' symbol recently adopted by extreme German nationalists, anti-Communists and anti-Semites. When questioned, one soldier explained that they were of the blond German race and hated Jews everywhere. They wanted to round them all up and put them in concentration camps, but first they were off to fight the Spartacist army. First the Communists, then the Jews.

Stan then teamed up with another journalist, Frederick Augustus Voigt, a fluent German speaker and correspondent for *The Manchester Guardian*. They travelled to Essen in the Ruhr Valley, at the heart of the national strike, where workers were demanding nationalisation of the coal and potash industries. Known as the Red Army, they had already defeated the government and the Freikorps troops in the area, and were in control of Düsseldorf and Elberfeld as well as Essen – this despite the fact that, under the terms of the Peace Treaty, the Ruhr Valley was designated a neutral zone between the Allies and Germany. At the same time the French had begun to make preparations to occupy parts of the region.

Stan reported that looters in Essen were being shot on the spot by the Red Army and that people were becoming increasingly nervous about the chaos and what it portended for the future. She attended a meeting of the Ruhr Workers' Council and witnessed the majority of members voting to continue fighting for their demands.

Hiring a car and sticking a red flag on the bonnet, she travelled to Wessel to talk to the workers' army there. 'It seemed customary to lie down in a ditch when a shell sounded as if it were coming our way, so we conformed to usage.' Progress was also slowed by 'the necessity of showing one's pass to every over-wrought boy with a rifle who thought we ought to be shot as spies'.[5]

Voigt believed that Stan thrived in these dangerous circumstances. He noted the same ambition and fearlessness that had so impressed Käthe Kollwitz. She loitered, he wrote, 'in unhealthy places in a manner likely to arouse the suspicions of the trigger-happy military and strode into strife with a gleam in her eye'.[6] She possessed a confidence that nobody would hurt her because she was a woman, a belief that would later prove illusory.

For more than a week, heavy fighting between government troops and workers continued in and around Essen; Stan reported that the latter lacked guns and ammunition. On April 5th, to her surprise, many of the Red troops returned from the front to pick up their wages. The HQ of the Council of Workmen's and Soldiers' in Essen was based at the Hotel Kaiserhof where the Council of Ten, of which Stan was an observer, were meeting. To her alarm, soldiers burst into the room, demanding to be paid. On being told that all bank funds in Essen had been smuggled out of the city in Red Cross boxes for safety, the furious soldiers locked the council members, including Stan, in the meeting room until the money could be found. She later wrote how the ensuing fiasco had amused her. The door had foolishly been left open after someone came to check on the prisoners and so the captives were able to flee. The wages were not, on this occasion, paid.

The next day, Stan wrote, somewhat portentously, that 'this may be the last time for some days that I shall be able to communicate from Essen with the outside world', as the police force had been dissolved and no one knew what would happen next.[7] She noted that the workers' army, fearing mass reprisals, had begun donning civilian clothes as soon as they knew that government troops were on their way. The following day the *Reichswehr* (government army) marched into the city, patrolling the streets, questioning and detaining anyone who looked suspicious. Stan reported that the troops who had surrounded Essen on behalf of the Socialist Republican government were the same troops who had earlier fought in the Kapp Putsch against the government. In the meantime the French, unhappy that the Peace Treaty terms had been violated, occupied Frankfurt, Darmstadt, Hanau and Homburg.

Foolishly, Voigt wired his newspaper that he was proceeding to Barmen, Düsseldorf and then on to Berlin. The *Reichswehr* troops interpreted this message as proof that Voigt was a workers' spy, and he and Stan were promptly arrested. Taken to the *Reichswehr* headquarters, they were interviewed by a Lieutenant Linsermaier, who according to Stan was a 'small, evil looking man, wearing a black monocle'.[8] Voigt was beaten, called an English swine, and Stan could hear the soldiers shout: 'Strike the dog, teach the Tommy' and 'Teach this Englishman how to behave in the presence of a German officer'. Angrily, she demanded they stop this ill-treatment, assuring them that Voigt was a newspaper correspondent, not a spy.

Despite being threatened with execution if she did not behave, Stan persuaded one of the guards to take her to Dr Luther, Mayor of Essen, whom she had found quite personable at an earlier meeting. He pulled strings and Voigt was released, though forbidden to leave Essen. Stan, now also released from custody, spent the rest of the day ringing all her contacts in Berlin who might be able to help him gain his freedom of movement. She never knew if it was her dogged persistence that ensured his release later that evening, or the involvement of the British Government, but it was not long before Lord Kilmarnock, the British Chargé d'Affaires in Berlin, demanded an apology from the German government over the episode. It was not to be the last time that Stan found herself involved in an international incident.

* * *

A few weeks before Stan's arrest in Germany, Marguerite had attended an open meeting of the Moscow Soviet at the Grand Opera House on March 6th 1920, and listened to Lenin as he addressed the audience. She found it disappointing. Lenin was surprisingly short, he had a quiet 'unemotional, almost monotonous manner of delivery', and he looked, she thought, more like a middle-class businessman than a statesman.[9] At the beginning and end of every speech, the Grand Orchestra played the 'The Internationale'.

Marguerite also observed a closed meeting of the annual Russian Communist Party Convention. It was there that she witnessed the beginnings of the split between Trotsky, who supported government decentralisation, and another member of the Politburo who favoured centralisation: a coarse, ruthless, smallpox-scarred former seminary student from Georgia named Loseb Dzhughashvili, better known as Joseph Stalin. Marguerite had managed to get a ticket through Angelica Balabanova, Secretary of the international Communist movement, the Third International, founded in March 1919. This would have been an invaluable contact for any American spy interested in links forged between American Socialist organisations back home and the Third International. She had gained Balabanova's trust and was privileged to sit on the stage with other journalists. Marguerite considered Balabanova, unlike Lenin, a superb speaker. Originally born into a wealthy family near Kiev, Balabanova became involved in the Italian labour movement in the early 1900s after studying in Brussels and Germany. Emma Goldman, meeting Balabanova around the same time, found her 'not possessing' and in poor health, but with 'large and luminous' eyes that radiated 'sympathy and kindness'.[10]

Balabanova was only one of a number of prominent women whom Marguerite met. International Women's Day had first been established in 1913 as women across Europe held peace rallies against the imminent war. Alexandra Kollontai, another prominent Bolshevik, persuaded Lenin to introduce the celebration as an annual event in Russia. On March 8th 1920, as offices were closed in Moscow and speeches arranged throughout the day, Marguerite was able to accompany Kollontai as she gave talks at different venues throughout the city.

Kollontai came from an aristocratic family, as did so many of the Bolshevik leaders, and had used her position as People's Commissar for Social Welfare to found the women's department. When Marguerite went to visit her in her room in the National Hotel in 1920 she was ill but clad in a green velvet boudoir gown trimmed with sable and matching velvet slippers. She explained her concern with children's education and the need to rid the new Russia of the paternalism that, in her eyes, had hindered imperial Russia. Furthermore, she advocated free love and the raising of children in communes; she saw little use for relationships other than for the procreation of the human race. Marguerite kept to herself her disagreement with Kollontai's ideas.

Also in March of 1920, Marguerite met Francis McCullagh, another member of the spying community when he was billeted at the guest house. Born in 1878 in Northern Ireland, McCullagh had worked as far afield as Ceylon (Sri Lanka) and Siam (Thailand); he was a veteran war correspondent, having covered the Russo-Japanese War of 1904-5, the Portuguese Revolution of 1910 and the first Balkan war of 1912-13.

During the Great War he had joined the Royal Irish Fusiliers and fought at Gallipoli, Serbia and Macedonia, later joining the Expeditionary Force in Siberia as an intelligence officer in 1918. On November 14th 1919, the day before the Bolsheviks defeated the White government's leader in Siberia, General Kolchak, the 35-year-old McCullagh had fled Omsk disguised as a peasant. He was finally captured at Krasnoyarsk on the 6th of January.

Posing as a civilian journalist rather than registering as an Army officer, McCullagh was granted permission by Commissar Sverdlov to travel to Ekaterinburg to interview Trotsky about his plan to convert the Army into a labour force. McCullagh had lived in Ekaterinburg in 1918 and had been shocked by the propaganda posters in the city: a priest depicted as a leering spider with a web around a family, Kolchak seated drunkenly on a throne with fat businessmen bowing before him while a corpulent, bibulous priest blessed him, Denikin's bull-necked, red-faced officers shooting women and children, and the British soldiers in India blowing Hindus from the mouth of a cannon. He saw children playing amongst the frozen naked corpses of Kolchak's soldiers and numbers of starving horses left over from the White Army, wandering around the streets until they dropped dead, whereupon their carcasses were moved to a large, open field, skinned and tanned for leather; these were, he reported, horrific sights.[11]

McCullagh was even more disturbed by what he saw in early 1920 en route to Moscow.' In the dilapidated suburban stations which we passed,' he wrote, 'we saw gangs of wretched and sometimes villainous-looking men and women setting out into the country with bags to collect food and fuel from the villages. Among them were schoolboys, editors, teachers, poets, and sculptors.'[12] When he arrived, paperless, at Nikolayevsky (renamed Leningradsky) railway station he decided to camp out on the train, scrounging food until venturing into the city where he made contact with the Reverend Frank North, unofficially in charge of the British Red Cross, who gave him money for food. McCullagh had developed trench foot as a result of being unable to dry his boots, soaked through by the snow and sludge; and, as a final blow, he slipped in the dark, snow-filled streets and broke his glasses. He witnessed 'feeble old men and delicate women engaged in dragging along the street little sleighs laden with firewood.'[13] He heard stray bullet shots, and said it felt like something out of Dante's 'Inferno' – much worse than anything he had experienced in the First World War.

Tucked away in his wallet, McCullagh had kept an article that he had written for the *New York World* with his photo emblazoned on it. This enabled him to persuade Rosenberg at the Foreign Office that he was a journalist with *The Manchester Guardian*. Having heard of Marguerite from the Reverend North, McCullagh turned up at Marguerite's guest house.' I saw a frail-looking little man in a sheepskin coat and much-worn leather breeches,' Marguerite recalled. 'He looked like a peasant, so I was more than surprised when he spoke excellent English.' He couldn't directly contact *The Manchester Guardian* to back up his story as he was not permitted to use the wireless, so Marguerite suggested that she post a despatch to Associated Press in London, mentioning that she had met the correspondent for *The Manchester Guardian*, recently arrived from Siberia, in the hope that this would be spotted by the British Intelligence services. All went according to plan and McCullagh was sent verification of his press credentials. The Cheka, it seems, were oblivious to the fact that he was a British Intelligence officer.

If there was a group in society that the Bolsheviks hated more than capitalists, then that was the Russian Orthodox Church. Marguerite and McCullagh visited the Patriarch Tikhon, who had been under house arrest at the Donskoy Monastery since 1918.[14] Dressed in a long cassock of rich black silk, he wore a headdress of white velvet embroidered with pearls and, around his neck, 'a jewelled chain terminating in a superb cross, while on his index finger was his ring, which Mr McCullagh kissed devoutly.' Tikhon was 56 years old, a well-built man with a beaming smile, a head of grey hair and a bushy beard. Since the October Revolution, 60 bishops and several hundred clergy had been put to death as anti-Bolshevik sympathisers. The liquidation of Patriarch Tikhon would have been a step too far, even for the Bolsheviks, and he was to die of natural causes, still under house arrest, in 1925.

When Marguerite heard of an exhibition at the Kremlin on the history of the ROSTA (the Russian Socialist Telegraph Agency) which was only open to party officials, she and McCullagh decided to see if they could sneak in. The ROSTA had offices all over country and was the propaganda tool of the Communist party; this would give the two spies an invaluable insight into Bolshevik communication links. The Kremlin, however, was one of the most difficult places in Moscow to penetrate, as Lenin, Trotsky and other party officials all had apartments there. Marguerite, however, managed to bluff her way through the gate by saying that she and McCullagh had an appointment with the propagandist Karl Radek. The exhibition was located in a room in the Commissariat of Justice, which they found easily. No one made any attempt to stop them, so they wandered around the buildings and courtyards of the Kremlin's interior. As they crossed the great square between the Commissariat of Justice and the Cavalry Corps they spotted Leon Trotsky. Marguerite recorded watching 'a broad-shouldered man of middle height slightly inclined to stoutness at the waistline, but erect and military in his bearing.' She later noted that he had 'grey-green eyes, a prominent chin, brought still more into relief by a dark chestnut goatee, and close-clipped dark moustache.' She chased after him and, speaking in French, asked him about the People's Army. Without giving them much information he responded politely, asking her about America and her impressions of Soviet Russia. When the conversation came to an end Trotsky kissed her hand and bade her a pleasant visit.

Pleasant meetings with Trotsky aside, the relative freedom of movement and of contact that Marguerite had enjoyed in Moscow for the past couple of months was about to be circumscribed. In early April 1920, on the pretext that there was no longer any room at the Haritonevsky Guest House, Marguerite, Francis McCullagh and Dr Anna Karlin were moved to the Hotel Savoy. Although much closer to the Foreign Office, the Savoy was by no means luxurious. There were no sheets, mattresses were infested with bugs, and washing facilities inadequate. Marguerite was also aware that some of the guests staying there were under surveillance. She was later remembered having 'an uneasy suspicion that all was not as it should be.'

Chapter Nine

The Death Ship

On Good Friday, April 2nd 1920, as Marguerite was walking home to the Hotel Savoy during the early hours of the morning from the Foreign Office, a friendly young Bolshevik guard stopped her. After confirming her name, he then took her to the Lubyanka. Francis McCullagh and Dr Anna Karlin also were arrested by the Cheka. McCullagh's first impression of Lubyanka was that its exterior was similar to that of Harrods or Selfridges. 'Far from resembling a gloomy prison like the forbidding fortress of SS. Peter and Paul [in Petrograd], it is light and airy in style of architecture, and there is not a single iron bar on any of its exterior windows.'[1] He noted the inscriptions on the windows which still advertised a dentist, music shop and bank. The sign over the doorway advised: 'It is prudent to insure your life' – a now ironic relic of the days when the building was the headquarters of the Russian Life Insurance Company.

Lubyanka might not have looked forbidding from the outside, but the Moscow Cheka was headquartered there and the prison was described by inmates as 'the death ship' because of its peculiar construction of inner courtyards and buildings. Executions took place in the 'engine room', once the archive of the insurance company. According to the Russian journalist Georgi Popoff, 'the persons condemned to die, most of whom show an incredible submissiveness and resignation to their fate, are pushed naked through the corridor door into the hold; thence they are made to descend the iron ladder into the "engine room", where they are delivered into the hands of the executioner.'[2] Prisoners were then shot with a revolver, often at the back of the neck in order to mutilate the face and make it unrecognisable.

On arrival, Marguerite was searched, photographed and her thumbprints taken. She was then led to a small, dingy room with a whitewashed window and a plank bed, and given mouldy black bread and a poor imitation of tea. A peephole in the centre of the door was opened every thirty minutes.

Later, she was escorted to a room to be interviewed by Solomon Grigorevich Mogilevsky – who reminded her of a black puma – and Viacheslav Rudolfovich Menzhinsky, the head of a special section of the

Cheka, who spoke twelve languages but was described by his enemies as a dilettante and hypochondriac.

The 'black puma' soon informed Marguerite that they had been watching her and were well aware that she was an American spy. Mogilevsky claimed that they had her reports, and to prove it she was shown a copy, word for word, of a despatch that she had sent to the MID. Marguerite immediately knew there must have been a security breach within the agency and that the Cheka were most probably aware that she had been a spy since her Berlin days. Indeed, on March 15th, a cable had been sent from Colonel William Godson in Geneva to the MID, that raised the alarm. Marguerite's boss, Brigadier-General Churchill, then cabled the military attaché in Warsaw to warn 'B', [3] but it is not known if she had received the warning.

Marguerite was questioned at length about Francis McCullagh. Although the Cheka appeared to accept her denial of any knowledge that he was any more than a journalist, the interrogations continued. Eventually, Mogilevsky told her he was prepared to grant her liberty under certain conditions. She must make no attempt to leave Moscow, and it was essential that she report to Mogilevsky once a week to pass on information about any foreign visitors that she encountered. If Marguerite did not accept these conditions, she would be charged as a Polish spy. As Russia was now on the cusp of war with Poland and, as she had crossed illegally into Russia via Poland, she was in danger of execution.

To spy for one's own country, even against one's own countrymen, as Marguerite had done in Germany in the Robert Minor case, was one thing. But to spy against one's own country and its allies for a foreign power – a foreign power in whose cause she did not believe – was quite another. The consequences of such treachery, she must have known, would be severe. The notorious spy for the Germans, the Dutchwoman Mata Hari, who allegedly sent thousands of Allied soldiers to their graves, was shot by a French firing squad in 1917. Moreover, if Marguerite agreed to spy for the Russians, there could be terrible repercussions – torture and possible death – for anyone whom she informed on to the Cheka.

The decision, apparently, did not weigh heavily on Marguerite. The world that she had been desperate to leave behind suddenly beckoned. 'Like a drowning person who sees all his past life in a second, I saw the image of Tommy waiting in vain for me in Switzerland. I thought of my friends, my secure peaceful life in Baltimore. In that moment I renounced everything that hitherto made up my existence. It was finished – and I felt as if I had already died and been born into a new nightmare world.'

She looked Mogilevsky directly in the eyes and answered so calmly that she wondered about herself: 'I accept your proposition.'

Within 72 hours of their arrests, Marguerite, McCullagh and Dr Karlin were released. Marguerite spent two weeks at the Hotel Savoy before being returned to the Haritonevsky Guest House.[4] She was now a 'double-agent'. Her first assignation with Mogilevsky was at the Alexandrovsky Gardens at 4 p.m. Entrance to the gardens was through the magnificent cast-iron gates built to commemorate the Russian victories over Napoleon. Marguerite walked with Mogilevsky as if they were long-lost friends, passing on the most trivial gossip she thought she could get away with in the hope that this would satisfy the Cheka.

In the meantime, she sent messages or ciphers via diplomats warning people to keep away from her.[5] She also contacted the American Consul at Helsinki to say that she thought her life was in danger. This was passed on to the Associated Press bureau in London who informed the MID. A message was sent recalling her to America to work on the Presidential election, and Krasin, who was at the time in London, was asked to assist in getting her exit papers. These efforts were to no avail as Marguerite was to be detained indefinitely along with other Americans so as to pressure the United States administration into recognising the Bolshevik government.

Whether or not it was particularly wise under the circumstances, Marguerite nevertheless began assisting the British priest, Frank North, in sending food packages to British officers who had been captured at Omsk and had been taken to Moscow's Andronowski monastery, now being used as a prison. North was the head of St Andrew's Anglican Church, and as there was no official British representation in Moscow, he took charge of affairs of the British citizens in the city. Previously, he had been curate at St Thomas's Anglican Church in Petrograd, whose tower has been used by the Bolsheviks during the October Revolution to fire at passing counter-revolutionaries whilst North and his family sheltered in the basement of the parsonage next door. He had never learnt Russian, but his wife, Margaret Caird Birse, whose Scottish parents had worked in Petrograd as representatives of the cotton merchants, Hubbards, spoke the language fluently. When food shortages in Moscow were acute in 1919, Frank North had opened a soup kitchen for the poor and served up millet and horse meat, and anything else edible that he could get his hands on.

Presumably in anticipation of the information that Marguerite would report to him, Mogilevsky gave her and Reverend North permission to visit the British officers at Andronowski Prison and take tea with them on Sunday afternoons. The officers were housed in the former monks' quarters with a piano in an adjacent room they could use. They were treated far better than detained Americans and were even driven to the opera or theatre once a week and permitted to shop, if accompanied by a guard.

Marguerite soon had new company at her lodgings. In December 1919, 249 suspected Communists and anarchists had been herded onto the *Burford*, a ship that became known as the 'Soviet Ark', and exiled from America to Russia under the terms of the 1918 Anarchist Exclusion Act. They were not allowed to take their wives or children with them and most were never to see their families again. When the deportees began arriving in Moscow, some of them – including two of the most famous, Emma Goldman and Alexander Berkman – were lodged in the Haritonevsky Guest House.

Emma Goldman was only one of three women in the group from the *Burford*. Born in Lithuania, she had emigrated with her sister to the United States in 1885. After meeting and falling in love with Alexander Berkman, she became involved in anarchism and was eventually imprisoned for two years in 1917 for encouraging people to refuse to register for the draft. Berkman, also a passenger on the 'Soviet Ark', had been born in Lithuania, but was raised in Petrograd by his Jewish parents. Emigrating to New York after the death of his parents, he became an anarchist soon after arrival in 1887. Berkman was notorious for his attempted assassination of Henry Clay Frick, manager of the Carnegie Steel Company's factory. In 1892, steelworkers had struck for better pay and conditions in what became known as the Homestead Strike. Frick dealt with the strike by hiring 300 armed guards from the Pinkerton Detective Agency to break up the picket lines. Several were killed, and when the strike was broken, Berkman resolved to visit Frick in his office and kill him. Despite shooting him three times and stabbing him in the leg, Frick did not die, and Berkman was to spend fourteen years in jail.

When Goldman and Berkman arrived in Moscow they were given the room next to Marguerite at the Haritonevsky, probably so she could spy on them for the Russians, but they also would have been of interest to the MID. Marguerite described Berkman as a 'quiet little man with a big domed forehead brought more into prominence by his baldness, with kindly, somewhat near-sighted grey-green eyes, rather owlish in expression behind his huge horn-rimmed spectacles.' Years of life in prison had left him in ill health and, when he suffered a stomach attack, Marguerite prepared him some light food and lent him her hot-water bottle. When Berkman recovered, he and Goldman accepted a job collecting information on the revolution for a proposed museum. Provided with a car and a guard, they set off on a tour of the Ukraine, along with another American journalist, Henry Alsberg of the London *Daily Herald*. However, Goldman was to become disillusioned with the new Bolshevik state and would grow increasingly homesick for America.

Marguerite was to remain in Moscow, presently confined there by the Cheka.

* * *

Meanwhile, Stan had continued to provide articles from Germany for *The Daily News*. She tracked down and interviewed Ignatius Timothy Trebitsch-Lincoln, Kapp's former press censor. Trebitsch-Lincoln, according to Stan, was capable of talking himself into or out of any situation – rather like herself. He was of particular interest to the British, having once been a British MP. A Hungarian Jew who converted to Christianity when he came to England, he became a missionary in Canada, held a curacy in Kent, and got elected as a Liberal MP for County Durham in 1910, before retiring after nine months due to lack of funds. Rejected by the British Secret Service, he instead became an agent for the Germans. Emigrating to the United States in 1915, he was extradited to England on charges of fraud, and when convicted spent three years in Parkhurst Prison on the Isle of Wight. On his release in 1919, Trebitsch-Lincoln immediately travelled to Germany where he became involved with Dr Kapp and the Kappists – and where he began his next career.

On the 13th of April, Stan paid a visit to Colonel Neill Malcolm, Chief of the British Military Mission in Berlin, and told him that Trebitsch-Lincoln was openly discussing organising a new putsch and making Gustav Bauer, who had resigned as Chancellor the previous month, either President or Chancellor. Malcolm wrote in his diary that Stan had reported Trebitsch-Lincoln saying 'that putting up Kapp was the greatest mistake.' Trebitsch-Lincoln assured Stan that his party had the support of Winston Churchill, received through Cologne.[6]

According to Malcolm, this was the second time the British Government had been unfairly implicated in backing unrest in Germany. He wrote in his diary regarding the Kapp Putsch: 'A most unpleasant feature of the whole affair has been a fairly general effort to implicate the British Government and to say that the whole thing was known to, if not engineered by, the British Military Mission. Of course there is not a word of truth in this, but some colour is lent to it by the fact that I have met Lüttwitz on several occasions.' Malcolm added that despite Lüttwitz knowing the truth – that the British had not backed him – he was still prepared to swear in a court of law that there had been direct assurance of support.

On May 3rd 1920, Stan provided a major scoop to *The Daily News*. Captain Hermann Ehrhardt had been ordered to hand over his defeated 2nd Marinebrigade to General von Bernd. This development was deeply resented by the nationalists and anti-Communists, so the date had been kept secret. However, Stan was tipped off by one of her many Socialist contacts and, pretending to be a relative, walked into the Munsterlager, a military training camp near Munster in North Rhine-Westphalia, where the ceremony was being held. The heath on this occasion re-sounded with the sounds of boots and songs of 6,000 troops loyal to Captain Ehrhardt. The 2nd Marinebrigade made a fearsome sight. 'A swastika on our helmet,' they had sung, 'and a black, red and white band – we are called the Ehrhardt Brigade!'[7]

A few days earlier, she had managed to interview Captain Ehrhardt, who, despite his relatively lowly naval rank, commanded the thousands of shock troops who had so effortlessly captured Berlin in March. She described him as 'a square-set man of medium height with a sunburnt face and a blunt, straightforward manner'. He was blunt indeed, inform-ing her that the dissolution of his brigade would mean 'Bolshevism in Berlin'. Ehrhardt blamed the failure of the Kapp Putsch on Jewish under-secretaries of state who provoked strikes and paralysed the machinery of the state. 'We neglected to shoot these under[-]secretaries – a fatal mistake,' he told her. He also blamed the cowardice of the middle class, who were delighted with the coup 'but stayed at home and rubbed their hands with glee, instead of coming forward openly to help us'.[8]

Ehrhardt was in equally bellicose form in the Munsterlager, thanking his troops for their loyalty and expressing the hope that he and they would soon be reunited 'for the sake of the Fatherland'. Readers of *The Daily News* were left in no doubt where his men's loyalties lay, because Stan reported that a company officer called out: 'Eyes right and look at the captain, not the general,' as Captain Ehrhardt and his successor, Gen-eral von Bernd, reviewed the brigade.

Entranced, Stan took out her notebook and began to record the pro-ceedings. She was quickly spotted by one of the Marinebrigade officers. 'This is simply unheard of,' he declared as he examined her papers. 'The speech is to the brigade only. Withdraw 500 paces immediately!' But Stan, as ever, had connections. Another officer whom she had met in Berlin also spotted her and he allowed her to stay in the parade ground and listen to Ehrhardt as he introduced his successor.

The men in steel helmets marching through the Munsterlager had crushed the 'Red Terror' in Germany. But there was one place where the Reds remained undefeated. That was, of course, Russia – and that was where Stan, who always wanted to be at the heart of the action, planned to go next.

* * *

In late-April 1920, Marshal Piłsudski pre-empted Lenin's plans for a Communist Poland (which would have provided a gateway to Germany) by invading the Ukraine. Russia and Poland were at war and as a consequence, Marguerite Harrison's 'controller', Solomon Grigorevich Mogilevsky, was now preoccupied with greater matters than an American journalist/spy. Reckoning that she now had a greater latitude to act, Marguerite continued to file reports to the MID and mix with the residents of and visitors to Moscow. She ate in illegal restaurants and in people's homes, met Diemen Biedny, the poet employed by the propaganda department, at Domino, the poets' club on the Tverskaya. She visited the Tschoukin and Tretiakov art galleries and, with Ivan Axionov from her boarding house, attended the opera, where she heard Feodor Chaliapin sing, and watched plays by Tolstoy. She talked to the German Socialist politician and a co-founder of the Spartacus League, Clara Zetkin, and described her as a 'fat little German Hausfrau in appearance, and always wearing a black silk dress, with a lace collar and a large cameo broach. Her cheeks are as ruddy as winter apples and her grey hair is parted and drawn to a demure little knot on the back of her head.' She also met delegations from China, Persia, Afghanistan, Italy and Germany, as well as Irish members of Sinn Fein, Indian nationalists and Djemal Pasha, the Turk from Anatolia who opposed the British-controlled government in Constantinople. But, Marguerite's situation was taking a toll on her and she wrote, 'I was miserably lonely and homesick and the strain of waiting for the inevitable dénouement was very great.'

In early May 1920, Reverend North and his family were expelled from Russia. Prior to their departure, the Cheka had published an alleged confession by Mrs North, accusing her husband of handling money for the counter-revolutionaries. The purpose seemed to be propaganda, and they were both allowed to leave before the case came to trial. Safely back in London, North was interviewed by the American military attaché, Colonel Oscar Solbert, about what he knew of Marguerite. North told him that it was widely thought that she was sending derogatory information about the Soviets through irregular channels. He suspected this was why all the men and women in his party were stripped naked at the frontier and roughly searched for hidden papers.[9]

Marguerite had taken over from the Reverend North the task of supplying 28 imprisoned British officers with food packages. Mogilevsky must have approved of her doing this, almost certainly with the understanding that she would inform on them. In order to supply the officers, she exchanged American dollars on the black market, sold more of her belongings, and used money donated by foreigners who had left Russia. She also assisted a Mademoiselle Charpentier from the French Red Cross, supplying food to the French and a few American prisoners. On Monday and Thursday mornings the two women would visit the Soukharévka market, buy food, spend the afternoon cooking it over Marguerite's kerosene stove, then set off to distribute food parcels to the foreign prisoners at Butyrka, Lubyanka and Andronowski prisons.

Mademoiselle Charpentier had received a note from a Polish prisoner indicating that one of his fellow inmates was an American. A further note arrived from the man in question, a Corporal Mosher, who claimed that he was indeed American, having served as a pilot with the Lafayette Escadrille during the war, later joined the American Expeditionary Force and then volunteered for the Kościuszko Air Squadron in the Polish army. He was taken prisoner by the Bolsheviks near Kiev at the end of July after his plane was shot down. Charpentier told Marguerite who, well aware of the appalling conditions in the Polish prisoner of war camp, sent him a food package and asked what else he needed. Mosher replied quickly: a blanket, pillow, clothing, toilet articles, food and, most importantly, a pipe and tobacco.

Corporal Mosher, it transpired, was none other than Merian C. Cooper, the dashing man Marguerite had met few months earlier when they had chatted and danced together at a ball in Warsaw. He had taken the name Mosher which was written on the underpants he had acquired from the Red Cross. Fortunately, Cooper was soon transferred to Andronowski Prison where conditions were far better. As with Marguerite and Stan Harding, Merian Cooper and Marguerite Harrison's paths would cross again.

Constance Grace Lesslie 'Stan' Harding

The Lesslie family home in Toronto, Canada, where Stan was raised

*The Baker family mansion, Ingleside, built by Marguerite's father
in Catonsville, outside of Baltimore, Maryland*

Marguerite Elton Harrison, née Baker.

The German artist, Käthe Kollwitz

Edward Gordon Craig with his wife (Mina Loy) and children

(Top left) *British artist, Stephen Haweis;*

(top right) *American radical journalist, John Reed;*

(left) *arts patron, Mabel Dodge;*

(above) *art historian, Bernhardt* (later, Bernhard) *Berenson*

Designs for soft pear wood carvings
by Edward Gordon Craig;
Beast (top left), Eve (left) *and*
Beauty (above) *for which*
Stan Harding was the model
during their tempestuous love affair in
Florence in the early years
of the 20th century

(Left) Albert Ritchie, Marguerite's brother-in-law and lover;
Van Lear Black, friend of Marguerite's and Chairman of The Baltimore Sun

Joseph Ames, of Johns Hopkins University, Marguerite's
supporter and stepfather-in-law.

(Left) Brigadier-General Marlborough Churchill, head of the American MID;
Brigadier-General Ralph Van Deman, previous head of the MID

Leaders of the National Assembly in Weimar where a new constitution for Germany was written and adopted. (Left to right) *Justice Minister Dr Otto Landsberg; Chancellor Philipp Scheidemann; War Minister Gustav Noske; President Friedrich Ebert; Work Minister Dr Rudolph Wissell*

Pro-government defensive position, Berlin, early 1919

The Freikorps in Berlin, January 1919, during the Spartacist uprising; the tank is a captured British Mk IV

Spartacist militia in Berlin, early 1919, during the uprising

(Above) *Karl Liebknecht and Rosa Luxemburg, 1909*
(Left) *Clara Zetkin* (left) *and Luxemburg, 1910*

Family scavenging in Berlin, early 1919

Chapter Ten

A Completely Crazy Plan

On April 27th 1920, a British delegation from the Labour Party left Newcastle upon Tyne for Russia to report on Socialism in the making there and to see if there were any grounds for the negative reports in the Western press. The party of fourteen arrived in Moscow via Petrograd in early May for their six-week visit. Amongst the delegation was Philip Snowden, the former Labour MP who had lost his seat in the 1918 election largely due to his pacifist views. He was accompanied by his wife Ethel, a leading campaigner for women's suffrage who, as the party departed English shores, proclaimed to a journalist that the Russian Revolution was 'the most important experiment of the time'.[1] A fellow delegate was Clifford Allen, a member of the Fabian Society who in 1914 published *Is Germany Right and Britain Wrong*? He had served sixteen months in prison during 1916-17 for refusing military service. Dr Leslie Haden-Guest, also in the party had served in both the Boer War and the Great War, and had pioneered hygiene clinics as a school doctor for the London County Council. Another member was esteemed mathematician and philosopher, Bertrand Russell – though Marguerite was not impressed: 'In spite of his profession of Socialism, Russell was essentially an aristocrat … He could not mix with the proletariat and there was always an air of aloofness about him.' She noted that the Snowdens, on the other hand, arrived with open minds, and that Clifford Allen was a dreamer and idealist. Another delegate was George Young, the journalist she had met back in Berlin in 1918, and who had first introduced her to Stan Harding.

The Bolsheviks left no stone unturned, or opera box empty, to please their British comrades. As Emma Goldman bitterly observed, the Labour Delegation 'was entertained royally with theatre, operas, ballets and excursions. Luxury was heaped upon them while the people slaved and went hungry.'[2] Dr Haden-Guest added that despite being treated in a royal manner wherever they went, 'it was interesting – but fatiguing and after a point boring beyond belief.'[3]

When the delegation was to take a cruise on the Volga, Mogilevsky ordered Marguerite to join the delegation on their trip. She entertained, apparently, few scruples about spying on the British for the Russians.

From Moscow, the party of 40 that included delegates, interpreters, journalists and secretaries went in luxury by rail to Nizhny Novgorod, and then by steamboat to Saratov. The train and steamboat were equipped with white, starched linen sheets, electric lights and offered three good meals a day. Saratov, a major city in southern Russia, was home to the Volga Germans. The German-born Catherine the Great had encouraged Germans to emigrate and farm Russian land, and they had maintained their own culture, language and traditions.

Told that they had the freedom to see whatever they wanted, in reality the delegation was always accompanied by anything from six to twenty Bolshevik minders. And, according to Ethel Snowden, the delegates were regularly used in Soviet propaganda, including having their photos taken sitting on podiums while watching countless parades lasting as long as four hours whilst the workers, university graduates, boy scouts, girl guides and young gymnasts proceeded past.

A few days after the party had boarded a boat to Saratov, Clifford Allen was stricken with pleurisy and pneumonia. Marguerite helped greatly to nurse him and it was planned that once they reached Saratov, the delegation would return to Moscow by train. But when they arrived, Allen suffered a haemorrhage and could not be moved. Dr Haden-Guest, with help from Bertrand Russell and Mrs Snowden, took over the nursing duties as they sailed on to Astrakhan, where the Volga River meets the Caspian Sea. As Marguerite was not permitted to travel to a Cossack region, she returned with the rest of the delegation to Moscow.

Once back in Moscow, Marguerite soon gave Mogilevsky the information she had gleaned from the British delegates. That evening, while sending despatches to Associated Press from the Foreign Office, the translator Mikail Rosenberg told her he had received an application to visit Russia from a Mrs Stan Harding, correspondent for *The World*. What, he asked, did she know of her?

Marguerite suspected that the Cheka knew that she and Stan had shared a hotel room in Berlin. She remained composed and, thinking quickly, told him the truth, recommending that Stan be refused a permit on the grounds that she was not a serious journalist. Sensing professional jealousy, Mogilevsky challenged her and, finally, was not persuaded by her objections. Marguerite then spoke with Walter Meakin of *The Daily News* in the hope that he would discourage Stan from her proposed visit. As the weeks were to pass with no sign of her 'friend', Marguerite concluded that Stan must have successfully been warned off.

* * *

The call for a correspondent with Socialist leanings in 1920 was to get into Russia to report the 'truth' about the Bolsheviks. Stan was no different: 'At this time my prejudices were far from being anti-Soviet… I thought that anyone who took an interest in politics must see this experiment for himself before forming an opinion.' Evidently, she had hoped to go to there as early as 1919, and by 1920 had an 'overwhelming wish' to see Communist Russia.[4] After witnessing Stan's exploits during the Spartacist Uprising, Käthe Kollwitz observed that 'she has the completely crazy plan of going to Russia ... Of course, she doesn't want to stay there, she wants to write for *The Times* and the *Daily Mail* from there. This work runs her down terribly, but I like the way she goes at it immensely, with so much energy.'

Getting into Russia, however, would not be an easy task. Although Walter Meakin, a member of the British Labour Party's delegation to Russia, was already in Moscow reporting for *The Daily News*, most journalists were refused entry visas. But Stan was confident that she would secure the necessary paperwork. Indeed, in early June 1920 she managed to convince James Tuohy, European editor of the *New York World*, who had been unable to get visas for his regular correspondents, to hire her instead. He even sent her a sample of the type of copy he was after.

News out of Russia was patchy at this time, and the Bolsheviks were extremely wary of the outside world – with good reason, especially as far as the British were concerned. After the Brest-Litovsk Treaty had been signed between the Germans and Russians in 1918, Winston Churchill, then Minister of Munitions, had despatched British troops to Northern Russia. At the time, the Allies were concerned that supplies sent to aid the Russian war effort and which were now sitting in Russian ports would likely find their way into German hands. The detachment of 170 Royal Marines at Murmansk was joined in late-June 1918 by further British troops, along with thousands of American, Canadian, French, Australian, Greek and Japanese soldiers who now supported the White Russians and the anti-Bolshevik resistance. Additionally, the British also were to supply significant amounts of matériel, and 'advisors' to the White Armies fighting the Reds and the anarchist Greens in the south of the country.

The Bolsheviks were convinced that the British had been behind a plan to assassinate Lenin and overthrow the government. On the 30th of August 1918, a military cadet assassinated the head of the Petrograd Cheka, Moisei Uritsky, sending shock waves through the ranks of the Bolsheviks. The next day, Dora Kaplan from the Socialist Revolutionary

Party fired shots at Lenin, seriously wounding him in the arm, jaw and neck. The Bolsheviks were quick to fill the newspapers with propaganda stories of nefarious British plans. Nearly two years later, the Bolsheviks were as wary as ever, and it was this world of treachery and suspicion that Stan hoped to enter.

* * *

Despite having letters of introduction from prominent Socialists in Germany, Stan Harding was unable to make any headway in getting permission to enter Bolshevik Russia. Arriving Copenhagen, she found that the Swedish Embassy and the Estonian Legation refused to grant visas for British journalists en route to Russia without recommendation from the British Embassy – which presently was rejecting all requests. Maxim Litvinov, the Bolsheviks' roaming ambassador, met Stan in Copenhagen and handed her a letter of introduction enabling her to travel on via Stockholm to Reval (Tallinn) in Estonia. She would be the guest of the Soviet Legation People's Commissar for Foreign Affairs, Georgy Chicherin. She was greeted on arrival by a man named Gie, 'a fat Jew,' in her words, who was an assistant to the Soviet Economic Commission in Reval. He told her that Chicherin's invitation and permission to travel to Russia had arrived, 'and you will go on the first diplomatic train.'[5]

In Reval, Stan met members of the British Labour Delegation on their way home from their Volga cruise and their gruelling tour of Moscow's finest operas and theatres. She found that not everyone had been impressed with the Bolsheviks. Bertrand Russell told her that Bolshevism was danger to Socialism. Stan found that her enthusiasm 'to see Soviet Moscow shivered in the draught of his criticism, but my hope remained that out of this chaos a new and better state of society would arise'. Russell warned her that, from Reval on, she would be surrounded by both Bolshevik and anti-Bolshevik spies, and that she should proceed with the utmost caution. Another delegate asked if she was not afraid to travel into Russia on her own. 'No,' she replied, 'whom should I be afraid of? I shall not be up to any counter-revolutionary intrigue and the Bolsheviks are intelligent enough to know that.'[6]

There was, of course, much to be afraid of. In England, Lord Emmott had been asked by the British Foreign Secretary, Lord Curzon, to chair a committee on Russia. It was to investigate the conditions under which British subjects were recently imprisoned or detained in there, and to assess the country's economic and political situation. The Foreign Office suggested that Emmott interview some of the 800 British refugees recently returned to England on the SS *Tagus* and SS *Dongola*. By the time Stan had set off for Moscow from Reval, Emmott and his team had interviewed over 40 Britons, including Marguerite's Moscow acquaintances, Reverend Frank North and Francis McCullagh. The report was to be published later in the year in a White Paper consisting of three volumes entitled *Minutes of Evidence Taken before the Committee to Collect Information on Russia*. Accounts of harrowing experiences at the hands of the Cheka were to make for distressing reading.

Stan did not question why she had received her visas so quickly when other foreign journalists were refused them, or why she had been invited to join the diplomatic train heading for Moscow. She blithely assumed all was natural – a consequence of what had been, all her life, the ability to push her way almost effortlessly through doors that were closed to others.

There was something else that should have triggered warning bells that all was not as it seemed. In Reval, members of the British Labour Delegation told her that Marguerite Harrison was under suspicion by the Bolsheviks, that she had spent 70 hours in prison, and now went to see Chicherin every evening. 'I also knew positively,' Stan later wrote, 'that she was working for the American State Department – that is to say I knew positively that she was doing secret service work.'[7] But, characteristically, Stan ignored these cautionary details and rushed forward.

On the 24th of June 1920, Stan Harding, with 'Pass' stamped in her passport, crossed the border on a train from Estonia into Russia, heading east towards Petrograd, 360 kilometres away, and then on to Moscow. She occupied a clean, well-kept sleeping car with an 'absolutely filthy' washroom devoid of towels and other amenities.[1]

Stan was soon approached on the train by a man who introduced himself as Solomon Grigorevich Mogilevsky. She took him to be nothing more than a helpful, courteous official from the Foreign Office. In reality, of course, the 35-year-old Polish Jew was head of the Cheka in Moscow – and the man who had turned Marguerite Harrison into his spy. Stan realised later that Mogilevsky was on a very specific mission to Estonia. 'I have reason to believe,' she later claimed, 'that Mogilevsky was sent specially to Reval to meet me for the purpose of accompanying me to Moscow.'[2] He was joined by his interpreter, Julius Rozinsky, who, having lived in London for many years, spoke impeccable English.

Stan found Mogilevsky very attentive and helpful: he brought her towels for the washroom, purchased strawberries when they arrived at the last station on the Estonian border, and in general 'danced attendance' on her.[3] When the train reached Yambourg, the passengers disembarked for a bout of rousing propaganda: they listened to recitations by a revolutionary poet, to a rendition of 'The Internationale', and to recordings of Trotsky's stirring speeches played on a 'magnificent gramophone' onto which a girl laid the record 'reverently in position.'[4] When Stan went into a station bookshop, she saw that there was virtually nothing in stock except propaganda and a few books on agriculture. Another stop on the journey allowed Stan and the other passengers to murmur appreciatively over the sight of a locomotive that had been finished by volunteer workers on – as the happy coincidence recorded on a plaque stated – May Day.

Mogilevsky took pains to engage with Stan during their journey. As the train puffed and shunted its way through the flat landscape with its endless screens of trees, he was critical of the British and the blockade. 'Your country paid for the shells,' he would sternly inform Stan as they passed shell-holes – of which there were plenty – by the sides of the tracks.

When the train stopped at Gatchina, Stan was permitted to interview soldiers while Mogilevsky translated, but she thought the replies sounded suspiciously well-rehearsed. Still, her enthusiasm for the new political experiment did not waver. 'Of course,' she later stated, 'I was still thoroughly pro-Bolshevik, without being a Bolshevik.'[5] She and Mogilevsky sat up late into the night, under the midnight sun, talking about German politics. He was, she decided from these discussions, 'hopelessly ignorant of European politics', thinking, for example, that the Italians had not entered the war until 1918.[6]

On the 25th of June the train at last neared Petrograd. It took a full six hours to crawl into the station, all the while allowing other trains to come and go. Looking out of the window, Stan saw the people of Petrograd, who were 'most fearfully badly dressed', which she attributed to the effects of the blockade.[7] Everyone appeared ill-nourished. She witnessed a poignant scene: a woman hurrying past the station fell while carrying a pint of milk, which broke. 'She burst into tears over this accident,' Stan wrote. 'That showed one what a disaster that sort of accident was in Russia.' Petrograd was, she concluded, a place of 'generally fearful misery'.[8]

The delegates arriving for the Third International Conference finally disembarked and were escorted to meet the President of the Petrograd Soviet, Grigori Zinoviev. Stan asked if she could join them as she had a letter of introduction to meet him, but Mogilevsky refused to let her off the train. She was also refused permission to interview Emma Goldman, who was visiting Petrograd. 'I thought it would be a rather good story for the New York paper to have a chat,' she said. But this, too, was denied. Rozinsky warned her: 'You see, you have not yet got your Sovietski passport, and if you go out by yourself you are liable to arrest.' Eventually, Rozinsky accompanied her for a walk down Nevsky Avenue, Petrograd's main thoroughfare – a 'very dreary stroll in the rain' past buildings with 'an indescribably filthy appearance'.[9]

Before the October Revolution, Nevsky Avenue had been spectacular. Buildings bordering the street included the superb Stroganov Palace; the neoclassical Kazan Cathedral, an eighteenth-century indoor shopping complex containing over 100 shops; and the Passage, a department store completed in 1848, its three storeys encased in an arching glass ceiling. However, in 1920 there was little left of the Nevsky's former glory. Most of the shops were closed and, as Stan stumbled into one of the 'numerous great holes made in the roadway by the removal of wood for blocks for firewood, and went nearly up to my knees in a puddle of water,' her spirits fell. 'Trudging down the middle of the Nevsky I hunted in my mind for an expression that would do justice to the flea-bitten appearance of the buildings, attacked apparently by some strange architectural blight.' She thought the people looked preoccupied and sullen, like those she had seen in Berlin after the Armistice.

There was, however, time for an outing: Rozinsky escorted Stan to Pavlovsk, a town some 30 kilometres from Petrograd. Before the revolution, Pavlovsk had been the country seat of the Grand Duke Konstantine and was a summer retreat for the bourgeoisie, many of whom, Stan noticed on her 'fearfully crowded train' from Petrograd, were still very much in evidence; or at any rate, she saw many people who were better-dressed than those in Petrograd. She witnessed them in the audience when Rozinsky took her to an open-air ballet theatre where they watched a performance of 'awfully good dancing'. Afterwards she watched these relics of the old Russia 'strolling around a pond, in a sort of enchanted way'. However, she felt pity for this leisured class, still clinging to their old ways – 'trying to do the old game' – while a great social and political experiment was happening in their own land.[10] She and Rozinsky arrived back in Petrograd in the middle of the night, and the desolation of the city was made even more eerie under the pale light of the midnight sun.

The following day, along with the delegates of the Third International, Stan boarded the train for the 700-kilometre journey to Moscow. The cars shunted along, she joked to Rozinsky, 'like an archbishop on a tri-cycle'.[11] On arrival, the delegates were 'whisked off in a motorcar' while Stan remained on-board with Mogilevsky. Foreign guests were put up in the Metropole, National or Savoy hotels, in the vacated palace of a Russian sugar king on the Sofiyskaya Naberezhnaya, or in the German factory owner Roelich's villa in Haritonovskaya Street. Stan was taken by Mogilevsky to Roelich's villa, renamed Haritonevsky Guest House, which she later learnt was nicknamed the 'House of Suspicion'. She would very soon discover that Marguerite Harrison was also billeted there.

Chapter Eleven

The House of Suspicion

The 'House of Suspicion' was guarded outside by a pair of soldiers and patrolled inside by what one of the guests, the fur dealer Hector Boon, called a 'rat-faced commandant who padded about the house in noiseless boots'. All was presided over by Ivan Axionov, described by Boon as a 'mustache-twirling, beard-combing, smirking, Iscariotic apology for a man'.[1]

At arriving at the Haritonevsky Guest House on June 27th 1920, Stan was surprised to be told that it was full. 'I was asked,' she later testified in London, 'if I would mind for one night having a room made up with Mrs. Harrison.'[2] This arrangement did not rouse any suspicion in Stan's mind, so she agreed, although she knew from the Labour delegates that Marguerite was suspected by the Bolsheviks, not least because of her cover as a journalist for *The Baltimore Sun*. 'That was a mistake on her part,' Stan later sniffed – the *Sun* was simply not big and important enough, she believed, to send a correspondent to Moscow.[3]

A young Russian woman, fluent in English and 'about twenty', Stan thought, was assigned to help her unpack. Stan, who suspected her of being a spy, learnt that the woman's brother had been shot by the Bolsheviks in Siberia, and that she was on her way back to Petrograd to determine if her parents were still alive. When Stan asked the woman to find her someone who could translate for her, she was asked if she preferred a Communist for the work. Stan replied that she would rather have someone without political bias – an answer that would later be used against her.

At the guesthouse she met Hector Boon, a British-born businessman based in New York who had spent the past few months trying to recover a consignment of 5,000 white fox skins confiscated by a bandit chief in Eastern Siberia. When he told her that he was writing a series of articles on his tribulations for, coincidentally, the *New York World*, Stan was sceptical. 'That seemed to me very suspicious and very funny, and I said to him: "How odd that the paper should not have mentioned to me that they had another correspondent in Russia."'[4] Yet Boon was telling the truth, and his articles about Russia would be published by the paper during the following January. They were highly critical of the Bolsheviks, whom he called 'a gang of thieves', 'the enemies of mankind', and a 'militant minority which is exploiting and terrifying 99 per cent of the Russian people'.[5]

Boon vented his frustration to Stan, even though Julius Rozinsky was present in the room (indeed, Boon later claimed that Rozinsky never left her side). As he launched into a long and bitter diatribe against the Soviet government and 'the results of Soviet misrule', Stan desperately tried to introduce him to Rozinsky who, she told him emphatically, was from the Soviet Foreign Office. When Boon heedlessly continued, she blinked at him frantically to get him to shut up. She felt 'rather uncomfortable' and, after fifteen minutes of anti-Soviet monologue, turned to Rozinsky for his opinion. 'I say they are all lies,' he said, beaming at Boon, who, undaunted, continued his assault.[6]

A lunch then followed ('soup, potatoes, meat – plenty of them') with ten other guests, all silent and strained, in 'an extraordinary atmosphere of suspicion'.[7] After coffee, Rozinsky invited her for a walk through the old financial sector, where Stan noted that all the banks had been closed down. They crossed the river to Red Square and strolled towards St Basil's Cathedral with its four distinctive onion-shaped domes.

Marguerite Harrison was at the guesthouse when Stan returned. There were no fond embraces. The American 'greeted me rather formally,' Stan recalled, 'of which I was glad, as I knew that she was suspected, and thought that if she greeted me very warmly some of the suspicion with which she was regarded might be diverted to me'.[8] An apologetic Mogilevsky appeared, and informed Stan that more suitable accommodation had been found, much nearer the city centre. 'You see, you will probably be going every evening to the Foreign Office, and it will be difficult to get cabs.'[9] She agreed, saying she would pack and move on the following day, but Mogilevsky replied: 'Do come now. I have a car.'[10] Taken by surprise, Stan, claiming she was tired, requested a quarter of an hour to rest before leaving. Spotting Marguerite in the billiard room, she asked her to accompany her to their room in the hope of discovering why she was being moved.

Here the two women's stories differ. In Marguerite's version of events, when they were alone Stan had greeted her enthusiastically. 'My dear,' Stan said, 'I am going to get us both out of this mess.' The implication was that she knew Marguerite was under some sort of pressure from the Bolsheviks. By Stan's reckoning, Marguerite seemed nervous and unwilling to spend time alone with her. No sooner were they together than Marguerite offered to get her a cup of tea 'and darted off again'. Stan then sent a maid to fetch the American 'to come back and chat with me while I was resting'.

Marguerite maintained that when she returned to the room, she said to Stan: 'I do not want to seem to want to speak to you alone. The situation is very critical' – at which point she once again left. Stan later reported that Marguerite's behaviour had not worried her, but that the fraught atmosphere of the guesthouse had made the American nervous.

After meeting Marguerite, Stan then sought out Hector Boon. 'Why did you run down the Soviet like that? Did you not see me blinking at you?' she asked. Boon replied that he did not. Nor, it seemed, was he concerned about possible retribution. Indeed, some weeks later, threatened with prison by the Bolsheviks, he was to tell them that if they dared proceed, Leonid Krasin, the Soviet representative in London, would be tossed into an English jail. It was a bluff, but enough to warn off the Russians.

Stan assumed that she was being shifted to another hotel 'to be removed from the contamination of Boon's anti-Soviet ideas'. She would be surrounded instead, she expected, by Soviet propaganda.[11] Mogilevsky reappeared to speed her along with her packing – 'my chauffeur will not wait'[12] – and within minutes she was ushered into a waiting car where Julius Rozinsky joined them. As they left the guesthouse, members of the luncheon party and the porter's children silently watched them go. Even so, Stan was not unduly concerned about her departure until they had crossed the river and arrived at Lubyanka Square. Here, Mogilevsky turned towards her and announced sternly: 'Madam, I have to tell you that you are under arrest.' Stan Harding had been in Moscow for fewer than 24 hours. Shocked and confused, she was taken into Lubyanka Prison, headquarters of the Cheka.

* * *

Mogilevsky had reason to be suspicious of any British woman travelling in Russia. The British had widely used women as spies during the Great War; indeed, some six thousand had served as members of the British Intelligence community during the previous decade. The British War Office at its counter-espionage headquarters in London had even used Girl Guides for war work, entrusting adolescent females with secret reports and memoranda.[13] British Intelligence had also recruited numerous female spies abroad, among them the famous traveller and archaeologist Gertrude Bell, the Belgian Gabrielle Petit, and Sarah Aaronsohn, the 'Jewish Joan of Arc'. No code of gallantry protected women spies from imprisonment and, sometimes, execution. Petit was shot by a German firing squad, and Aaronsohn killed herself while in Turkish captivity after being caught with a carrier pigeon fitted with an encrypted message for British Intelligence.

Stan was taken to a guardroom, stripped, and her clothes, including the seams and hems, examined, and then moved to a solitary cell furnished with nothing but a 'verminous plank bed – no chair'. She was lying on the floor when Mogilevsky appeared and asked if she was well enough to be interrogated. Anxious to hear his explanation for her arrest, she was then conducted upstairs to his study. 'By this time,' she later claimed, 'my blood was boiling.' Asking whether or not Chicherin had given permission for her visit to Moscow, Mogilevsky replied, 'Certainly, madam. We asked Chicherin to invite you because we wished to give you the choice between suffering the penalty of espionage in wartime or of disclosing the secrets of the British Organisation in Russia.' For Stan Harding was, he informed her, none other than the chief of the Secret British Organisation in Russia.[14]

'I am not,' she firmly told him, 'I never was, and I never will be in the British Intelligence Service.' Mogilevsky replied: 'Tell that to your grandmother.' The polite, solicitous tone that he had used on the train from Estonia was gone and he became 'fearfully rude'. Claiming that the Cheka possessed documents pertaining to her 'brilliant career' (as he much to her amazement called it), she was accused of having been an espionage agent in China at the time of the Boxer Rebellion. The claim was ludicrous, and Stan realised that Mogilevsky – who had a 'complete ignorance' of Chinese as well as European politics – must have received information regarding her voyage on the Upper Yangtze from one source in particular. 'I saw at once,' she later testified, 'that he had got a lot of details from Mrs. Harrison.'[15]

Had Marguerite informed on her to the Cheka, and if so, why? Marguerite's motives, Stan thought, were not that she feared that Stan would expose her to the Bolsheviks – because the Russians already knew that Marguerite was a secret agent of the American government. Rather, released from Lubyanka on condition she informed for the Bolsheviks, Marguerite was not only under pressure to produce results – to inform on others – but also fearful that Stan would see what she was doing and report her treachery to the British and Americans – 'as I certainly should have done.'[16]

The interrogation continued for several hours. Mogilevsky's questions confirmed her suspicions from his conversation on the train that he was 'stupid and ignorant – as I thought, fearfully stupid'.[17] Stan now understood that he had only a vague sense of her activities and even less of who she was. Mogilevsky told her that she had been working with a British Intelligence officer named Tuohy. To emphasise the fact, he waved a telegram found on Stan that Tuohy had sent her, outlining the type of 'copy' he required. And it was common knowledge, Mogilevsky added, that she was an accomplice of General Malcolm, chief of the British Mission in Berlin.

Still believing that she was caught up in a terrible misunderstanding, Stan politely corrected her interrogator. When the Boxer Rebellion ended in September 1901, she had just turned seventeen and was then visiting cousins in Canada. Immediately before that, she had been living in England with her family. Stan saw no reason to deny that she had known Marguerite Harrison in Berlin, but made it quite clear that it was only as a fellow journalist.

As for the telegram, that was easily explained: James Tuohy was the European manager of the *New York World* who had merely hired her to write on events in Russia for his newspaper. The claim was 'simply preposterous', the word 'copy' referred to newspaper copy, not to intelligence material. It soon became apparent to Stan that Mogilevsky had confused James with his son, Ferdinand Tuohy, the author of *The Secret Corps*, a book about the British Intelligence Service, and by his own admission a British agent during the Great War. She insisted she had never met Ferdinand nor was she aware of his book.

As for being an accomplice of General Malcolm, Stan admitted to taking tea with him in Berlin with the hope of gaining information for news stories; as had many foreign journalists stationed in the city during the Armistice. But she protested that there had been nothing out of the ordinary about their occasional conversations and lunches.

Mogilevsky was disbelieving, and then apprised Stan that the Cheka, having discovered her friend Marguerite to be an American spy, had been fortunate in making an 'arrangement' with her. Then came the bombshell – he suggested that Stan, too, might come to a similar arrangement with him in return for her freedom.

Stunned, she demanded to see Cheka boss Felix Dzerzhinsky, and Georgy Chicherin, from whom she had received her invitation to visit Russia. 'The Minister of Foreign Affairs does not concern himself with espionage,' she was told. 'Neither do I,' Stan replied. Mogilevsky assured her that she would not see Chicherin 'unless you come to terms with me'. He asked her to 'tell us your mission and denounce your accomplices'.[18] In vain she protested that she had neither a mission nor accomplices.

The gravity of her situation soon became very clear when Mogilevsky casually revealed the names of two more Entente agents who had come to an agreement with him. This information was highly sensitive, but he explained that he did not fear she would reveal their identities and their treachery to their home nations 'because you will never leave the cell where you now are except to suffer the penalty of espionage in war-time – unless we hold you in our power'.[19] That is, she would either be shot or, like Marguerite, become an informer.

Hour after hour, Mogilevsky went over the same ground, varying the wording of his questions in the hope of tripping her up. In the early morning Stan was finally returned to her cell. During her second interrogation there was an additional accusation of spying while she had been living in Italy. She denied this. After a third interrogation, with Stan unwilling to bend to Mogilevsky's will, he told her: 'Your case is closed. I have done what I can to save you, but you refuse to help me, and you have decided that you will remain faithful to the British Intelligence Service, and I can do nothing.'[20] She was then taken back to her cell.

* * *

For the first hours of her confinement, Stan was given only tea or coffee; but never knew which it was supposed to be: 'it was a sort of cross between the two'.[1] Later, she was given herring soup twice a day – or rather, the water in which herring had been boiled to make soup for the guards. What remained was a vile broth, with fins and eyes that floated on the surface. The only other nourishment was an occasional helping of porridge and some black bread.

She was alone in her cell, except for the lice that infested Lubyanka and brought the potentially fatal disease of typhus. Millions of Russians had died from it during and after the war. Victims experienced a rise in temperature, a fever, a rash on the chest, abdomen and wrists, weakness, delirium and coma, often swiftly followed by death.

Worst of all was the solitary confinement. 'Alone and without books,' she later wrote, 'one's only occupation was listening… listening with the acute hearing and exasperated sensibility that comes of solitary confinement. One listened to the sound of prisoners, like caged beasts at feeding-time, walking round and round their separate cells for half an hour or so before soup was brought, and to the sound of prisoners being taken from their cells in the middle of the night.' She heard the noise of a motor vehicle being started to hide the sound of executions, and the screams of fellow inmates gone insane in their cells. 'My position was similar to that of a miner who is entombed alive and knows that the only person who is aware of his whereabouts is one who wishes to prevent his rescue.' Clad only in summer clothes, Stan was terrified of being confined in her cell during the coming Russian winter where she would, literally, freeze to death.

She was, however, resourceful, and the solitude provided ample time to formulate a plan. She concocted a ruse to see Georgy Chicherin, thinking that if he knew of her incarceration he would order her release. During an interrogation with Mogilevsky, she fabricated a story that, under her guise as a journalist for the *New York World*, she had been instructed to collect secret information about Russia's raw materials. She invented a Russian contact – 'an anonymous and naturally fictitious man' – and told Mogilevsky that she would only reveal more if she could talk to Chicherin in person. Once she got to see him, she intended to 'make a hell of a row', indignantly demanding: 'Must I pretend to be a British spy, which I am not, in order to live free in Soviet Russia? Is that the condition of freedom in Soviet Russia?'[21]

Mogilevsky took the bait. Immediately he became very polite, telling her: 'I hoped that we should come to an understanding with you.' She was made to write up her account and sign it, but Mogilevsky then demanded more details, and told her that a condition of her release would be that she must spy for them.

Suddenly, Stan grasped that she had been invited to Russia for expressly that purpose. Crucially, the Cheka now had a signed document expressing her willingness to cooperate with them – a terrible lever they could use to extract more demands. One of Mogilevsky's constantly repeated mantras had been: 'Give us a document by which we hold you'[22] – a document that could, in effect, be used to blackmail her into working for the Cheka.[23]

The accusation of spying for the British – a charge that not even Mogilevsky credited – had merely been an attempt, she believed, to terrorise her into cooperating. Furious, she refused to give any more information about her mysterious contact unless she was taken to see Chicherin himself. Mogilevsky eventually agreed that she could see him if she made a fuller statement. She did so, but having never met him, insisted that a German Socialist editor, whom she knew to be in Moscow and who did know Chicherin, should accompany her.

The value placed on Stan Harding as a potential counter-espionage agent was revealed by the haste – less than an hour – with which both

Georgy Chicherin and the German editor appeared at the prison. 'It is Comrade Chicherin,' the editor confirmed. Stan then impulsively blurted: 'They are torturing me to make false confessions. You tell your colleagues that it is not true.'[24] Chicherin calmly replied that she could count on Mogilevsky's word, then left the room. However, Mogilevsky was furious, and once again she was locked alone in her cell.

In her oppressive isolation, broken only by further interrogations, Stan summoned back the summers she had spent alone on Italy's deserted Maremma coast. She became susceptible to images that appeared and disappeared before her eyes. At one moment, she was back in China, lying in a bamboo hammock on a junk roof; in another, she was in India on a moonlit evening, watching the throngs following an Indian temple ceremony until, 'swift as the click of a photographic shutter, it was gone'.

Once, after craning her neck to see a tiny patch of deep blue sky from her cell, she experienced a burst of Mediterranean sunshine flooding the cell. Overwhelmed by faintness, she let out a gasp and dropped to the floor as the image disappeared before her. She awoke with a soldier bending over her, reminding her to follow the rules of silence.

One vision in Lubyanka was all too real. A few weeks after Stan's arrest, Marguerite Harrison was summoned to the prison. She thought she was to be locked up again, but Mogilevsky had other plans. Marguerite's orders were to pass Stan in the corridor as the Englishwomen was being escorted back to her cell. 'I had no choice,' Marguerite protested, 'I left the room, and as I started to walk down the passage outside I saw Mrs Harding coming toward me, escorted by a soldier. Her head was held high and she looked angry and defiant as she gazed straight into my eyes without a sign of recognition.'

Stan was to later recall her thoughts in the wake of the brief encounter with Georgy Chicherin. 'There is no thirst like the thirst for justice, and from the moment I guessed the nature of the conspiracy of which I had been a victim, the wish to expose the lies which were suffocating me became the greater part of my will to live. Life without this vital justice was unthinkable, death without it unbearable.'

Now began a deep struggle of wills – between that of the Bolshevik State as personified by Solomon Grigorevich Mogilevsky, and that of Constance Grace Lesslie Harding, whose outrage at her unjust treatment would come to know no bounds.

Chapter Twelve

A Dust Heap of Lies

───◦◦◦───

Whilst Stan was firmly incarcerated in Lubyanka Prison; Marguerite remained at liberty – but under watch – at the Haritonevsky Guest House. During the six months that she had spent in Moscow, a number of fellow Americans had been imprisoned by the Bolsheviks. One of them, Merian C. Cooper, was the American pilot with the Kościuszko Squadron who Marguerite had met at a ball in Warsaw just before she travelled to Russia. His aircraft had been shot down over Russia in July 1920. Beaten by the Cossacks who found him, he was ultimately taken to Moscow and sent to a prison work camp there.

Also seized by the Bolsheviks was Weston Burgess Estes, a dentist and medical doctor from California who had served as a captain in Military Intelligence during the Great War. A friend of the radical John Reed, whom he met while mixing with – and possibly spying on – left-wing groups in America; Estes had secured a visa to enter Russia 'to study conditions there and to make motion pictures of what he saw'.[1] With him was John M. Flick, a journalist from the *Washington Star*. The pair arrived in Moscow in July 1920 and a few weeks later were arrested on spying charges. For many months, they, like Stan, subsisted on a grim diet of black bread and unappetising soups made of herring, cod heads 'and other piscatorial remnants'.[2] Estes was constantly threatened with execution, and Flick lost twenty-five pounds whilst on a hunger strike.

Another American imprisoned by the Bolsheviks in 1920 was Harvard-educated mining engineer Dr Alfred Wood Stickney. He had written his doctoral dissertation on pyritic copper deposits in Russia, and was working with the MID. Arrested in September, Stickney was held for two weeks while the Russians identified him. Released at the end of the month, he made his way to Riga, Latvia, from where he made an astonishing claim to the MID regarding Estes and Flick, both of whom were still imprisoned. He reported that the two Americans believed they had been denounced to the Cheka by 'B' – the code name for Marguerite Harrison. She was, they believed, 'under Bolsheviki compulsion'.[3]

If the men's suspicions were right, Marguerite had kept her promise to the Cheka by giving Mogilevsky the names of American Intelligence agents working in Russia. If so, her freedom was being maintained by the suffering of others.

* * *

Around the end of July 1920, after more than a month in Lubyanka and with seemingly no hope of release, Stan was to begin a series of hunger strikes. The first ended after several days when she was moved to a cell occupied by two women, Vera Ignatievna and Maria Vladimiorna, who both conversed with her in French. Vera had once been a leader in the counter-revolution but after capture became an informer. The French wife of a Russian aristocrat, Maria had played a minor role in Vera's organisation. Occasionally, other prisoners would join them in their cell: a Polish woman who had attempted to slit her wrists with a piece of glass, and an old woman who ranted and raved, believing, perhaps understandably in the circumstances, that she was being followed by spies. Each evening, Vera was taken away to report on anything she had overheard or gleaned.

Two weeks later, Vera and Maria were removed and Stan found herself alone again. 'Without books,' she recalled, 'one counts time not by days or weeks, but by hours, minutes, seconds.' She tried to practise the yoga she had learnt in India, but the lice made it impossible to perform the positions on the floor. Attempts at other Hindu exercises, designed to attain detachment, also failed.

Her misery was punctuated by further interrogations. On one occasion, Mogilevsky promised that she would be released if she were prepared to take a message to the British Prime Minister. Stan replied that she would do so, and signed a document to that effect. Unwisely, she confided to another prisoner – sent to spy on her – that the message she would give to the Prime Minister was that 'the present Communist Government is in the strangle-grip of the Cheka.'[4] Unsurprisingly, she was not dispatched to Downing Street.

Stan realised that the Cheka now had two documents that she had signed for them, both indicating her willingness to work on their behalf. If she died in Lubyanka without having the chance to tell her side of the story, her name might be forever blackened. The pressure was taking its toll: 'Back in my cell I once more went through hours of physical numbness and mental stress. I tried to think clearly, but the buzzing of flies and black thoughts in that cell destroyed all power of reflection.'

Her interpreter, Boris Bieloff, spun her a tale that his family were abroad and he was desperate to join them. Stan asked him to take a message to a journalist friend and in return, once home, she would arrange a visa and a job for him in England. Bieloff was, of course, an informer. Then she handed a note intended for the same journalist to a woman, Annetta Annsberg, but it was intercepted by Mogilevsky. Annsberg was not seen again.

Stan continued to ask to see Felix Dzerzhinsky, and to be relocated to Butyrka, a prison for political undesirables which supposedly had both better food and regular visits from a doctor. Both requests were denied, so she continued her hunger strike. After fourteen days, as her health declined, the prison commandant agreed to move her to a cell with others. In anticipation, she resumed nourishment, only to find on arrival at her new cell that there were no cellmates. This latest accommodation had recently been whitewashed and the commandant pointed to the walls, informing her that 'bugs might be crushed on the floor, but not on the walls'.

Stan resumed her hunger strike but feared the coming of October and the cold weather, certain that she would die of cold, and that Mogilevsky would do nothing to prevent it. She refused food for three weeks and became so weak that her eyesight began to fail. Fearing she was on the verge of death, Mogilevsky allowed her to have a cellmate. 'I went quite blind, and when my sight came again', she recalled, 'I recognised first a blouse of my own which I had given Vera Ignatievna.'

Stan resumed eating and her heath and situation improved. She had Vera to talk to, and she was even allowed books to read: Victor Hugo, Byron, Balzac and the *Bible*. Vera never let up trying to persuade Stan to admit her guilt and if Stan had not been so naïve she would have realised that Vera was in fact a 'stool pigeon' and had been placed in Stan's cell to make her confess.

But the Englishwoman was single-minded: she was a guiltless journalist, not a British Intelligence officer. As a consequence of her failure to get a result, Vera was removed – and Stan resumed her hunger strike. 'I knew the third, fourth and fifth days are physically the most trying,' she said, and so she braced herself for the difficult days ahead by urging herself on in the name of justice.

Solitary confinement gave her much time to think and Stan became ever more convinced that her former friend, Marguerite Harrison, had denounced her. 'One would not mind dying for a mountain that was high enough, or for a river deep and swift enough,' she recalled. 'But to die by this spy's [Marguerite's] trickery and be hidden for ever under a dust-heap of lies – that was different.'

It took another week of the hunger strike before, in September, with the cold weather approaching, Stan got her wish and was transferred to Butyrka Prison. It was about 4.5 kilometres from Lubyanka, on the main road leading north out of Moscow. The building was used in Tsarist Russia as a transit prison, but by 1920 up to 3,000 prisoners were crammed in together. A soldier was ordered to walk her there, but she was so weak that he was forced to commandeer a *droshky* (horse-drawn cart). Arriving at Butyrka, Stan was led to *Na Segreto*, the secret cells, and placed once again alone in a cell furnished only with a copper basin, a jug, and a rusty iron pail. It was, she wrote, like being shut up like a fly in a bottle. She knew in her heart of hearts that the situation would eventually drive her mad, so after a day she resumed her hunger strike. As a small concession, Vera, now also in Butyrka, was taken to Stan's cell at night, but the Russian woman was deeply unhappy with the arrangement, for she had been removed from an open cell where her movements about the prison were far less restricted.

The interrogations continued. Mogilevsky had been replaced by Comrade Lutzky, whose mother tongue was Yiddish. He possessed, she wrote, 'the eyes of a toad and the neck … of a vulture that telescoped in and out of the humped shoulders'. On one occasion Stan complained to Lutzky that Vera, who worked in the hospital during the day, was too tired to talk to her when returning to their cell at night. Stan thought she was doing Vera a favour, but Lutzky was furious as she had been instructed to spy on Stan. As a punishment, Vera was sent to an isolation cell for ten days.

With the September nights growing colder, Stan celebrated her 36th birthday in Butyrka and was warned that if she tried to look out of the window of her cell and was spotted, the guards would shoot her.

Annoyed that the Englishwoman was again on hunger strike and fearful of her dying on his watch, Lutzky sent her back to Lubyanka. Once again, Vera was summoned to share Stan's cell in an attempt to extract a confession. Vera begged, cajoled and encouraged Stan in every conceivable way to admit she was in league with Marguerite Harrison and working as a British spy, but Stan refused to budge.

Then, at the end of October, Stan noticed a change of attitude during her interrogations – a change that made her think her release could be imminent. Though still kept in isolation, she ended her hunger strike. The weather, however, had taken a turn for the worse, and she found herself unable to sleep in her thin summer clothing.

Stan's interrogations by Mogilevsky continued until she finally agreed to sign a statement regarding her activities in Rome and Berlin in 1918 in what she called 'an almost entirely fictitious account'.[5] In the statement she admitted that she had visited the British Embassy in Rome when seeking help to arrange a trip to Berlin in 1918 and was there asked to carry out intelligence work for the British. This plan, however, had come to nothing – 'it fell through completely'.[6] She later claimed that her statement to the Cheka was full of lies and disinformation, and her account to them of her relations with the British Military Mission were 'more or less fantastic'.

However, she did admit that she gave to the Cheka the names of agents in Sir Samuel Hoare's network: 'They asked for the real names, and I gave names which are something like the real names, and are of course names which would not hurt in any way. They are simply the names of the members of the Military Mission in Rome.'[7]

Whether giving the names of the agents could not 'hurt in any way' must be a matter of debate. True, they were not agents working in Russia, but they were important resources of British Intelligence. Later she would insist that no harm could have come from her divulging these names, although her reasoning was somewhat contradictory. First, she claimed that the Russians knew the names already. Second, she 'slightly altered' the names, such that Captain Baker became Captain Barker, and so forth. This precaution made little sense if, as she stated, the Russians already knew the names. Third, she was told: 'If we find out that these names are incorrect you go back to solitary confinement at once' – a statement that suggests the Russians did not, in fact, know the names she gave them.[8]

In any case, Stan had few compunctions about what she had done, later claiming: 'I bought my life with that document,' because it resulted in her transfer out of Lubyanka, and it also led to her being given a blanket to keep warm. She claimed that her actions might have been ill-judged, but she was, although ill, 'perfectly sane at the time'.[9]

She also gave the Cheka other information mixed with disinformation. She agreed that she had entered Germany against the advice of the British Legation in Berne, who had advised her to arrange her private business via the Swiss consular authorities. She disagreed, however, with the statement that she was asked by a journalist writing for an English newspaper to send uncensored news copy to him via an irregular channel. The journalist in question was Frederic Sefton Delmer of *The Daily News*, to whom Stan did sell stories, but she insisted that they were always sent the normal way, via cable. However, her signature was all that was needed to have her sent back to Butyrka, so she complied. She knew that what Mogilevsky wanted was a document from her that could be used to prevent her, once she was released, from telling the story of her incarceration or the methods of the Cheka. They wanted something that would prove her guilt so that 'my mouth would be shut'.[10]

Stan was sent back to Butyrka at the end of October and her second stay there was less oppressive. She was no longer in isolation and permitted to walk freely around the prison compound, to use a pre-Bolshevik library, and to chat with other prisoners. Prison-born babies, cats and dogs were aplenty. 'To me after those Lubyanka oubliettes, with their buzzing flies and black thoughts,' she said, 'this pestilential prison seemed almost a sanatorium.'

On arrival, Stan had been placed for a week in the quarantine tower. At the centre of the building was a corkscrew stairwell where women wandered around in tattered nightwear, fetching hot water for the day. One-by-one they would ask Stan if she was 'political' or 'criminal'. Throughout the day women came and introduced themselves to her, speaking in French. Time and again she was warned not to talk to the prisoner in cell number 1, as she was a spy. When Stan discovered that this spy was none other than her former cellmate Vera, she was shocked. However, she was reassured by the fact that the Cheka must have been convinced of her innocence 'because they saw that I trusted her absolutely and that I had always protested my innocence, and if I had been working for the British I should certainly have told her'.[11] When Vera asked her to share a cell, she happily agreed.

After her week's quarantine, Stan was placed in an attic with 70 other women from all walks of life – prostitutes, crooks, brigands, teachers, aristocrats, suspect intellectuals and women held hostage for their husbands who were serving the Bolsheviks. To Stan, though, there were only two classes of people in Russia in 1920: 'the living and the dead'. And, compared to the conditions and hardships on the outside, life in the attic was relatively good; it was warm, they were given adequate food, and hot water was available for washing. Once a fortnight they were taken to the vaults of Butyrka for 'a regular Russian bath, which was a great treat'. She joked that it could be called 'Butyrka-les-Bains'.[12]

Stan met two Americans whilst at Butyrka. One was the exotically named Xenophon Kalamatiano, a Russian-born Greek-American businessman who had been in prison for over two years and had sent her some mittens and a muffler, along with a warning about Vera. Kalamatiano had sold farm equipment to Russia before the Revolution and remained afterwards under an assumed name. He had been recruited by Samuel Northrup Harper, Professor of Russian Language at the University of Chicago, to gather information on the Bolsheviks for American foreign policy purposes. He had set up a spy network, worked with Sidney Reilly and George Hill, and he was planning a courier network to get information out of the country. Several days after the attempted assassination of Lenin, Kalamatiano and members of his network were arrested, and after his trial he had ended up in Butyrka. Stan whiled away many hours walking and talking with him. Years later he told Samuel Harper that Stan Harding, though 'a mighty fine lady', was 'something of an emotional and hysteric type'. He noted that she was 'on the edge of a nervous prostration ever since they put her in the Cheka on the day of her arrival and is apt to exaggerate.'[13]

The other American that Stan encountered at Butyrka was Royal B. Keeley, a consulting engineer. He had been invited to Russia by Yuri Lomonosov, assistant Bolshevik representative in New York, to evaluate the state of Russia's industrial and agricultural bases. In a brutally honest report he predicted famine, and stated that in his considered opinion Bolshevik policies were not supported by the peasants or factory workers. These home truths were not appreciated, and as a result he found himself as a guest of the Soviet penal system.

Stan's arrest by the Cheka had taken place three years after the October Revolution. It had been the attempt in 1918 on Lenin's life that triggered 'The Terror', when anyone opposing the Bolsheviks was liable to either be imprisoned or executed. Now, the country was in the latter stages of a brutal civil war. Butyrka was full of political prisoners and even had its own special wing dedicated to them. Stan decided that she was a political prisoner and requested to be transferred to the Socialist House within Butyrka. Many prisoners held there were from trade unions or cooperatives, having at one time or another criticised the Soviet, while some had been arrested in connection with elections or for talking to delegates from the British Labour Delegation that had visited Moscow earlier that year. The wife and children of Viktor Chernov occupied a cell in the Socialist House. Chernov, a Menshevik whom the British Labour Delegation had heard criticising the Bolsheviks at a meeting, was able to escape after his speech, but his family were not so lucky.

By the end of November, the weather was so bitterly cold that two prisoners attempted to get Stan's money back from the guards so that she could buy a fur coat and snowshoes. In the meantime, she had been lent a sheepskin coat to enable her to continue taking daily walks around the courtyard. Learning Russian was a priority, and a fellow prisoner helped her to read the Bolshevik newspapers *Izvestia* and *Pravda*. Lunch and supper typically consisted of potatoes turned black with age, but what Stan appreciated most at Butyrka was being able to talk and debate with other prisoners.

However, one day at the end of November when she was walking in the prison compound, a guard approached and without giving a reason, ordered her to go and pack her things. She guessed that she was either going to be released or executed.

Stan Harding was overwhelmed by a multitude of thoughts. She had packed so much adventure and activity into her 36 years. She had escaped her deeply religious family, travelled the world, witnessed wars and revolutions, and fallen in and out of love with both men and women. With the possibility of meeting a prematurely abrupt end, Stan could think only of how she had arrived at this point in her life.

Chapter Thirteen

Prisoner 3041

In September 1920, Mademoiselle Charpentier from the French Red Cross departed Moscow with most of the remaining foreigners, leaving Marguerite, still refused an exit visa, to provide provisions for the prisoners Charpentier had looked after, as well as her own.

Later that month, H.G. Wells and his nineteen-year-old son, George, a Russian linguist, arrived in Moscow for a two-week visit, having accepted an invitation from Lev Kamenev, who was in London with the Anglo-Soviet trade delegation. H.G., who had previously visited Russia in 1914, was shocked to see the devastation. 'Ruin; that is the primary Russian fact at the present time,' he wrote in his book *Russia in the Shadows*. He remembered the Kremlin of 1914 being 'a very open place, open much as Windsor Castle is, with a thin trickle of pilgrims and tourists in groups and couples flowing through it. But now it is closed up and difficult of access.'[1]

Mogilevsky forbade Marguerite from talking to Wells, but she was permitted – indeed encouraged – to meet another British visitor, the sculptress Clare Sheridan. Arriving in September, Sheridan was billeted at the same Guest House as Wells, on the Sofiyskaya Naberezhnaya. As she was a cousin of Winston Churchill, Mogilevsky instructed Marguerite to spy on her, although there is no public record of any report.

A few days before these two British visitors arrived in Moscow, the American journalist John Reed returned to the city from a conference – the Congress of the Peoples of the East – that he had been ordered to attend in Baku in present-day Azerbaijan. Since his idyll on Italy's Maremma coast with Stan in 1913, Reed had become well known in America through the publication of his first-hand account of the October Revolution, *Ten Days That Shook the World*. He had returned to the United States in April 1918, written for the left-wing magazine *The Masses*, and then been indicted on several occasions under the Sedition Act relating to his anti-war articles and political activities. He fled for Russia in early October 1919. Arrested in Finland for smuggling jewels and carrying false papers, he spent four months there in prison, where he was beaten and tortured, but finally had arrived in Moscow in late-June.

Marguerite had first met Reed in August and, although he was depressed and ill, she found him an 'intensely honest, rather fair minded person'. Indeed, he told Marguerite that he wanted to return to America to face the sedition charges against him. But his health was already broken and he contracted a fatal bout of typhus in Baku, dying on October 17th 1920, aged only 32. John Reed was to be placed in a silver coffin and, as a recognised supporter of the Communist regime, lay in state between marble pillars in Moscow's Labour Temple adorned with flowers and banners and guarded by fourteen soldiers.

Marguerite was, however, to see none of this pomp as she was awakened by a knock on her door at 2 o'clock on the morning of the 22nd of October 1920. She opened it to find three Russian soldiers, two men and a woman, armed with search and arrest warrants. She had been forbidden by Mogilevsky to visit the Hotel Metropole where Louise Bryant, Reed's widow, was staying along with other members of the Third International. However, as soon as she heard of Reed's death she had ignored Mogilevsky's warnings and rushed off to the Metropole to offer Bryant help and support. One of the charges against her would be that she was trying to get information out of Louise to pass back to the MID about the Communist Party both in Russia and in the United States.

The Russian soldiers proceeded to search her room, going through her bags, examining the linings of her clothing, and turning out the bed, carpet, chairs, letters and books in search of suspect material. Even the space behind the radiator was closely inspected. One of the soldiers slowly and deliberately counted her money – a considerable amount, totalling one and a half million roubles destined for feeding prisoners. Marguerite herself was then searched by the female soldier who examined every detail. She 'felt in my corsets, my stockings and my hair, went over every inch of my fur-lined coat to see if it concealed any papers.' Nothing incriminating was found, but knowing where she would be taken, Marguerite asked if she could gather together some toiletries, a change of underwear, her Army bedding roll, some chocolate and cigarettes, and of course her fur coat.

When she arrived at Lubyanka, Marguerite found herself in the same small room to which she had been taken when previously arrested. Her experience this time was not to be so cordial. Two guards sat at a large table strewn with papers while other unfortunates hung around the room, waiting to be processed. After an hour, Marguerite was handed a form to complete. She was then approached by a dozen soldiers, one of whom, egged on by his colleagues, took it upon himself to conduct an intimate search of her person. Protesting that she was an American, she was bluntly informed that her nationality would do her no good. 'I bore it patiently as I could, for I realised that the more angry I became the more entertainment my tormentors would derive from my indignation.' Marguerite did not elaborate on whether she was physically assaulted but when the ordeal was over, she was taken to another room and searched again in the correct manner that Bolshevik soldiers were told to follow. Her belongings were removed, her official mugshot was taken, and she was allocated the serial number 3041.

Eventually, a guard escorted her to her new lodgings, room number 39, a tiny space in which three other women were already billeted. Two of them lay on the floor while the third reclined on a rudimentary plank bed squashed between a table and a makeshift tin latrine. Marguerite recognised one of the women as being from the famous Moscow vaudeville club, La Chauve-Souris (The Bat). The second had worked at the Russian Foreign Office and had been arrested with hundreds of other employees in an alleged counter-revolutionary plot, while the third, who had fallen in love with a Hungarian prisoner of war, had subsequently been accused of helping Hungarians officers to escape. For this allegation she had been held for six weeks in solitary confinement.

Marguerite was not to spend long in room 39; soon she was summoned to an interview with Mogilevsky. Having realised that some of the information she had provided was worthless, he demanded more details about the people she knew: Russians, foreigners in Moscow, the prisoners to whom she had been delivering food. 'I fully realised the gravity of my position,' Marguerite later wrote, 'but I was determined to put a bold face on the matter before him.'

Her situation was dangerous on two accounts. First, the messages she had been sending to America included the names of Russian agents of the Third International, an international Communist party founded in Moscow in 1919 and subsequently established in the United States. Marguerite had resumed transmitting information following her first arrest in April, and in some quarters it was thought that she was taking too many risks. 'I trust Mrs. Harrison realises the danger she runs in sending such communications, and that the Consul has been sufficiently impressed with the need for secrecy,' W.L. Hurley of the State Department wrote to Colonel Cox of the MID. 'Otherwise,' he continued, 'she will not last long.'[2] Second, she had successfully concealed Francis McCullagh's true identity as a British secret agent. Either fact, if discovered, would have been enough to have her executed by the Bolsheviks.

Furthermore, there was much ill feeling towards the United States in Moscow at this time, due to Secretary of State Bainbridge Colby's continued refusal to recognise Soviet Russia. The precedent of referring to Russia's 'de facto' government had been set by Colby's predecessor, Robert Lansing, and was to remain in force until 1933. More concerned with Western European matters, Woodrow Wilson had left Soviet policy to Lansing and Colby, both of whom were anti-Bolsheviks, and this policy had continued under the Harding administration. As there were no official American representatives in Russia, the two men merely relied on reports from US legations in Stockholm, Helsinki, Viborg, Riga, Warsaw, Harbin and Constantinople.

Mogilevsky interviewed Marguerite for three hours. At first, the atmosphere was cordial and she was offered tea and cigarettes in between rounds of questions. However, when the session was over, rather than being returned to room 39, she was put into solitary confinement. Her cell, roughly 9-by-9 feet, was dark and cold, containing just a plank bed, a table and a tin latrine. Its only window had been whitewashed and the walls were covered with flowered wallpaper defaced by the previous occupants' scribblings in assorted languages. A boy arrived with a huge copper kettle, and Marguerite was handed a tin cup of tea made with apple parings and dried carrot.

Realising that her incarceration would become a waiting game, Marguerite was determined to keep healthy, mentally and physically. Sleep was difficult as her cell was opposite the entrance to the building with its constant stream of traffic. Guards tended to gather near the door, and Marguerite could hear them talking and laughing. She never revealed whether her knowledge of colloquial Russian was good enough to understand fully their conversations, but when the Russian journalist Georgi Popoff was later imprisoned in Lubyanka, he claimed that the volume and tenor of the profanities shocked him. 'The warders swore at each other, the prisoners at each other, and the warders at the prisoners. And what that meant,' he recalled 'can only be realised by those who know the peculiar objectionableness and obscenity of Russian oaths.'[3]

Marguerite also heard the 'frantic knocks from prisoners who demanded in loud voices to be taken to the toilet; occasionally there was the sound of women's voices quarrelling in another room, and I was continually haunted by the eye at the peephole.' The peephole was opened every thirty minutes, night and day: Marguerite became so used to the staring eye that she soon became oblivious to it, even when 'engaged in the intimate mysteries of the toilet'.

Each morning a woman arrived, handing Marguerite a broom; and, after shaking the bedbugs from her sleeping bag, she swept everything into a neat pile. To stay sane, she created a routine, giving herself a daily sponge bath regardless of the temperature of the water. Twice a day, she paced 500 times up and down her tiny room to stimulate her circulation. She made pick-up-sticks (jack straws) out of dead matches and a bent hairpin, and playing cards out of cigarette boxes. These innocent activities kept her occupied until they were discovered by a guard and confiscated. And she kept her mind focussed by reciting songs and poems under her breath and giving herself oral examinations in different languages.

Supper was served at 5 p.m. and the menu never changed – the inevitable fish soup with its floating eyes and bobbing fins. Marguerite detested it and held her nose as she ate the unpeeled, black potatoes that floated in the soup. The black bread was sometimes edible, though frequently adulterated with a substance that, she said, gave it the consistency of clay and the colour of dirty putty. 'I can well imagine, however, that strangers who were arrested almost immediately on their arrival in Moscow,' Marguerite wrote, perhaps in reference to Stan, 'would regard it as starvation diet.' But she knew from her many months of living in Russia that such was the food eaten by most free Russians since, as the *New York Times* had reported, the average Muscovite was forced to subsist on 'the equivalent of only 12 cents to a few dollars monthly'.[4] To survive on such a diet, prisoners needed to receive food parcels from the outside, and Marguerite worried how the other American and British prisoners for whom she had been providing supplies were coping without her assistance. For the first three weeks of her own incarceration, she received nothing until a friend from the Czechoslovakian Red Cross began sending her food, shoes, soap, thread and needles.

After a few weeks, Marguerite requested an interview with Mogilevsky and also asked to be removed from solitary confinement. Unusually, this second request was granted and she was placed in a cell housing between seven and twelve women. Although every prisoner had the right to make appeals in writing, in reality an appeal was a futile exercise, as the Russian journalist Georgii Popoff was to discover two years later. His cellmates complained how each had written petitions daily, sometimes preparing up to five copies, addressed to the council of the Cheka, the examining judge, and the President of the Soviet Union or the Revolutionary Tribunal. 'The results were always the same – not a sign of an answer.'[5] Marguerite's successful appeal raises the question of why she was moved so quickly while Stan had to endure several hunger strikes before she was transferred.

Marguerite's new lodgings were much larger than her previous cell; the walls were whitewashed and the windows sealed and viewless. Entering the vile-smelling room, Marguerite noticed bundles of belongings stuffed under the beds. The seven occupants were initially unfriendly, not only suspicious that she might be a spy, but also annoyed that yet another body was to be crammed into the narrow room. It was some time before one of the women – perhaps spotting a kindred spirit – approached her. Dressed in worse-for-wear Parisian fashion and wearing *láiti* (the prison-issue straw slippers), Madame Helena Solgoub, speaking in French, explained to Marguerite that she had been accused of being intimate with a White officer. Furthermore, her grand house, on which Tolstoy had based the home of Piotr, hero of *War and Peace*, was now being used for public lectures by the Commissariat for Education. Madame Solgoub introduced the other inmates: three clerks from the War Office who had been arrested in connection with a counter-revolutionary plot, the wife of a Lettish Communist, the wife of a naval officer, and a sixteen-year-old peasant girl from Archangel who had been arrested for gossiping about counter-revolution.

Inmates came and went every couple of weeks and on one occasion there were as many as fourteen women squashed into the inadequate space. There was, however, some semblance of order in the cell, as the occupants elected a chairperson who organised a cleaning rota; each day the cell was swept and tidied, and rations and food parcels shared. Once a week, the floor was scrubbed and the toilet cleaned.

Marguerite was infested with nits, but bedbugs and fleas carrying typhus were the biggest problem, and twice a day she would search for them in her underclothes. There were three cases of typhus during her incarceration, and after each diagnosis the inmates were forced to wait for two weeks before discovering whether they, too, would become infected. A doctor made the rounds, but chronic conditions were ignored and only basic remedies such as soda, castor oil and aspirin were available. Hysteria, Marguerite noted, seemed to be common: its victims were provided with valerian to help calm them. One woman, suffering from an advanced case of syphilis, fell into madness and was removed.

Prisoners were not expected to wear a uniform so those without suitable attire were provided with clothes from the prison stores. Several of the women in Marguerite's cell mended prison laundry, for which they were given needles, thread and, more importantly, a pair of scissors, which could be used for other things such as cutting stale bread, opening tin cans, and trimming hair and nails. Marguerite volunteered for sewing duties and began her mending by shaking out seams full of flea eggs that had remained despite boiling. When not sewing, the cellmates passed the time by making and playing games. Cards created from cigarette boxes were used in fortune telling, chessmen and checkers were fashioned from stale bread, and dominoes cut out of paper. Stage plays were performed, and an imprisoned ballerina from Petrograd demonstrated dances while her audience hummed the tunes. Marguerite taught Swedish exercises to her cellmates and when asked to give talks on foreign customs, literature and art, she readily agreed in return for the others sharing stories about Russia. 'Under such circumstances,' Marguerite reflected, 'you have either got to go under or live for things of the mind and spirit. There is no middle course.'

Marguerite fared much better in Lubyanka than Stan did. Unlike the Englishwoman, Marguerite was kept in solitary confinement for a mere two weeks. Later, through mixing with other prisoners, she became knowledgeable about the latest Bolshevik decrees and political developments relating to foreign governments. After her arrest in October 1920, the majority of prisoners with whom she came into contact were either political or connected to the alleged counter-revolutionary plot in the War Office: in one department alone, all 200 employees had been arrested, while naval officers thought to have been implicated in the same particular plot were also imprisoned, along with their wives. Next came Russians arrested for mixing with foreigners. When the Bolshevik government discovered that foreign delegations were smuggling letters in and out of the country, they issued a decree that made fraternising with foreigners illegal.

A steady stream of White Army prisoners continued arriving after the defeats of General Pyotr Wrangel's army in the Crimea during the summer and autumn of 1920. They were followed by large numbers of Latvian Communists who, badly scarred by inhumane treatment in Latvian prisons, had left their homeland thinking they would find asylum in Russia. Immediately after crossing the border, instead of being welcomed as Communists, they were arrested as spies. During the winter months of her incarceration, Marguerite witnessed the arrival of Cossack women, Socialists, Mensheviks, the Right Social Revolutionaries and Jewish Bundists. Lubyanka welcomed them all.

Chapter Fourteen

Freedom

After being ordered by a guard at Butyrka Prison at the end of November 1920 to 'pack her things', Stan learned the she was to be transferred back to Lubyanka for further interrogation. Beside herself with worry, her fellow inmates urged her to refuse to go. They would declare solidarity, they claimed, and organise a prison hunger strike. The guard was sent away, only to return with the message that she was to be processed for release. Some prisoners collected *sukari* (dried bread) for her that had been carefully hidden for emergencies. However, she remained fearful as to the true motive behind her transfer.

Stan felt that her recent interrogations had become less harsh and more sympathetic. What she did not know was that negotiations with the Bolsheviks by Lord Curzon and Prime Minister David Lloyd George were underway for the repatriation of all British prisoners before the Anglo-Soviet Trade Agreement, still under negotiation, would be signed.

Stan's incarceration first came to the attention of the British Foreign Office early in October after she was added to the list of British prisoners held in Russian jails. The list had been compiled by the British Red Cross in Finland who was sending food parcels to prisoners in Petrograd and Moscow. On the 13th of October, Stephen Tallents, from the British Consulate in Riga, sent a telegram to the Foreign Office in London reiterating the words of Hector Boon and Captain Campbell, both recently released from prison in Russia. They urged that strenuous official pressure be exerted by His Majesty's Government to secure the release of Mrs Harding and Miss Bowler (a nurse imprisoned eighteen months previously on a charge of espionage), both of whom were confined in 'vile conditions' in Moscow. They described the health of the two women as 'bad'.

However, Tallents expressed little sympathy for Stan's predicament. 'It is a pity that she is imprisoned in "vile" conditions. She went to Russia apparently in July, at a time when British subjects were not allowed to go there. She therefore did so entirely at her own risk; we cannot therefore make a very great stir about her.' Nevertheless, Tallents conceded that her case was 'an admirable stick for us to beat the Bolsheviks', since she had received Maxim Litvinov's permission to go to Moscow, yet was arrested within a few hours of her arrival. It was clear to him that Litvinov had acted in 'bad faith'.[1] And, there were concerns that agents acting under future trade agreements with Russia would have no guarantee of safety.

As Stan was a correspondent for the *New York World*, Tallents questioned as to whether she was an American citizen. Its editor, James Tuohy, was contacted and he confirmed that, although he had never met Stan in person and was unsure of her nationality, he had commissioned her to correspond for him in Russia because she had insisted it was possible for her to get the relevant entry visas whilst his regular correspondents could not.[2] Stan had only recently regained her British citizenship, and with the ink on her records probably still damp, communication between governmental departments in Whitehall was understandably not up to date.

Negotiations for the Anglo-Soviet Trade Agreement (which had begun in May 1920) were now in the third round of discussions; nothing would be signed until all prisoners were exchanged. The Soviets insisted that the release was to occur at the Finnish border and recommended that Captain Horrocks and Lieutenant Hayes, both Russian speakers, should go to Russia and organise the repatriation of all British prisoners. Hector Boon and Captain Campbell had urged that the Foreign Office needed to get every single British subject out of Russia because 'whenever His Majesty's Government took any action with which the Soviet Government disapproved, the remaining British subjects would be persecuted'.[3] The Foreign Office pointed out that matters were not entirely straightforward as some British subjects might wish to remain in Russia as they had no home to go to in England and feared unemployment or relegation to a workhouse.

* * *

Stan Harding's official release date was set for November 26th, but it took so long to complete the red tape and form-filling at Lubyanka that when she and her guard reached the train station, the locomotive was already in motion. The guard shouted at her to run alongside the train, throw her belongings aboard, and jump on. The other prisoner refused to follow suit and Stan then found herself in the precarious position of travelling alone without papers on a train filled with Red soldiers heading for Petrograd. Her last memories of her guard was of him 'stamping up and down the station platform and tearing his hair at the prospect of the six months' imprisonment which he would surely get for losing me.'

She spent three days in Petrograd before joining seven other British subjects at the Bjelo-Ostrow Finnish border on November 30th 1920. Most of the group spoke little or no English and were British only by marriage or birth. Asked at the border to fill out a form giving her reasons for leaving Russia, she wrote that her stay as a newspaper representative had come to an end.

The Finnish border ran along a stream, and at the end of a bridge the Chief of the British Red Cross in Finland greeted her and shook her hand. Immediately, all the released prisoners were taken to Villa Reisen in Terijoki, a former summer resort for Petrograd citizens, for debriefing and a medical examination. When the Moscow Political Red Cross had interviewed Stan at Butyrka in October they observed that she suffered from nervous attacks (similar to shell-shock) and a severe form of anaemia as a consequence of her arrest.[4] Unfortunately, no records remain from her medical examination by Dr Thure Gustaf Grönlund at Villa Reisen, but there is no reason to assume that her condition six weeks later was any better.[5]

The British refugees, including another 61 from Petrograd, were to be quarantined for two weeks at Villa Reisen. Terijoki (renamed Zelenogorsk in 1947) was known as the 'Riviera of the North' because of its long, sandy beaches, beautiful wooden villas and spas that were positioned on the Karelian Isthmus facing the Gulf of Finland. It should have been an ideal place in which to recuperate, but Stan could not relax. She insisted that she had important information to report and asked to have her quarantine cut to a week.

A letter dated the 1st of December from Major J.C. Fitzhugh to Mr Kidston at the British Legation in Helsinki claimed that she was 'of strong Socialist views and I think it would be as well for Boyce to interview her before her request is taken into consideration.'[6] Ernest Boyce was the British Passport Control Officer in Helsinki and hence a member of the Secret Intelligence Service.

Stan's request was refused. A few days later, Major Fitzhugh received word from the British Legation office in Helsinki that they had received a telegram from Lord D'Abernon, the British Ambassador in Berlin, informing them that Stan had asked to return to England via Germany. 'She is well known to General Malcolm and Lord Kilmarnock and I hope you will do what you can to facilitate her visas.'[7] Her papers were issued and she set off, weary and in ill health, to return to England via Berlin.

* * *

Whilst Stan had returned safely to England and was celebrating the Christmas of 1920, Marguerite remained locked up in Lubyanka. She was feeling particularly homesick for her family and friends, but she and her cellmates made the best of things. A few days before Christmas, while enjoying a rare treat – an excursion to the public baths – they passed Trubnaya Square where Christmas trees were being sold. A few of the prisoners picked up stray branches, smuggled them back to their cells, tied them together and arranged them in a bottle. This makeshift Christmas tree was decorated by Marguerite with ornaments made from the silver paper from her Red Cross soap wrappers. The prisoners even enjoyed a Christmas feast: a white towel was spread on the table and pooled resources from food parcels were laid out, among them a tin of American canned beef, two salt herrings, rice pudding, prison bread, butter, sugar and tea.

Later, Marguerite and some of the other women were moved to an attic cell. With its one boarded-up dormer window, this room was even stuffier than the previous one. 'The air,' she said, 'was damp, cold and permeated with the smell of fresh paint.' It was so cold, in fact, that no one could sleep, and the smell coming from the lidless tin toilet was appalling. 'By morning we were all gasping for breath, and had turned various shades of white, green or yellow, according to our various complexions, and were so weak we were hardly able to move.' They decided as a collective to write to the head of the Moscow Cheka, Vyacheslav Menzhinsky, requesting to have the window opened. Menzhinsky complied and ordered the window to be smashed open – but warned that anyone caught looking out of it would be shot.

Still anxious to remain healthy in the Moscow winter, Marguerite kept up her twice-daily exercises. But, as the months passed, the dire living conditions and poor diet caused her head cold to turn into a persistent cough along with a relentlessly high temperature that was not eased by the feeble remedies supplied by the doctor. Marguerite wrote to Menzhinsky, requesting a transfer. In mid-November a young guard came to escort her outside the prison to Lubyanka Square. 'The dazzling sunlight blinded my eyes, and I felt like a mole that has suddenly come up from months underground,' she wrote, and after the sepulchral sounds of the prison she found the noise in the street deafening. She could barely stand and was mildly alarmed when the guard explained that he did not have the authority to request transport and that she must therefore walk to her new lodgings – Novinsky Prison. Furthermore, he did not even know the way. Too weak to walk anywhere, Marguerite took the initiative and stopped a pedestrian to ask for directions. Glancing around to see if he was being watched – for he could have been arrested for talking to a foreigner – he pointed the way, explaining that her destination was more than 6 kilometres away. In her knapsack Marguerite had two cans of American corned beef, and with these as currency she persuaded the driver of a horse-drawn cab to take them to Novinsky Prison.

* * *

Novinsky Prison, halfway down a steep hill, its yard overlooked by a church, was used as a holding station for prisoners awaiting transfer to internment camps. Hundreds of women passed through each month prior to being despatched, usually, as far as possible from their families. 'When we arrived at the prison, I was very nearly all in, my head was spinning, my knees wobbled, and I felt I had a high temperature', Marguerite remembered. She was handed over to a female guard who directed her to the prison hospital. As she walked through the courtyard with its shrubs, benches and clusters of women sitting chatting while they knitted or sewed, a woman ran up to Marguerite and threw her arms around her. It was one of the prisoners who had passed through Lubyanka and who had come to know Marguerite well. Other women gathered around the American, clamouring for information about people they knew. A group took her to the prison nurse and vouched that she was 'clean' and wouldn't need to be quarantined.

Initially, Marguerite was to share a large, airy room with eleven other prisoners. They slept on hammocks hooked against the wall during the day. At the foot of each bed was 'a dog' – a small wooden chest in which to store belongings. A long table stood in the centre of the room with shelves underneath for provisions and utensils. On each floor there were two large bathrooms with modern plumbing, and prisoners were allowed to bathe every ten days. Marguerite noted that she was the only one to wash daily. Political prisoners were separated from criminals and allotted their own times for exercising in the yard. They were not permitted visitors, but by climbing the church bell tower that overlooked the prison, their visitors could conduct shouted conversations with them. As several of these went on simultaneously, it was hard to hear details and fights often broke out in the yard.

Life was much more relaxed in Novinsky than at Lubyanka, and the cultural activities, improvised by the inmates, were even more enterprising. After morning inspection at 7 a.m., most prisoners were permitted to wander freely between rooms until 9 p.m., and were allowed to exercise in the yard for two hours in the morning and three in the evening. The 24 Socialist prisoners who shared a room were allowed daily newspapers and, as Marguerite was friendly with several of them, they passed these on to her. Prisoners were allowed to use the library behind the church that held many classics in French, German and English as well as Russian. There were reading classes for the illiterate, organised by two visiting social workers who also distributed the mail. Impromptu dances were held in the yard, and a drama club performed plays every Sunday. Prisoners were also allowed to attend church services, and two women were appointed to clean the church brass daily. Mothers of babies born in prison were permitted to keep them until these little inmates reached school age.

But stealing was common; thieves, if caught, would be beaten by other prisoners while the guards obligingly turned a blind eye. Marguerite witnessed a flourishing black market where food and goods brought in from the outside were sold. A bread ration could be bought for 25 cigarettes or 10 fresh eggs. Playing cards were forbidden, but they were everywhere, used for gambling with anything from food rations to the clothes on one's back. And, although Marguerite did not elaborate, she mentioned the prevalence of 'unnatural forms of prostitution'.

Marguerite had never fully recovered from her severe cold, and as her fever worsened she was removed to the hospital where, for the first time in eight months she slept in a proper bed with a mattress, albeit one made of straw. The diagnosis was tuberculosis. She shared a room with a buxom, ruddy-faced peasant girl whose innocent looks belied her habit of stealing anything she could lay her hands on. The food in the hospital was of a higher standard, and included regular offerings of sugar or honey, butter, coffee, dried apples, meat broth, and even caviar. Despite the lack of medicines, Marguerite received daily injections of arsenic, then a common 'cure' for tuberculosis. She described the nurses as 'kindness itself'.

* * *

On November 2nd 1920, some ten days after Marguerite had been arrested by the Cheka, the MID in Washington received a secret telegram from Reval reporting her probable arrest. When news of this became known in America, her friends quickly mobilised. Father-in-law Dr Ames; former brother-in-law and 'special friend' Albert Ritchie (who had been elected Governor of Maryland in January 1920); and editor Frank Kent – all of them influential men – immediately lobbied the MID to secure her release. Since the United States had no diplomatic relations with Russia, nothing could be done through official channels, but Marguerite was not forgotten and her situation frequently made newspaper headlines in the *New York Times* and *The Baltimore Sun*. From American shores, matters must have looked grim. In 1921, the *New York Times* would report the execution of 61 prisoners by the Cheka in Petrograd, some of whom were reputed to be 'agents of the American Intelligence service'.[8]

Previously, in the summer of 1920, Harold Carlson, a Chicagoan held in Russia with his wife and two children, had managed to smuggle a letter out of the country which made its way to the MID. He wrote of their plight and of his disappointment that the American government was doing nothing to rescue them: 'An American passport does not seem to afford the same protection and consideration as for instance a British or a Swedish one.'[9] He warned that the American prisoners were in dread of the harsh winter, with scarce food, fuel, and winter clothing. American canned food, Carlson lamented, was being handed out by the Danish Red Cross to other foreign nationals while the Americans received none.

In September, another expatriate, Dr Herschel C. Walker, had written to the American Chargé d'Affaires in Stockholm, voicing alarm that Americans were being used as forced labour, citing the daughters of a Mr Hopwood, a former manager of Kodak in Russia, who had been compelled to clean apartments, cut ice and move railroad ties.

In January 1921, Dr Ames, Governor Ritchie and Frank Kent joined forces with Secretary of State for Maryland, Philip Perlman, and travelled to New York to take up Marguerite's case with the Soviet Representative to the US, Ludwig Martens. A Bolshevik of German descent (his German-born father had run a steelworks in Kursk, where Martens junior was raised), he was a colleague of Lenin's and a man who, it seemed, could pull strings. Marguerite had visited him in New York in late-1919, in hope of gaining a Russian visa as a journalist before her second trip to Europe that year.

But, Dr. Ames, in a letter to General Nolan at the MID, reported that the meeting had not been particularly successful: 'To my mind he [Martens] is nothing but a blond German liar. He denied all knowledge of the situation – indeed seemed surprised that there was any situation, but promised to send a cablegram to Moscow asking for information.'[10]

---

* In 1922, Fridtjof Nansen would create the Nansen Passport for refugees. By the early 1940s, the 450,000 passports he had issued were recognised by 52 countries.

Dr Ames then called on Fridtjof Nansen,* the Norwegian explorer and diplomat who lately had been overseeing the return of prisoners of war from Russia, to ask if he could provide any help. And, though Marguerite had worked as a volunteer typist for him when he visited Russia before her arrest, there was nothing that even the intrepid polar explorer could do. Marguerite, it seemed, was destined for a long incarceration.

Moreover, Marguerite Harrison would soon be the subject of both official and public scrutiny in Britain and America through Stan Harding's coming crusade for personal justice and revenge.

PART THREE

1921-1924

Chapter Fifteen

Probably Undesirable to Call Attention to Her

⸺∞⸺

Early in 1921, Stan Harding's mission to clear her name, seek compensation and wreak revenge on Marguerite Harrison would bring her to the heart of the British establishment and government. Some eight months earlier, in May 1920, the government had appointed a committee to collect information on Russia, including the treatment of British subjects by the Bolsheviks. The findings were to be used by the British Foreign Secretary, Lord Curzon, as background for his negotiations over the proposed Anglo-Soviet Trade Agreement. Chaired by Lord Emmott, the four-man committee published a White Paper in February 1921 that, amongst other findings, detailed the experiences and observations of more than 40 Britons recently released from Russian prisons. Taking an adversarial stance toward the Bolsheviks and making some robust demands, the White Paper cautioned the Bolsheviks to desist from issuing propaganda 'directed toward the destruction of the political and economic order existing in other countries'. It also deplored the 'state of administrative incompetence and corruption' into which the departments of the Soviet Government had fallen. And it quoted Leon Trotsky: 'Russian Socialist society is on the way to ruin.'[1]

The committee was to be disbanded before the publication of the White Paper until Lord Curzon suggested that the latest batch of British prisoners released from Petrograd, Siberia, and Azerbaijan should be interviewed in order to compare their treatment with that of earlier prisoners.

Summoned to Whitehall by the committee, Stan arrived for the interview at Carlisle Place, near Victoria Station, on January 3rd 1921,[2] and might have expected a sympathetic audience from Lord Emmott and his colleagues: Conservative MP Sir Ellis Hume-Williams, judge Sir Ryland Dent Adkins, and Labour MP Major David Watts Morgan whose battlefield heroics in the war won him the DSO and a CBE (which in turn won him the nickname 'Dai Alphabet').

She must have been disappointed that Lord Emmott alone would take her evidence as the three other committee members had failed to keep the appointment. Nevertheless, she seized the opportunity to recount her version of events and recalled in graphic detail her arrest within 24

hours of arriving in Moscow and the following six months of imprisonment. She also told of how the Cheka had accused her of being the head
of British Intelligence in Russia as well as having collected information
for them during her travels in China in 1911-12 and in Germany before
the Armistice in 1918. The charges, Stan claimed, were based on information given to the Russians by the American Marguerite Harrison
from conversations the two women had had when they shared a hotel
room in Berlin in 1919. Not only had Harrison falsely denounced her
as a British secret agent, Stan told Lord Emmott, but also her interrogator, Solomon Mogilevsky, had made it clear that he had come to an
arrangement with the American: in return for her freedom, Harrison
had agreed to spy on foreigners visiting Moscow. He had hoped that the
same arrangement could be made with her. However, being less accom-
modating – as well as (in her own estimation) more principled and
courageous – she had refused. However, Stan admitted to giving the
Cheka the names of the agents working with the British Military Mission
in Rome. The minutes of the interview reveal that Lord Emmott made
no judgment. His questions suggested that he was more interested in
prison conditions and train schedules than the guilt or innocence of the
various parties.

Two months later, on March 3rd 1921, Emmott wrote to Lord Curzon
to enquire whether it was worth incurring the expense of printing a supplementary report containing the most recent evidence, given that he
had found little difference between prison conditions experienced by
the later arrivals – they were still bad, but no better or worse. 'The case
of Mrs Stan Harding stands by itself,' Lord Emmott concluded. 'It must
be admitted that her treatment in prison, including, as it did, many
weeks of solitary confinement, differs from that of other prisoners
whom I have examined. At the same time I am not without fears that
Mrs Stan Harding may have made statements which might have aroused
the suspicions of the Bolsheviks and even led them to believe that she
was or might become a secret service agent.'[3] Emmott was referring to
Stan having concocted the story that would gain her a meeting with
Chicherin in Lubyanka, as well as her claim that she would deliver a message to Prime Minister David Lloyd George – ruses that had backfired
in Russia.

An internal Foreign Office memo covering Emmott's letter to Lord
Curzon suggested that there was no need to publish further material on
the subject. 'The most interesting of these new cases is that of Mrs Stan
Harding,' it stated, 'but we are so vague about her position and whether

or not she was an agent of some kind, that it is probably undesirable to call attention to her.'[4]

Stan, however, had every intention of calling attention to herself and would repeat the story of her harrowing experiences in Russia to politicians, civil servants, professional organisations, journalists and anyone else of influence who would listen and could be of help. Beginning a relentless publicity campaign, she made her grievances news and soon the case was being raised in Parliament. Captain Wedgwood Benn, Liberal MP for Leith, posed a Parliamentary question, asking the Under Secretary of State, Cecil Harmsworth, whether the allegation that Mrs Stan Harding was a British Intelligence agent was correct. Harmsworth, younger brother of the newspaper magnate Lord Northcliffe, replied categorically that the allegation was untrue.

Much would hinge on Stan's efforts to have it officially confirmed and publicly accepted that she had not spied for the British; at stake was her hope of a public rebuttal of Marguerite Harrison's allegations, the support of journalism organisations in Britain and America, and the hope for compensation – initially from the Russians and subsequently from the Americans.

* * *

But Stan's single-mindedness in the pursuit of her mission and the hopes for its success would be accompanied by an inability to place her case proportionally in the wider context of international relations. When she returned to Britain in January 1921, the Anglo-Soviet Trade Agreement was near to signature after a year of negotiations. Its importance both to Britain, who needed raw materials and new markets, and to Russia, whose devastated infrastructure required imports of most kinds, may explain why an attempt was made to intimidate Stan into ceasing her protestations.

'A civil note, bearing a famous address, awaited me one morning,' she recalled. The famous address was Scotland Yard, to which she was invited for an interview. Matters did not go as she had expected, since a young officer threatened her with five years' penal servitude under the Official Secrets Act if she continued with her campaign against Soviet Russia. Stan was understandably upset but was consoled by a friend who reassured her that this was unlikely to happen. Sometime later, Stan was informed, reliably or otherwise, that the young man who interviewed her at Scotland Yard had exceeded his instructions and spoken out of turn. She was told by Scotland Yard that he had suffered shell-shock during the war, and that he was 'no longer with us'. The threat may have given her momentary pause but she would soon be back indefatigably lobbying her case.

Despite Prime Minister David Lloyd George's full support, Lord Curzon bitterly opposed any cooperation with the Bolsheviks, and it was in Curzon that Stan was to find a champion. Charismatic, grand and often pompous, Curzon had been the Viceroy of India. In his role as Foreign Secretary, he had supported British military intervention in Russia, and when it became clear that the Bolsheviks could not easily be defeated, he had been amongst the voices calling for a full-scale military intervention against them.

But Britain had incurred huge debts as a result of the war, British workers were striking for better pay and conditions, India wanted autonomy, and Sinn Fein was causing trouble in Ireland. A war-weary nation with its own internal conflicts understandably did not have the stomach for another major foreign conflict.

Dire events in Russia during the previous year had brought the Bolsheviks to the negotiating table. Although, in the autumn of 1919, the southern anti-Bolshevik forces had been routed and by the end of 1920 all the main White Armies defeated; the Polish-Soviet War had gone disastrously for the Soviets. During 1920, Lenin had grasped that the much-desired world revolution was not going to ignite in the near future. The Spartacist Uprising in Germany had ended in defeat and the Hungarian Communists, led by Béla Kun, were deposed when Romania invaded Hungary in 1919 and overthrew the Soviet Republic there.

Internally, Russia was experiencing famine, and economic failure was widespread. Lenin was aware that, if the Bolshevik State was to survive, it was in the interest of Soviet Russia to continue to foment revolution outside Russia. On November 23rd 1920 he had informed the Council of People's Commissars that they must 'remove the opportunity for the enemies to create an alliance among themselves for a struggle against us; to keep on interfering with their policies, to prevent them from winning.'[5] Lenin wanted it to appear that his New Economic Policy would open trade links with the outside world; privately, however, he was merely seeking a temporary breathing space, while at the same time cannily exploiting conflicts of interest between Britain and France, Britain and America, America and Japan, and the Entente and Germany.

Lenin would not have needed to work too hard to stir up bad feeling between Britain and America on the subject of Russia. Warren G. Harding had been elected President in November 1920, with a mandate of a return to 'normalcy' that included renewed isolation. Charles Evans Hughes became the new American Secretary of State, and the ensuing foreign policy was wholly opposed to any form of relations with Soviet Russia. The American government refused to recognise the Baltic States or the Republics of Georgia and Azerbaijan, but made exceptions for Poland, Finland and Armenia on historical grounds. The new President and the Secretary of State had not, therefore, appreciated Lloyd George's negotiations to open trade links with Soviet Russia. Nevertheless, The Anglo-Soviet Trade Agreement was signed on March 16th 1921; and the conditions of its adoption would directly affect both Stan Harding and Marguerite Harrison.

* * *

Having put the threat of imprisonment under the Official Secrets Act behind her, Stan Harding applied for membership of the National Union of Journalists (NUJ), with the aim of gaining their backing for her cause. On June 1st 1921 (whilst Marguerite was still incarcerated in Moscow), the General Secretary of the NUJ, Henry Marriott Richardson, wrote to the Intelligence Department of the Foreign Office in Whitehall requesting confirmation that Mrs Stan Harding was not a British agent. Having made their own enquiries, the NUJ had discovered the Russians' insistence that they had proof that Stan was an agent. If true, Richardson wrote, her application to join the NUJ would be turned down.

Edward Wise, a civil servant at the Board of Trade, was also contacted by the NUJ; he in turn relayed to Howard Smith of the Foreign Office that 'Mrs Stan Harding, who is in a highly nervous condition, is very anxious for her position to be cleared, and it will be doing her a kindness if we can reply categorically that she was in no way employed by us in Russia'.[6] The official reply from the Foreign Office was to refer Richardson to the Under Secretary of State's Parliamentary Reply to Captain Wedgwood Benn three months earlier, which had stated that 'it was untrue Mrs Harding was working for British Intelligence'. She received her NUJ membership card.

While Stan was doing her best to mobilise powerful allies in London, in America, Marguerite also had influential friends keeping her name in the press and lobbying for her release. In May 1921, her newspaper boss, *The Baltimore Sun* publisher Van Lear Black, had persuaded Maryland Senator Joseph I. France, a Republican, to make a fact-finding trip to Russia for the US Congress – no easy feat considering America's antipathy towards anything to do with Soviet Russia. Senator France was described by *The Baltimore Sun* as a man with a 'commanding appearance and manner which attracts and holds his audience. His gestures, while forceful, are at the same time graceful and appealing'. As Joseph France had long been advocating the resumption of diplomatic and economic relations with Russia, it was thought by Marguerite's friends that once in Moscow he would also be able to raise the subject of her incarceration and advocate for her release during the discussions. Keen to help, he set off for Europe on May 21st, taking with him Mark Watson, assistant editor of *The Baltimore Sun*. Watson, however, got no further than Riga, having been refused an entry permit on the grounds that he was a foreign correspondent. Senator France was allowed entry.

Concurrently, events unfolding in the central Volga region would have a profound effect on Marguerite's incarceration. Due to a combination of drought and crop failure in the summer of 1920, and subsequent farm mismanagement under the Bolsheviks, Russia was about to experience the worst famine in its history.

The first official acknowledgement of the impending disaster appeared in *Pravda* on 26th of June 1921, describing the situation as worse than the famine of 1891. On that earlier occasion, Marguerite's father had sent one of his steamships filled with food for the starving victims and had later been presented, by way of gratitude, with a silver tea service by Tsar Alexander III. On June 30th, *Pravda* reported a mass exodus of refugees from the afflicted areas; while in early July two separate appeals from Moscow, aimed at Western ears, were despatched from the Patriarch Tikhon and the writer Maxim Gorky. These telegrams were sent to Fridtjof Nansen, then back in Norway, and were passed on to the relevant quarters. The *New York Times* printed Gorky's appeal: 'I ask all honest European and American people for prompt aid to the Russian people. Give bread and medicine.'

One of the few people in a position to deliver food aid on such a massive scale at this time was a staunch anti-Bolshevik named Herbert C. Hoover. Orphaned at a young age, Hoover had earned immense wealth as a mining engineer in Western Australia and China. He had also acquired a reputation as an innovator, a skilful administrator and an astute manager of money. When 200,000 American tourists were stranded in Europe on the outbreak of war in August 1914, many of them short of funds, they had gathered in London where Hoover, whose headquarters was in the City, assisted in caring for their immediate needs and in getting them home.

After hearing of the plight of the starving Belgians early in the war, Hoover had founded the Commission for the Relief of Belgium (CRB), with the aim of providing food aid. All the warring parties were unhappy with the programme, but ships sailing under the CRB's own flag delivered their cargos which were deemed to be the personal property of the Ambassador to Belgium of the then-neutral USA. The CRB was highly efficient and was run on the same strict accounting and administrative lines as Hoover's mining companies. His staff consisted of his business associates along with Rhodes Scholars studying at Oxford University. With financial contributions from the United States, England and France, as well as from private individuals, he amassed $880 million for CRB's use over four years. He was to maintain supreme authority over the operation throughout.

When the war ended, Hoover accompanied Woodrow Wilson to Paris for the peace talks. He was made Director General of Relief for the Allies, and in 1919 was appointed principal executive of the Allied Supreme Economic Council. Later that year, Hoover suggested that a separate US government organisation should be created, with its own funds for European relief. Called the American Relief Administration (ARA), its 1,500 staff members were selected from demobbed Army and Navy officers. Through the ARA, Hoover organised $1 billion of food aid destined for countries bordering Russia.[7]

Herbert Hoover certainly possessed an incredible track record in the international food-aid distribution, and if past experience was anything to go by, he would be successful in getting supplies to millions of starving Russians. However, he agreed to help only if certain conditions were met including stipulations that only American aid workers were to administer distribution within Russia and that all American prisoners be repatriated. Despite the Soviets being well aware that Hoover had secretly supplied the counter-revolutionary armies with food during the Russian Civil War, on the 28th of July 1921 Lev Kamenev agreed to Hoover's terms.[8] The Bolsheviks were desperate.*

* * *

Marguerite knew nothing of the negotiations by Herbert Hoover and Dr Ames, so when summoned by the head of the American Bureau of the Cheka on July 23rd 1921, she was surprised to a see a well-dressed

---

* By August 1922, American kitchens would be feeding 10½ million Russians with white bread, beans, corn grits and cocoa every day.

man in American attire walk into the room. Marguerite recognised him as Senator Joseph France and momentarily wondered if the he had 'run amok and turned Bolshevik'. However, France reassured her that she was likely to be released. He had spent the previous weeks in negotiations with Lenin, Trotsky and Kamenev, and ultimately it was Hoover's stipulation regarding American prisoners that would secure her freedom. At that moment, Marguerite could not believe that her release was imminent, and 'resolutely put the idea of freedom out of my mind and returned to the prison routine'.

Four days passed before she was ordered to pack her bags for her return to Lubyanka for processing. However, Marguerite was ill, and her temperature remained so high that the nurse refused to let her go, telling the guard to return for her the next morning. As she drifted off to sleep, still unconvinced that she really was to be released, the door of her hospital room flew open and two guards and a female attendant burst in. Without a word they began examining her belongings, removing all printed and written material. The following morning, before the arrival of her escort, Marguerite wandered around the prison saying her goodbyes: 'Suddenly I realised that a close tie was about to be broken. Prison friendships,' she explained, 'are about the most real things in the world.'

When she reached Lubyanka later that day, processing her exit took several hours. After a final cross-examination, Marguerite was given a release number, 2961. She had been allowed to leave Russia earlier than the other American prisoners, probably thanks to Senator France. Mogilevsky came to say goodbye, insisting that he had nothing personal against her and hoping she would return to Russia one day under different circumstances. That evening, with only seven minutes to spare, she caught the train leaving for Riga, in which Senator France was already aboard. 'The senator was horrified when he discovered that he was to occupy the upper berth at night,' Marguerite recalled. She, for her part, didn't mind in the least because her months in prison had taught her that 'privacy, like everything else, is relative'.

On arrival in Riga, she was met by the American Military Attaché, Colonel Worthington Hollyday, and his wife. Marguerite was wearing a dirty khaki suit and a man's shirt and shoes – a far cry from the glamorous socialite – and was desperate for a bath. Mrs Hollyday lent her some silk underwear and a luxurious tea-gown. Marguerite was unable to eat much of the food she was offered as her stomach had shrunk due to malnourishment. Cables of congratulations started arriving and she made arrangements to meet her son Tommy in London. And, of course, she immediately set to work on her report for the MID.

After four days of recuperation, Marguerite was accompanied to Berlin by Senator France and Mark Watson, who had remained in Riga. In Berlin, Merian C. Cooper was the first person to meet her off the train. Since escaping Russia in April 1921 when working in a railway prisoners' gang, Cooper had been plotting ways of arranging Marguerite's escape. Never one to miss a chance for adventure, Cooper claimed that he had got as far as bribing one of the guards at Novinsky Prison to smuggle her out, and had hired a Polish aeroplane to rendezvous in a nearby meadow to pick her up and take her to Poland. He may have been disappointed that her 'escape' required no such derring-do on his part.

After a few days in Berlin, Marguerite and son Tommy sailed on the *Rotterdam* to New York, arriving in August, where they were met by Van Lear Black who had gathered her friends aboard his yacht to sail them back to Baltimore.

The eighteen months had been difficult but enlightening. Although she had suffered physically and materially, Marguerite felt she had gained by her experience in other ways. 'I knew the heart of Russia, and no one in these troubled times of transition can ever know it unless he lives with the Russian people both in and out of prison.'

The Baltimore Sun of July 31st 1921 had carried a story of Marguerite's alleged espionage and counter-espionage, but concentrated more on her exciting Russian experiences as a female journalist. Shortly after returning to the States she was debriefed in Washington by her Military Intelligence Department boss, Brigadier-General Marlborough Churchill, and J. Edgar Hoover, the soon-to-be appointed deputy head of the Bureau of Investigation.

Chapter Sixteen

America Will Protect Its Agent

While Marguerite had assumed a version of her old life, this was not so for Stan Harding. She remained angry and bitter at what she believed had been a betrayal, and for revenge was determined to expose Marguerite's treachery. In the summer of 1921, Stan was to gain a powerful ally and advocate in the person of Lord Robert Gascoyne-Cecil. The 56-year-old son of the great Victorian Prime Minister, the Marquess of Salisbury, and a direct descendant of Queen Elizabeth I's ministers Lord Burghley and Robert Cecil, he had been the Under-Secretary of State for Foreign Affairs from May 1915 to January 1919. A supporter of women's suffrage, the League of Nations and Esperanto (he wanted the League to adopt Esperanto as its official working language), Cecil was fiercely devoted to the cause of peace. Also, he abhorred Bolshevism and its dialectical materialism which he believed was destructive to the spiritual nature of mankind.

Cecil empathised with what he regarded as the unfairness of Stan's treatment by the Bolsheviks and probably also saw her case as a complaint substantial enough to use for public criticism of the Soviets. Following on from Wedgwood Benn's enquiries, on the 14th of July he submitted a Parliamentary question to Under Secretary of State, Cecil Harmsworth, asking if he was aware that Mrs Stan Harding, a British subject, had been invited to Moscow, imprisoned on her arrival, accused of working for British Intelligence, and pressured to enter the espionage service of Soviet Russia on threat of execution. 'Has the British government made any application for redress for these injuries to the Soviet Government, and if so, with what results?'[1]

Harmsworth replied that no representation had been made to the Soviet government because 'the lady went to Russia on her own responsibility with safe conduct from the Bolsheviks at a time when it was well known that His Majesty's Government gave no passport facilities for that country.'[2] It was not stated in the Emmott Report, he added, that Harding had not been under sentence of death.

Dissatisfied with this answer, Cecil submitted a supplementary question to Harmsworth, asking on what grounds the British government was refusing to assist Stan in seeking redress from the Soviets, on whose invitation she had visited the country. Harmsworth reiterated his earlier answer and added that she she had entered Russia 'at her own risk'. Harmsworth maintained that although she had not forfeited the rights of protection that His Majesty's Government exercises on behalf of all British subjects, 'His Majesty's Government cannot be blamed if her assumption [that she would be safe] proved ill-founded.'[3] His advice was that Stan should lodge any claims at the Russia Claims Office at the Board of Trade, and that redress would be discussed with the Soviet Government before normal relations could continue.*

Harmsworth soon found himself confronted with further Parliamentary questions. In August, John Erskine, Assistant Parliamentary Secretary to Viscount Long, and two Conservative MPs, George Balfour and Sir Ernest Wild, submitted questions pressing for Stan's grievance to be made into a special case and urging that representations should be presented to Chicherin, demanding an apology and compensation. (Stan had in mind the sum of £10,000 – approximately £430,000 today.) Harmsworth replied in the House that he had nothing to add to the answer given to Lord Robert Cecil.

The Foreign Office was anxious not to jeopardise the recently signed Anglo-Soviet Trade Agreement. An internal memo dated August 15th 1921 noted that no useful purpose would be served by presenting Stan as a special case, reiterating that it was important not to become involved in any controversy with the Soviets. The suggestion was made that someone at the FO should have a quiet word with Lord Robert Cecil, explaining the situation. 'The argument about becoming involved in controversy with the Soviet Government is not one that would appear suitable for public discussion.'[5]

Nonetheless, the Parliamentary questions kept coming until Harmsworth was able to state in the House, this time in reply to Sir Harry Brittain, Conservative MP for Acton, that the British agent in Moscow finally had been instructed to make strong representations to the Soviet Government on the matter. For in early September, the Foreign Office had written to Robert MacLeod Hodgson, the diplomat and official agent at the British Commercial Mission in Moscow, requesting

---

* Given his official position, Harmsworth would have known that between 1917 and 1920 there were 309 British claims registered with the Russian Claims Department. They included six claims from representatives of people who had died in Russian prisons, six from people who died soon after release as a result of their imprisonment, and seventeen people who had been permanently disabled.[4]

him to bring Stan's case to the attention of the Soviet Government. When Stan learned of this development she wrote to Harmsworth: 'I think that I quite insufficiently expressed my appreciation and wish to do so now.' She concluded the letter: 'Thank you again and hoping to make no further demands on your time and attention.'[6]

Stan's claim was immediately dismissed by the Soviets. On behalf of Georgy Chicherin, Maxim Litvinov sent a reply to Hodgson insisting that he had personally advised against Harding entering Russia, but that she had refused to listen and had obtained a visa in Reval. This was not completely true, as Litvinov had given her a letter of introduction to Gukovsky, head of the Soviet Mission in Reval, who had then informed her that she had permission from the People's Commissary for Foreign Affairs – that is, from Chicherin – to enter Russia.

Litvinov also pointed out to Hodgson that Stan Harding was arrested in June 1920, long prior to the conclusion of the Anglo-Soviet Trade Agreement, and that the authorities had reason to believe that she had travelled to Russia with the intention of collecting information for Russia's enemies. They would not, therefore, consider any redress unless Britain were to consider similar Russian claims.[7]

A Foreign Office internal memo discussing Litvinov's reply stated that if more Parliamentary questions on the matter were raised, Harmsworth should report that the Soviets refused to acknowledge Stan's claims. This, they hoped, would be the end of the matter.

* * *

When James Madison drafted the First Amendment of the American Constitution, enshrining free speech and freedom of the press, he suggested that if it could 'be so arranged that every newspaper, when printed on one side, should be handed over to the press of an adversary, to be printed on the other, thus presenting to every reader both sides of every question, truth would always have a fair chance.' Unfortunately, he understood human nature only too well because he added: 'But such a remedy is an ideal.'[8]

Stan now wanted to fill in the adversarial side of the newspaper sheet and attempted to open a new front for her campaign in America. In September 1921, she sent her story, including defamatory allegations about Marguerite's 'dark and mysterious activities', to the New York World, the newspaper that Stan had represented during her trip to Russia. Afraid of being sued for libel by Marguerite Harrison, they refused to publish.

Learning of Stan's approach to the New York World, an outraged

Brigadier-General Churchill, Marguerite's MID boss, wrote to Colonel Oscar Solbert, the American Military Attaché in London: 'In view of the fact that Mrs Harrison has on occasion been of assistance to the British authorities, amongst other things helping Mr [Reverend] North, the Foreign Office representative in Moscow, Mr Hurley of the State Department is of the opinion that possibly the Foreign Office might be approached on the subject of closing Mrs Harding's mouth and preventing her from injuring Mrs Harrison, in whom we all have the greatest confidence.'[9]

Soon afterward, in October, a Mr Le Clercq from the American Embassy in London paid a visit to Esmond Ovey at the Foreign Office to press the American position and seek cooperation. Although not always sympathetic to Stan Harding, Ovey pointed out to Le Clercq that perhaps she had good reason to criticise Marguerite Harrison. He read out a copy of a telegram of the 6th of January 1921 to the Hearst Press in Berlin sent by Louise Bryant, the American journalist and widow of John Reed whom Marguerite had consoled in Moscow. It stated that the Cheka knew Harrison had been a professional spy since May 1917 when she had entered the service of the Department of Justice, Baltimore section, and later transferred to Military Intelligence. When Marguerite was arrested the first time, 'realising seriousness of situation considering evidence against her as military and political spy confessed everything [stop] Offered information and future services to Soviet Government [stop].'[10]

The telegram also alleged that Harrison had provided the Cheka with information on British and American spies in Russia, and that she was responsible for many foreign correspondents being refused entry visas. More importantly, Bryant's telegram claimed that Marguerite was responsible 'for arrest of many of her compatriots [stop] In some cases gave correct information in others absolutely false [stop] Logical conclusion double existence led to her own arrest.'[11]

Ovey was treading into awkward territory. He knew that no country would admit to the use of secret agents. Le Clercq was told 'unofficially' that, as Harding was at the time employed by an American newspaper, the British government would not support her claim for compensation. She must, therefore, obtain support from the American government, but Ovey knew well that the United States would not support Harding if she continued to make allegations against their own spy.[12] Le Clercq left the meeting claiming he would look into the matter, but both parties were satisfied with the outcome of the conversation.

Stan at this time was leading a peripatetic existence, moving between various London addresses. She lived for short periods in a flat in Ryder Street, St. James's – a smart block of Victorian mansion flats – and another in Stratford Place, north of Oxford Street. But she also made use of her bohemian connections and talent for cultivating influential friends in the arts. She could often be found at Anderton's Hotel in Fleet Street, a refuge for journalists where the London Press Club met, and at the Lyceum Club in Piccadilly, a women's club founded in 1902 and open to female artists and writers. She also stayed in the attic rooms above Harold Monro's Poetry Bookshop off Theobalds Road in Bloomsbury. Founded by Monro in 1913, the shop sold and published poetry, and poetic luminaries such as W.B. Yeats and Ezra Pound declaimed their verses amid the stacks. Wilfred Owen and Robert Frost, among other impecunious poets, had at different times passed through the attic rooms occupied by Stan.

One of Stan's friends and supporters at this time was Jessie Grosvenor, the widow of Richard Grosvenor, a barrister, businessman and cousin of the Duke of Westminster. The 65-year-old Jessie had lived a full life. Her 1898 marriage to Grosvenor, her second husband, had broken the heart of the writer Samuel Butler who first met her when she worked as an actress on the London stage. Jessie, the smitten Butler had exulted, was like 'an Easter Monday or some other Bank Holiday'. When the American Embassy requested that Stan visit them to discuss her charges against Marguerite Harrison, it was this formidable and respectable woman that she asked to attend the meeting with her.

In early November 1921, the two women were met at the Embassy (then at 10 Grosvenor Gardens, near Victoria Station) by the American military attaché, a West Point graduate named Colonel Oscar Solbert. Stan presented her case to the Colonel and, according to Stan, Solbert eventually offered her 'hush money' amounting to £10,000 – the same amount that she was claiming as damages from the Russians – if she refrained from making statements about Marguerite Harrison. 'What have you to gain by attempting to publish these things?' Solbert queried.

Solbert then claimed that the American government had control over certain sections of the British press, and in particular over *The Times* through its Managing Director, Sir Campbell Stuart, who during the war had served as Deputy Director of Propaganda in Enemy Countries. 'If you send your story to *The Times*,' Colonel Solbert blithely informed Stan, 'Sir Campbell Stuart will ring us up and we will say, Drop it, don't touch it! America will protect its agent.'

Stan recounted this interview to the Foreign Office and they advised her not to attempt to publish her story in the immediate future, as they were endeavouring to secure compensation for her from Russia. This was not what Esmond Ovey at the FO had told Le Clercq of the US Embassy although, of course, Stan did not know this. So, for the time being she agreed to back off, but soon sensed that her demands were being swept under the carpet.

As 1921 came to a close, Stan wrote again to Cecil Harmsworth, reminding him that her treatment in Russia 'had so injured my health and capacity to work as to be practically equivalent to ten years off my health; while the false accusation is a hindrance to my career.'[13] She repeated her demands: an apology and statement from the Soviets that she was not a British agent, together with £10,000 compensation for loss of health and earning capacity. She even managed to arrange a meeting with Harmsworth. The Under Secretary of State, described by a journalist as 'a rather charming man ... with hogged moustache and a general savour of tweeds about him, very quiet in a solid way, and extremely courteous',[14] was not impressed by Stan. No doubt she belaboured him employing the same anxious rhetoric as in her letters, and Harmsworth concluded that she was in both physical and mental distress.

Two more letters were sent to the Foreign Office urging the government to do more on Stan's behalf, the first from the National Union of Journalists, and the second from Ernest Wild, MP; both accused the government of being neglectful. Replies were quickly dispatched, reiterating that strong representations were being made in Moscow. Despite such assurances, the wheels in Whitehall ground extremely slowly; it took Lord Curzon two months to reply to Robert Hodgson's letter from Moscow of the 29th of September 1921 regarding Litvinov's refusal to grant Stan compensation. 'I cannot accept M. Litvinov's reply in justification of the incident,' Curzon wrote on December 3rd.[15]

Once again, Curzon instructed Hodgson to inform Litvinov that unless a satisfactory reply was forthcoming, 'they will be compelled to communicate to the press the whole correspondence on this lamentable affair. Mrs Stan Harding's case has excited widespread interest and sympathy in Parliament and in the press in this country, which His Majesty's Government fully share.'[16] But the Foreign Office was tiring of the whole affair. 'Mrs Stan Harding is the bane of our lives in the Northern Department,' an internal Foreign Office memo lamented a few days into 1922. 'She is continuously calling or writing to urge us to take further action.'[17] The civil servant was referring to Stan's latest letter pressing the Foreign Office to send yet another telegram to Hodgson to push her case. On this occasion she even offered to send it at her own expense. 'This suggestion is not made in a misplaced effort on my part to be facetious,' she explained, 'but merely to meet the objection.'[18] Her offer was declined, but she was informed that Hodgson was returning to London shortly, and that her case would be discussed with him.

In the meantime, Chicherin had replied to Curzon's December communiqué, reiterating that the Russians would not consider Harding's claims unless the British considered their claims, in particular the case of Mr and Mrs Babushkin, the Russian Consul and his wife. They, along with the consular staff, had been arrested by the British on October 25th 1918 in Meshed, Persia; the couple claimed still to be suffering from injuries sustained during their arrest and detention.

The steady stream did not abate. Letters urging action on Stan's behalf continued to arrive at the Foreign Office, including one from Adelaide Broadhurst of the National Political League, asking when the Foreign Office was to publish the facts of Stan's case since the Soviets had ignored the Foreign Office warning they would do so if they did not respond to their demands.

Stan now had the bit firmly between her teeth, writing to one of her champions, Lord Robert Cecil, informing him that the Foreign Office had refused her access to Hodgson. Cecil immediately wrote to Harmsworth, requesting that the terms of the note sent to the Soviet Government should be made public. Harmsworth was not satisfied with this and replied: 'We feel it will do little good and there seems to be nothing else we can do for Mrs Harding.' However, he now felt that there seemed to be no alternative but to publish the official correspondence pertaining to the matter so as to bring clarity to the debate.*

Harmsworth did not repeat details to Cecil of a Foreign Office internal memo written a few days earlier: 'A threat to withdraw the British mission (which I think Mrs Harding has suggested) is impossible, as apart from the weakness of her case, it would, I think, be generally agreed that our interests would materially suffer from such action, which is quite uncalled for. Mrs Harding is not the only sufferer.'[19] Harmsworth merely politely reminded Cecil that Harding should register her claims with the Russian Board of Trade.

---

* A ten-page booklet published by His Majesty's Stationary Office, *Correspondence with the Russian Soviet Government respecting the Imprisonment of Mrs. Stan Harding in Russia. Russia No. 1*, would appear later in the year.

In March 1922, yet more Parliamentary questions on the subject were lodged, from both Sir John Butcher and Sir Harry Brittain. Sir Harry was founder of the Association of American Correspondents in London and President of the British International Association of Journalists; as such, he was keen to forge good relations with Americans but also to uphold the profession of journalism.

Meanwhile, the bombardment continued. On March 9th, Harmsworth received from Stan a rambling letter deploring the long interval before the Foreign Office replied to Litvinov's September letter. In her opinion, the government had not taken her case seriously enough and the Russians would have reacted more positively to her requests had the letter been sent directly to Chicherin. The letter only confirmed the opinion Harmsworth had already formed of Stan that she 'seems to be in as much distress, physically and mentally, as when I saw her some months ago'.[20]

* * *

In April 1922, the Genoa Conference convened. Thirty-four countries met to formulate economic strategies to rebuild a devastated Central and Eastern Europe and to negotiate a relationship between Soviet Russia and the capitalist world. Characteristically, Stan wanted her campaign for compensation to be on the agenda. Five days before the conference was to begin, she and a small deputation from the Institute of Journalists and the National Union of Journalists arrived at the Foreign Office to demand that her case be raised at Genoa as a test of the good intentions of Soviet Russia.

Once again, the British government found itself in an awkward situation in which domestic political turmoil could have a detrimental effect on its foreign policy.

On April 7th, Harmsworth wrote to Stan, assuring her that Lord Curzon was extremely sympathetic and was anxious to do everything he could for her. 'If the question of recognition of the Soviet government arises, and if the British delegates are in a position to state and discuss the conditions upon which it would be given,' he wrote, 'an occasion might very well arise for putting forward your case, and demanding compensation.'[21] But, much to Stan's disappointment, the occasion did not arise. More than likely, the British delegates at Genoa had no intention whatsoever of bringing up Stan's battle for compensation with the Russians. There were much more important issues to sort out – in particular, oil concessions.

The Genoa Conference duly ended on May 19th without agreement. It was followed a month later by The Hague Conference – a continuation of Genoa – about which the New York Times warned: 'Let us avoid falling into the error of the Paris and Genoa Conferences of figuratively beginning with a flourish of champagne and ending with a headache'.[22]

If Stan harboured hopes that her case would be raised at The Hague, once again the British delegates undoubtedly had no intention of tossing that particular spanner into the works. They had agreed in a private meeting on June 20th that miscellaneous claims to be brought up at the conference would not include personal claims.[23] In early July, the head of the British delegates, Sir Philip Lloyd-Greame, confirmed that he was unwilling to raise Stan's case with the Russians as they would retaliate by raising similar cases against the British.[24]

The American Secretary of State, Charles Hughes, had refused to attend The Hague Conference, which ended on July 19th. The Germans, having signed an agreement with the Russians at Rapallo to annul any claims against each other, had not been invited, while France and Belgium adamantly refused to sign any agreement unless all their demands were met. Guarantees from Russia for the return of nationalised property to former foreign owners was sought. The Soviets resolutely declined. Thus a conference ended once again without agreement, and Stan was no nearer to gaining compensation.

When it became abundantly clear that her case was not being pressed at the conferences, the Under Secretary of State was confronted by a consequent onslaught of Parliamentary questions. The first, on July 12th 1922, from the Conservative MP for Kensington South, Sir William Davison, asked if Stan's case had been raised at The Hague. Was the Under Secretary of State aware that the chief Russian negotiator at the conference was Litvinov, the very man who had signed Stan's safe conduct to Russia? Should he not therefore, Davison continued, be approached to resolve the settlement?

An internal Foreign Office memo from Ovey's office had stated that little good would come of approaching Litvinov yet again, since he had repeatedly denied offering Stan safe conduct. And on at least one occasion, Ovey had lost his temper with Hodgson over the matter and concluded: 'Nobody has been treated with greater consideration than Mrs Harding, our only fault lies in having tried too much.'[25]

Chapter Seventeen

The Bane of Our Lives

After arriving back in the USA in August 1921, around the time Stan Harding was attempting to mobilise the National Union of Journalists for her campaign, Marguerite immediately set to work on the manuscript of a book that would be published later in the year as *Marooned in Moscow: The Story of an American Woman Imprisoned in Russia*. She also returned to her old job as a correspondent for *The Baltimore Sun*, but soon felt a rising frustration with the isolationist mentality of her fellow countrymen and the small-mindedness of President Harding's administration. She wrote of how she was 'shocked beyond measure' at the activities of the Ku Klux Klan and the growing spirit of intolerance. 'I was bitterly disappointed at the indifference of the average American to foreign affairs.'

Marguerite also embarked on a six-month lecture tour, probably in conjunction with the publication of *Marooned in Moscow*... 'My audiences,' she later admitted, 'were interested in me not because of what I had to tell them, but because my name had been in the headlines of the newspaper and because I was suspected of all sorts of dark and mysterious activities.'

But the lure of international travel and politics soon returned. Armed with commissions for articles from *Cosmopolitan* and Hearst's *International Magazine*, she set off for a working tour of Japan, Korea and China in June 1922, initially sailing from Vancouver to Yokohama.

After arriving in Yokohama, Marguerite made her way to Tokyo and was surprised at how cosmopolitan the city was. The Japanese women wore 'gay cotton crepe kimonos with babies tied on their backs, modern young people in European clothes walked arm-in-arm, old-fashioned wives toddling after their husbands, flamboyant geisha and bobbed Japanese flappers.'

Marguerite's knack of making influential friends and moving in higher circles did not fail her. It was not long before she was being entertained by the aristocracy and politicians, including the Foreign Minister. She even secured an interview with the newly appointed Prime Minister, Baron Tomosaburo Kato. Kato's background was impeccable: he had been born into a samurai family and graduated second in his class at the

Imperial Japanese Naval Academy. He had recently returned to Japan after leading the country's delegation at the Washington Naval Disarmament Conference, and would soon be appointed Prime Minister. Marguerite gained his confidence to such an extent that she was permitted to take motion pictures of herself playing with his children.

'Few foreigners have been received in Tokyo with as much enthusiasm as was Mrs Marguerite Harrison and she left a vivid and pleasing impression on a people more than hard to impress,' observed one expatriate American living in the city.[1] As well as charming the Baron, Marguerite captivated the Japanese people. However, her spectacles were not entirely rose-tinted, and she would warn in a July 1923 article for *The Atlantic Monthly*: 'Japan's goal for the immediate future is economic imperialism; and her eventual goal is the domination of the yellow races in the Far East.'[2]

But it was not just the Japanese whom Marguerite captivated. The American Military Attaché Charles Burnett informed Colonel Stuart Heintzelman at MID headquarters that an Englishman, Major Basil Winders, had fallen 'head over heels in love with her, and while in that state, gave up information'.[3] Winders suggested that Marguerite join Vickers Secret Service, an offer Burnett advised her to accept, as it would be useful for the MID to be aware of Vickers' plans. Even though her recent activities in Russia were presently the subject of gossip, speculation and condemnation, and her future as an intelligence officer appeared to be over, she was on the cusp of slipping again into the world of espionage.

During the war, the British steel manufacturing company, Vickers Ltd, had continued to make ships and armaments, although the contracts they had had with Turkey, Germany and Russia ceased. Shortly after the Peace Treaty was signed, Douglas Vickers MP took over as Chairman and the company began concentrating on civilian products – locomotives, railway material, boilers, turbines, merchant ships and even furniture and soft toys. Their only armament work was for the Japanese. In 1919, Douglas Vickers had asked Basil Winders to return to Tokyo to report on rival competition, especially that of the Americans.

It was not unusual for businessmen also to be working for the secret services, so when in March 1920, Winders, who had been a Vickers representative before the war, told the British Military Attaché in Tokyo that every Japanese aeroplane could be used for military purposes, a memo was sent to the Foreign Office asking whether he was trustworthy. The reply stated that he was 'a clever, little fellow who walks rings around the Japs, however, regard Winders as a useful source of information, but treat him with caution'.[4] This assessment was partly due to Winders having been caught up in a scandal in 1913, involving high-ranking Japanese naval officers taking bribes from foreign firms. Even though Winders had worked for the British Naval Intelligence in Scandinavia during the war, Vickers Headquarters confirmed to the Foreign Office in Whitehall that he was not their special 'representative' in Japan, meaning that he was not working in any capacity with the secret service.[5]

After Marguerite had been entertained for a month or so in Tokyo, she wanted to visit 'Japan's Alaska', Sakhalin, a large, elongated island perched in the North Pacific. The choice of destination may not have been entirely innocent. The Japanese and Russians had been quarrelling over its sovereignty since 1845, and for many years the Russians had occupied the north of the island, establishing coal mines, schools, churches and a penal colony, whilst the Japanese held the south. By 1920, the Japanese had encroached into Northern Sakhalin and were also in control of parts of Siberia in mainland Russia east of Lake Baikal, and the Trans-Siberian railroad from Vladivostok to Manchuria. Much to the anger of the Soviets, they had supported the Whites against the Bolsheviks.

The Allies were wary of Japan's expansionism in Russia and were relieved when it was agreed at the 1921-22 Washington Conference that they would leave Siberia and the northern part of Sakhalin. The Japanese Foreign Office, distrustful of the Russians, made Marguerite an offer she could not refuse. Provided that she was accompanied by Dr Matsujiro Honda, a man she found 'extremely agreeable', they would permit her to visit Sakhalin if in return she would later provide them with confidential reports on the political and economic conditions of Siberia.[6] No evidence survives of the precise terms of the offer or whether she accepted them, but at the end of July she was allowed to set off for Sakhalin.

On the island, Marguerite made a point of visiting Russian peasants, many of whom were descendants of convicts, residing in the interior of the island. She concluded that although they were cut off from the revolution during the civil war, they were, in fact, materially much better off under Japanese administration.

From Sakhalin, Marguerite sailed to Nikolayevsk-na-Amure on mainland Siberia. 'Most of the roads I followed were bloodstained roads,' she wrote. 'Grim reminders of the World War and Revolution; others fresh with traces of bloodshed since the peace; still others that were reddened almost as I passed.'[7] She was not exaggerating, for the region had a bloody history. During the Russian Civil War, the Japanese had occupied Nikolayevsk until Yakov Triapitsyn, an anarchist with Bolshevik connections, led 4,000 troops in the sacking and burning of the town, killing over 6,000 citizens, and 700 Japanese soldiers and their families. Triapitsyn was later captured by partisans and handed over to the Bolsheviks, who duly executed him. However, the Japanese did not think that this went far enough and repeatedly demanded compensation – hence their disinclination to vacate Sakhalin.*

Throughout her trip Marguerite met several American military attachés. She was unaware that Stan's actions in London had caused Marlborough Churchill to write confidentially to the American military attachés in Tokyo, Peking, and Chita in Siberia to warn them to be cautious in dealings with her. They should 'politely decline to give her anything in writing in the way of endorsements or to indicate to anyone except the officials of the American Embassy that she was ever in our service.'[8] Although Churchill added that as far as he knew, 'Mrs Harrison was a woman of great refinement and excellent education and thoroughly reliable,' it seems some employees at the MID were unsure of Marguerite's true allegiances and had monitored her lectures back in America.[9] They were now keeping an eye on her and her travels, just as were the Russian secret police, the GPU (the State Political Directorate who had replaced the Cheka in February 1922).

Moreover, Stan Harding's campaign in Britain had now spread to Asia. On August 24th 1922, the *Japanese Advertiser* ran a story carrying Stan's claim that Marguerite was a Bolshevik agent. Those, who a few weeks earlier were so impressed by her, now reacted with shock. Marguerite refused to comment, but the whispers of mistrust were heard a few days later in Washington when the Japanese Chargé d'Affaires, Saburi, called on D.C. Poole at the State Department to enquire whether Stan Harding's allegations were true. The Japanese, extremely suspicious of Bolshevism, were particularly concerned about the allegation that Marguerite was a Bolshevik spy. Poole reassured Saburi that the State Department did not think this was so.[10] This did not stop the warnings from Washington arriving on Lieutenant-Colonel Charles Burnett's desk at the American Embassy in Tokyo. 'Use extreme caution when dealing with Mrs Harrison,' he was advised in September 1922. 'The subject probably is a patriotic American, but has learned so much inside infor-

---

* The Japanese were to withdraw from Northern Sakhalin in 1925.

mation in many countries and has had such frequent personal contacts with many different national leaders that quite unconsciously may some day make a serious mistake.'[11]

The allegations against Marguerite had by now spread to Peking. One anxious American diplomat there sent a memo to the American Secretary of State, William Phillips, enquiring whether he should confiscate Marguerite's passport if the opportunity arose. Phillips replied that he doubted the newspaper allegations were true, but advised him to be discreet and reserved when dealing with her.[12] Marguerite was by this time no longer officially on the MID's payroll; she did, however, pass on information, such as a report on gold-mining in Siberia, that she thought might be useful to American military attachés.

Marguerite continued with her travels, trying as best she could to ignore Stan's allegations and the stir they were creating. From Nikolayevsk-na-Amure, she took a paddle steamer to Khabarovsk. From there she headed for Vladivostok, where the remnants of the Whites under the command of General Dieterichs were stationed. Marguerite interviewed the general and compared him to Felix Dzerzhinsky, both of whom she thought were fanatical in their beliefs.

From Vladivostok Marguerite took a steamship to Korea, and spent some time in Seoul. The Japanese had taken over Korea following the Sino-Japanese war of 1896, and Marguerite thought that as a consequence, Seoul looked like a thoroughly modern Japanese city with its 'broad boulevards, handsome public buildings and prosperous shops'. During her brief sojourn in the city, she was escorted around schools and institutions by the Japanese governor, General Sato.

Seoul was her staging post for Changchun in China, where the Russo-Japanese Conference on Japanese withdrawal from Siberia and Sakhalin was being held. Before leaving Japan, Marguerite had persuaded the Japanese newspaper, *Chugai Shogyo Shimpo*, to commission her to report on the conference, which, by the end of September, had disintegrated into squabbling over compensation for the massacre of Japanese nationals in Nikolaevsk. Marguerite's behaviour at the conference attracted a good deal of attention. She was openly friendly with the Russian delegates, upsetting the Japanese. And, as one magazine reported, she had even sat next to the Soviet diplomat and negotiator Adolph Joffe at dinner, quite obviously enjoying his company.

While in China, and always on the lookout for good copy, Marguerite arranged to interview the Manchurian warlord, Marshal Chang Tso-lin, on his views on the Japanese occupation and the future of China and

Manchuria. Face-to-face with a 'slender little Chinese in a long, black satin coat, wearing a small skullcap,' she reported that he 'stooped slightly as he stood with his hands tucked in his sleeves wearing a meek, almost deprecatory smile under his drooping black moustache'. Vehemently anti-Communist, he supported the restoration of the Qing dynasty. Six years after meeting Marguerite, he would be assassinated by the Japanese in retaliation for his failure to stop the advance of the Kuomintang Nationalists in 1928.

Marguerite then visited Mukden, Harbin, and Peking, but her heart, it seemed, remained in Russia. It was in October of 1922, she claimed, that she decided to extend her journey by returning to America via Soviet Russia. In Tokyo, she had acquired a visa to visit the Siberian city of Chita (then under Japanese control) and thought, due to Lenin's softening of relations with the West, that it would be possible once there to acquire the appropriate visa for Russia.

* * *

The National Union of Journalists (NUJ) and the Institute of Journalists decided the time had come to publicise Stan's case directly to America. Initially, in the spring of 1922, they had written to the Association of American Correspondents in London in the hope that they would pursue the matter. However, the Americans were unwilling to take any disciplinary action against Marguerite, and so British journalists published articles in *Truth, The Times, The Daily News, The Westminster Gazette* and *The Manchester Guardian*. On August 23rd, the Socialist newspaper *Truth* printed a letter from Henry Marriott Richardson, General Secretary to the NUJ: 'In this country a journalist who acted as a political spy or even as a police informer would not be permitted to be a member of my union. I do not think that American journalists are less careful of the honour of their profession than we are,' he wrote. 'And I trust that now you have called their attention to the facts they will hasten to make what amends they can to the victim of the base designs of one of their number, even though they are unable to do more than prevent Mrs Harrison continuing to receive the respect that which decent journalists are entitled to.'[13]

John Steele, correspondent of the *Chicago Tribune* and secretary of the Association of American Correspondents in London, agreed to forward Stan's case to its members. 'Personally,' he said in his reply, 'I hardly see what we can do. The facts are simply that Mrs Harrison is a "wrong 'un," has already been fully exposed as such, and I cannot see that what she has done reflects in any way on the journalistic profession.' He did not think she had ever been a professional journalist 'but simply a person who was hired by a news organisation for a particular job that had turned out badly, and was repudiated by her own organisation.'[14] This infuriated Stan because Marguerite had been a staff correspondent for eight years on *The Baltimore Sun*. Additionally, she had been given commissions as a Moscow correspondent from the *New York Evening Post* and the Associated Press. These organisations failed to criticise or repudiate her.

Marguerite had written articles during the war portraying herself as an ordinary American widow and mother doing her bit for the war effort such as when she donned 'womanalls' and worked in the steelworks. However, there was nothing ordinary about Marguerite. She had always been a member of the East Coast establishment with connections that enabled her to move in the upper echelons of both European and American society, and the many important and powerful men she knew were often willing to offer her help whenever she needed it. But she was also popular with ordinary Americans who had read her articles supporting the war effort. Later, her reports from abroad were exciting and sold copy, and she became known as an intrepid journalist who went to places where no other woman dared travel.

Stan, on the other hand, with her intense, forceful character and relatively humble background, had few, if any, family connections in high society. It was easy to dismiss her as an angry Socialist pursuing a jealous vendetta against a fellow journalist. In the political climate in America, which feared Socialism, she stood very little chance of getting her voice heard with any degree of sympathy or effectiveness.

American journalists might have had their hands tied with regard to publishing Stan's case, but their professional integrity was jeopardised by their refusal publicly to condemn, or at the very least to air, the allegations that Marguerite had been working for Military Intelligence under a journalistic cover. A direct result of Stan's very public feud with Marguerite was the founding in 1922 of the American Society of Newspaper Editors (ASNE). One of the founding members was Herbert Bayard Swope, executive editor of the *New York World*, who had commissioned Stan to go to Russia. The following year, the American Code of Journalist Ethics, devised by Henry John Wright from the *New York Globe*, was introduced. The canons were based around responsibility, freedom of the press, independence, sincerity, truthfulness, accuracy, impartiality, fair play and decency. It stated that 'a journalist who used his power for any selfish or otherwise unworthy purpose is faithless to a high trust'. However, many journalists agreed with Swope when he argued that the code lacked teeth and was a meaningless gesture unless provisions were in place to censure, suspend or expel members for gross misconduct and violation of ethics. Although the code of ethics lacked teeth, there was, however, recognition that something needed to be done to prevent journalists abusing their role.

While the debate concerning these moral issues was underway, President Harding, formerly prominent newspaper editor, was invited to speak to the first ASNE annual dinner event in 1923. He urged the need for responsibility and decency. 'There are certainly times when news of international importance cannot be given to the public,' he lectured the journalists and editors. 'Don't you see how important it is to omit the things that tend to destroy faith in society?' Yet this was a man who, ironically, had acted neither decently nor responsibly in one celebrated case. Early in his presidency his government had taken over the naval oil reserves at Teapot Dome in Wyoming and leased out the oil rights to his colleagues without debate or open competition. These actions had caused a huge scandal in the press, which may explain why he was so keen for ASNE to omit news when he deemed it necessary.

* * *

As the summer of 1922 ended, David Lloyd George's coalition government was showing serious cracks. Its death knell was sounded by the Chanak Crisis in September and October, which resulted from Kemal Atatürk's determination to depose the Sultan and establish an independent Turkish Republic. Under the Treaty of Sèvres, agreed in August, British and French troops had been stationed near Chanak to guard the neutral zone of the Dardanelles Straits. However, Turkish troops defeated the Greek forces and recaptured Smyrna. Lloyd George threatened war against the Turkish nationalists. But in Britain and her colonies there was no stomach for further fighting, and the Conservatives refused to comply. After a vote of no confidence in the House, a general election was fixed for the 15th of November 1922.

Shortly before polling day, Stan and the Institute of Journalists published an appeal in *The Times* addressed to all Parliamentary candidates, seeking their support for Stan's campaign for compensation and the clearing of her name. The Canadian-born Andrew Bonar Law led the Conservative party to victory, and elected to keep Lord Curzon in place as Foreign Secretary but replaced Cecil Harmsworth as Under Secretary of State with Ronald McNeill. McNeill was a diehard Ulster Unionist with extreme views and a mercurial nature (he once threw a bundle of papers at Winston Churchill, hitting him in the head). McNeill was considered a surprising choice by some, but his appointment gave Stan some hope since he was a former journalist, and had edited the *St. James's Gazette* from 1900 to 1904, after which he worked on the eleventh edition of the *Encyclopædia Britannica*.

McNeill soon got a taste of what Harmsworth had endued during the previous year. Within two weeks of the election, Sir Robert Burton-Chadwick, a Conservative MP, submitted a Parliamentary question to the new Under Secretary of State, adding another dimension to Stan's compensation claims – Mrs Marguerite Harrison's role in Stan's imprisonment. Had His Majesty's Government taken steps to secure redress from the United States for the misdeeds of its agent, asked Burton-Chadwick? McNeill's official reply stated that reports had reached the government about Harrison and her alleged role, but sufficient evidence had not been forthcoming to prove how far they were accurate. An internal Foreign Office memo noted that 'we rather suspect that they [Stan's accusations] may contain a certain element of truth and that the matter had been mentioned to Mr Le Clercq at the American Embassy, but no further action has been taken.'[15]

On December 13th, Stan, Burton-Chadwick and a deputation from the NUJ, the National Institute of Journalists, the National Council of Women of Great Britain and Ireland, and the Society of Women Journalists, descended on McNeill's office in Whitehall. They made several demands in addition to seeking mere monetary compensation for Stan from Russia: the Government should take steps to establish beyond any doubt that when in Russia she was not a spy, instigate a public enquiry into the role Marguerite Harrison had played in Stan's false denunciation, and publicise the case both in Britain and in America.

Stan remained convinced that if the American public were made aware of the facts as she saw them, they would support her campaign for compensation from the United States, especially as she had witnesses prepared to testify against Marguerite under oath, including John Reed's widow, Louise Bryant, and two Americans who had been imprisoned in Moscow, Weston Burgess Estes and Alfred Wood Stickney.

McNeill's replies were indistinguishable from the assurances previously given by Harmsworth. He insisted that he 'strongly sympathised' with Stan's case but reiterated that the Foreign Office had done everything possible to gain compensation for her from Russia. As the Soviets had stubbornly refused to comply, she must, as advised on many occasions, register her complaint with the relevant department until diplomatic conditions become more favourable.

Regarding Mrs Harrison, McNeill stressed that there was no evidence that she was a spy – other than Stan's word and the allegations contained in the telegram from Louise Bryant – and therefore no action could be taken against the United States regarding a private American citizen. If such an action was to be undertaken against the United States government, it was likely that the Russians would wash their hands of any responsibility in the matter and blame America.

McNeill said he did not see how the British government could do any more in publicising her case; a White Paper had been published on the correspondence between Soviet Russia and Lord Curzon; and the British representative in Russia had endorsed statements that she was never an agent of the British Secret Service. He added that he failed to see what benefit more publicity would have for her.

If there was an enquiry, McNeill continued, much of the evidence would have to be collected in Russia, which would be impossible. 'It could only be hoped, though the hope was only a very unsubstantial one,' McNeill said, that at some future date 'the Soviet government would be induced to recognise their liabilities in this and similar cases and to grant the compensation which was justly due.'[16] A scribbled note on the minutes of this meeting stated: 'This is satisfactory. I hope that Mrs Stan Harding will cease worrying the Foreign Office.'[17]

Naturally, this hope was a vain one. Stan left McNeill's office muttering about the Americans having offered her 'hush money', and that if her case was good enough to be offered that, it was good enough for compensation. The rest of the deputation went off to enjoy the Christmas of 1922 with their families, whilst Stan scuttled away to her modest digs and plan her next move. Mrs Harding was not going to be silenced so easily.

Chapter Eighteen

Back in the USSR

In July 1922, when Marguerite had obtained her visa for Chita, a city some 1,000 miles to the west of Vladivostok, it was still under Japanese control. [1] Now, in September, plans for its (peaceful) reoccupation by Russia were underway and as a known American secret agent, Marguerite might reasonably have assumed it would be dangerous for her to travel to there. Nevertheless, she was making plans to journey across the Gobi Desert to Chita in a battered Ford motor vehicle owned by a fur trader.

People who knew Marguerite well, such as her beloved Aunt Josephine Livezey, did not understand her desire to return to Russia. Senator France, who previously had helped negotiate her release from prison in Moscow, was appalled, particularly as he had pledged to People's Commissar for Foreign Affairs, Georgy Chicherin, that under no circumstances would she return to Soviet Russia. Marguerite later justified her actions by saying she had been homesick for the 'sound of Russian voices, for the broad sweep of the Russian wheat fields, for the homely little villages with their wooden izbas, for the childlike, lovable people with whom I had lived so much.'

She added that she understood that if she were to suddenly find herself once more in Soviet Russia, it would be awkward for her, having been deported from Moscow only fifteen months before with 'serious charges still pending, but I felt that my credentials would prove that I had had no intention of committing any irregularity.' [2] In fact, Marguerite's credentials included the recent preparation of confidential reports for the MID and, presumably, the Japanese Foreign Office as well.

The Japanese stood by their word and began withdrawing from Siberia in the autumn of 1922, and Chita and the Far Eastern Republic were peacefully incorporated into Soviet Russia. In the meantime, supposedly unaware of this development,

The trip was a dangerous one. Leaving Peking (Beijing) they stopped first at Kalgan (Changkiakow), the last modern city before reaching Mongolia's capital city, Urga (Ulan Bator). Four bullocks dragged the car, which often hung perilously over the mountain ledges, through the Hanibar Pass in the Great Khingan Mountains. On the other side of the pass, they travelled through the Gobi Desert, following the old Silk-Route until reaching Urga, and from there on to Chita. It had been a rugged journey of some 1,400 kilometres.

When they arrived in the city on November 19th, the Japanese had withdrawn and it was now under Russian sovereignty. Marguerite later told Colonel Naylor, Director of the MID, that she had entered Chita in absolute good faith when it was part of the Far Eastern Republic, but when she arrived, as Naylor sceptically recorded, 'lo! and behold! she was in Soviet Russia and not in the Far Eastern Republic.'[3] Naylor was right to be suspicious of Marguerite's November 19th arrival there, not least because she had attended both conferences that had discussed the Japanese withdrawals. She would have been well aware, when setting off in the battered Ford, that Chita would in all likelihood be in Russian hands by the time she arrived, and that she therefore would be liable to arrest.

A few days after her arrival, Marguerite was arrested at gunpoint while walking down the street by the GPU. Four days later, she was put on the Trans-Siberian Railway to Moscow and hence to Lubyanka Prison. She had placed herself in the precarious position of entering Russian territory without a visa issued by Russia. The question is: why had she done it? She had been told never to return to Russia, and yet return she did, despite the grave danger.

* * *

Marguerite's 4,000-mile trip to Moscow, escorted by a GPU agent and a soldier, was to take eight days. The train was comfortably heated, and Marguerite, with her usual charm, came to an agreement with the guards that if she made no attempt to escape or talk to anyone, she would be allowed to visit the bathroom unaccompanied. 'After four days together, we were the best of friends.' Meals were provided twice-daily, for which she paid the equivalent of $2 and typically included consommé or thick vegetable soup, beefsteak or roast mutton with rice or potatoes, a green vegetable and either blancmange or American canned fruits for dessert. There was even coffee.

Arriving in the middle of the night at Novo-Nikolaevsk – originally founded in 1893 when the Trans-Siberian Railway was due to be routed across the River Ob, and some 1,750 miles east of Moscow – Marguerite was taken by sleigh to a small office adjacent to the prison where she spent the night sleeping uncomfortably on the floor. Next morning she was led to the prison through the kitchen where the 'smell of half-rotten vegetables, putrid meat, *mahorka* [Russian tobacco], and dirty human beings, was indescribable'. She believed the small room to which she was taken as – even including her experiences in Lubyanka – the most horrible sight she had ever seen in her life. Its occupants were hardly visible due to poor light and boarded-up windows; when her eyes grew accustomed to the gloom, she made out four women lying motionless on plank beds. The room was damp and cold, heated only every third day, while the floor crawled with vermin. The women had been billeted there from one to four months with no fresh air or exercise. Marguerite was so appalled that she immediately distributed her limited supplies of soap, food, tea, white bread and chocolate.

Marguerite was lucky, remaining in the cell only for a day before a rough-looking guard arrived to take her back to the train. She recalled how he kept his 'pistol cocked and planted it in the small of my back, which made me decidedly uncomfortable', and was relieved to be handed over to her original guards, though this reunion did not prove a pleasant one. The next morning the guard's assistant woke with a swollen face and a high temperature. Never without her supplies of aspirin, Marguerite tended him, but the swelling grew worse. His skin turned red with purple blotches and he rapidly became delirious. Although a doctor was sought at every station, it was three days before one could be found. The unfortunate man was diagnosed with erysipelas, an extremely contagious skin disease caused by Streptococcus bacteria. Ordinarily he would have been placed immediately in isolation but, as this was impossible, both Marguerite and the guard were forced to remain with him in the carriage until they reached Moscow.

It was a relief for all when the sick guard was carted off to hospital. She and the remaining guard were instructed to wait for a car at the station. The guard suggested that they eat at the station's government restaurant – an establishment to which his party card allowed them entry. Waiters in black coats and white aprons, and white cloths over their arms, greeted them, and Marguerite was surprised to find that the tables were covered in white linen decorated with vases of artificial flowers. There was a buffet laid out with sandwiches, fruit and pastry, and even chocolate and cigarettes were available behind a locked glass cabinet. This was a definite improvement on her earlier Russian experience.

As they had travelled the 4,000 miles across Russia, Marguerite noted unmistakable traces of the civil war: piles of wrecked and burned freight cars, freight depots in ruins, and impoverished, ill-nourished people at the stations. But when they arrived in Moscow, the city appeared to have improved considerably since her last visit. Trams that had been out of action due to fuel shortages were now running. The streets were cleared of snow and the street lamps lit. Chauffeur-driven cars passed frequently, whereas eighteen months earlier the only civilian vehicles in use were those that had been requisitioned. Very few shops had been open before, now many welcomed shoppers with electric signs illuminating their doorways. She watched with interest as carts and wagons made deliveries, remembering how just a short time ago food was obtained either on ration cards or illegally, and dragged home on sleighs or carried on backs.

Little, though, appeared to have changed in Lubyanka. Marguerite recognised some of the guards in the reception office before being directed to the general waiting area – another familiar scene – that was packed with prisoners waiting to be processed. There she remained for three days until her name was called and she was ordered to pack her clothes. With eight other prisoners she was to be taken to Butyrka, the prison where Stan had previously spent many months. 'I would have preferred the Novinsky where I had stayed for so many weeks in 1921,' she recalled wistfully, 'but anything was better than the Lubyanka.' In Butyrka she was marched up to the women's section 'a big, high-ceilinged apartment with cement walls and stone floor where I found eleven other women, all politicals except two'.

Marguerite discovered that there was less freedom than in Novinsky, but prisoners were allowed to exercise, and books and newspapers were available. 'After dinner the women prisoners on our floor were turned out for exercise into a small court opposite a wing of the men's prison, with a high wall at each end,' Marguerite recalled. 'Round and round we walked on the hard-packed snow, stopping every now and then to exchange remarks with the women in the three upper tiers.' She was delighted to discover that the food was also much better than before. The dreaded herring soup was still on the menu, but this was complemented with a nourishing purée of black beans. Many prisoners also acquired food from relatives outside the prison and shared it out.

Each evening there was impromptu entertainment – games, dancing, singing, political discussions. 'My elementary knowledge of palmistry was called into play and I had to tell the fortunes of everybody in the room,' Marguerite explained. Hearing of her skill in predicting the future, people kept turning up to have their palms read. This was of course against the rules, but Marguerite got around them by telling a delighted female warden that she would acquire a 'second husband and a large sum of money within three years'. Marguerite could only hope, for her own sake, that she would be released before the three years were up.

Every morning at 10 a.m. various prisoners were selected and taken to the Lubyanka for cross-examination. Marguerite's name was called on the third morning. With twelve men she was escorted in the vehicle notoriously known as the 'Black Crow'. Accompanying her was a Polish officer accused of espionage, a Greek, and a Persian, whilst the rest were Russian. After an uneventful day spent waiting without interrogation, Marguerite was returned to Butyrka, still in the dark as to why she had been arrested. 'I began to hope against hope that some outside influences were at work and that I was perhaps going to be freed after all.'

Marguerite's health had never fully recovered from her first stint in prison, and she now began to deteriorate physically. When her name was called for yet another trip back to Lubyanka and was ordered to pack her things, she knew this time that it was serious. Endless waiting seemed to be the Russian way of life, and the hours ticked slowly by as she waited in anticipation for her transport to arrive. In the meantime, her head hurt and her body temperature rose. When she eventually arrived at Lubyanka, another day was wasted in the reception room waiting in vain to be processed. Finally, she was led through the inner court and up four flights of stone stairs to the commandant's office. After her baggage had been searched, she was escorted to an attic room on the fourth floor, 'just around the corner from the one I had occupied in 1921.'

Marguerite found conditions in Lubyanka improved – her room was clean and free of vermin, the food was much better, there was more of it, and she was allowed to take a bath every two weeks. In addition, she was permitted to buy almost anything from outside. On the other hand, she found that discipline was far stricter than before, and recalled how one of the Polish prisoners in her room smashed the plank beds and windows in a fit of anger, resulting in everyone's cigarette ration and books being removed. The guards, she noted, seemed much more hostile.

The Pole in question was supposedly an anarchist, but in reality was an informer, attempting to get the others to talk to a male prisoner in an adjoining room. 'For a time she pestered me with the most disgusting attentions. I did not dare to offend her,' Marguerite said, and 'I was obliged to restrain my feelings and refuse her advances as tactfully as possible'. Marguerite was perplexed as to why this woman had been employed as a provocateur because she was inept and 'so transparent that she gave herself away almost from the first'.

* * *

Marguerite's father-in-law, Dr Ames, was not so quick to galvanise support for her release this time round. Disturbed by press reports of Stan's allegations that Marguerite had falsely denounced her, Ames wrote for clarification to Colonel Naylor at the MID. He received a reply that files had been consulted and no evidence could be found that would 'prove or disprove' Stan's charges. He was told that the MID had instructed the American military attaché in London to investigate Stan's allegations and, after a meeting with her, could find no proof. 'The best evidence as to why Mrs Harding was arrested,' Ames was informed, 'is contained in the British pamphlet entitled "Correspondence with the Russian Soviet Government Respecting the Imprisonment of Mrs Stan Harding". From this it is inferred that Mrs Harrison was not concerned in the arrest and imprisonment of Mrs Harding.'[4] What Dr Ames was not told was that Stan had been specifically advised by the Foreign Office not to mention Marguerite's role when claiming compensation from the Soviets. They assumed that, if she did, the Soviets would quickly wash their hands of any responsibility and blame her arrest on the Americans.

By Christmas, Marguerite was extremely ill. 'All my physical and mental strength seemed to have left me,' she noted. 'The strain of waiting for something to happen sapped my vitality and at the end of the month I was so weak that I scarcely noticed the passage of time.'

In early January 1923, Marguerite was at last summoned for cross-examination, only to find herself face-to-face with her old adversary, Mogilevsky. She wasn't surprised to see him; the only puzzle is why he had taken so long to interview her. The sole record of their interview is Marguerite's version of events, which probably do not tell the entire story. What seems clear is that she had deliberately contrived to enter Russia and get herself arrested. The question is whether in doing so she was acting on the wishes of the MID and the Americans, or at the behest of the Bolsheviks, with whom she had earlier, of course, come to her notorious agreement to pass on information on foreigners living in Russia.

Had she struck a deal with Mogilevsky in 1921, agreeing before her release to return with further information? In her version of events, Mogilevsky greeted her jovially as if they had parted only the day before. Dumbfounded, she asked him why she was there. Because you are an American spy of course, he replied. Moreover, she had entered Russia without permission. He then continued to explain that, when she had agreed two years ago to work for the Soviets, she had double-crossed them. However, Mogilevsky still thought that she could be exceedingly useful if she were to work seriously for Russia. With this in mind, he gave

Marguerite a detailed explanation of how he had arranged for her recent arrest. Now, he had travelled all the way from the Caucasus to make her an offer she could not refuse. And, if she were to agree, she would be set free tomorrow.

The offer was that she should remain in Russia and inform, not on the Americans or British – she had proved untrustworthy in that department – but on Russian nationals. He reasoned that the Russians would trust her as a foreigner. In return, she would be offered a comfortable apartment, all her living expenses, and a salary paid in gold equivalent to $250 a month. In addition, they would allow her son to come to Russia and live with her.

Marguerite was dumbstruck. 'I stared at him horrified. I no longer felt weak or even ill. Anger had given me new strength,' she later recalled. In a renewed burst of energy, she adamantly refused his offer, informing him that she would prefer to die in prison. 'I shall never work for any government, my own or yours,' she declared. After taking a moment to digest her words, Mogilevsky politely but firmly informed her that if this were the case he would not intervene in the charge of espionage against her. Casually, he reminded her that she would be either sentenced to death or, if lucky, to ten years in Siberia.

Marguerite rose to her feet, forcing herself to look unconcerned, though she was trembling in every limb. Escorted back to her room, she was unable to sleep that night, her thoughts returning to Mogilevsky. From the beginning they had been enemies, matching their wits in verbal duels. 'I had always felt an unwilling admiration for Mogilevsky – he even attracted me in a curious fashion, and during our long talks together I had seen something of the human side of his character. I sensed that I had appealed to him in much the same way and as I lay staring into the darkness I wondered what the motive was that had impelled him to follow my movements after I had left Russia, and to scheme and plot to get me back again to Moscow.'

A few weeks later, Marguerite was summoned to the Foreign Espionage section of the GPU and cross-examined by a man named Roller, an Austrian assistant to the section's head, the Lithuanian Adolf Pilar von Pilchau. Her interview continued for a couple of hours every day, and each time she was offered tea and cigarettes. Marguerite claimed that she became weaker and weaker. 'I had no appetite whatever, and I spent most of the time lying on my plank bed in a stupor.' Then, out of the blue, she was summoned not to Roller's office, but to that of Pilar von Pilchau, a man who had much personal experience in counter-espionage in Lithuania. He informed her that he had an order for her release. Marguerite was convinced she had misheard. 'I knew that people in a weakened state were subject to hallucinations, and I was quite sure that this was what had happened to me.' But he repeated the statement and handed over her release papers. 'My hand shook as I took them and I realised that I was not dreaming.'

Roller then entered the room, and she was dismissed. 'In all my experiences with the officials of the Cheka I had made a point of resolutely suppressing any emotion, but it was only by a superhuman effort of the will,' Marguerite explained, 'that I refrained from bursting into tears.' Unable to speak, she bowed acknowledgement and was led back to her room to pack. Before she knew it, she was standing, completely dazed, in Lubyanka Square. 'Everything looked surprisingly natural and normal and the sharp air acted like a tonic.' It was February 17th 1923 – and Marguerite, once again, was free.

She decided to head for the home of Eugenia, a friend she made when they had shared a room in 1920 at Novinsky Prison. When Eugenia saw the American standing on her doorstep she screamed in excitement and the two of them sat up until the early hours of the morning, swapping news and chatting. It would be several days before Marguerite was able to clear the red tape and acquire the necessary exit visas.

She soon discovered that it was Colonel William Haskell, from the offices of the American Relief Administration (ARA), she had to thank for her release. The American Vice-Consul in Chita, a man named Thomas, had informed Washington as soon as Marguerite was arrested, and the news had immediately been passed on to Haskell in Moscow. The Soviet Foreign Office had no record of her arrest or her location, and had it not been for one of the Russian staff working for the ARA who happened to see Marguerite whilst visiting the Foreign Office on official business, she might have remained incarcerated. Haskell confronted Maxim Litvinov, now head of the Western Section of the Foreign Office, and demanded her release. At the time, the ARA were feeding up to 11 million Russians daily and so, in order not to upset the Americans, release papers were quickly signed.

Chapter Nineteen

Very Definite Proof of Her Real Character

Despite her treatment at the hands of the Russians, Marguerite insisted that she was sad to leave the country. Looking back at her days of incarceration in Moscow she wrote that she had 'admired the tenacity and courage which had enabled the Soviet leaders to bring order out of chaos and to establish their autocracy on a firm basis'. In social terms, though, she felt the Russians were oppressed. 'Individualism and independent thinking were ruthlessly suppressed in the young people; they were being turned out by the thousands from Communist schools and institutions with precisely the same ideas.' Everyone, she claimed, was forced into accepting the Marxist view of the world.

Marguerite took the express train from Moscow to Riga. There she was debriefed by American agents who were still unsure of her allegiances. The military attaché, Major Albert Loustalot, reported back to Washington that 'Mrs Harrison is advocating the recognition of Soviet Russia by the American Government'. Meanwhile, her father-in-law was still trying to get to the bottom of the truth of Stan's allegations. He wrote to Colonel Naylor, Director of the MID, requesting that he speak to Colonel Solbert, who had interviewed Stan in London.

Marguerite arrived back in the United States early in March 1923. There were two matters that she urgently needed to discuss with the MID. First, she was convinced there had been a leak in MI-2. During her recent interrogation in Moscow, a conversation that she had had in May 1922, with Major Robert Eichelberger of the MID, was repeated to her verbatim. She claimed even the time, date and place were disclosed.[1] Marguerite demanded that her old boss, Marlborough Churchill, arrange a meeting for her with his replacement, Colonel William Naylor, to discuss the matter.

Second, whether Marguerite was tiring of a life of subterfuge, or whether she felt betrayed by the MID; she was determined to come clean publicly about her role as an American secret agent in Germany and Russia. She wanted to be able to discuss Stan's allegations openly, and she would need the MID's permission to do so.

Churchill, who had stepped down from his post due to ill health, agreed to write to Naylor. In the past, he said, 'we have of course done everything in our power to conceal this fact in order to protect her, but in her opinion, matters have come to such a pass that she would prefer to have her connection with us known.'[2] Churchill did not seem to see this as a problem and suggested that, if Naylor agreed, he would willingly make the statement: 'Mrs Harrison did excellent work for G-2, and I have every confidence in her.'

But not everyone in the MID, it seems, shared that confidence. Accompanying Churchill's letter, an unsigned report dated March 29th 1923 and titled: 'IN RE: Marguerite Harrison' landed on Naylor's desk, and it included some extremely damning remarks about this particular agent. On her second trip to Europe in October 1919, Marguerite had apparently made many friends on the steamer. Anyone expressing sympathy for Russia was 'denounced by Mrs Harrison in her reports to Washington, causing some of them considerable trouble afterwards'. The report described her illegal entry into Russia via Poland: 'By ingratiating herself here and at other points through which she passed, she managed to collect a lot of military information of various kinds.' The fact that she found this easy convinced her it would be the same in Moscow. The Muscovites, however, were much better informed. By the time she was arrested, not long after her arrival in the city, 'very definite proof of her real character' had reached the Russian authorities and on investigation of her papers and other effects, left no doubt as to her being a professional military and political spy in the employ of the American MID.'

The report also stated that, when confronted by the overwhelming mass of evidence against her, Marguerite made a full confession. There then followed the superlative euphemism that being a lady of 'practical inclinations', she offered to enter the service of the Russian government. To appear willing, she gave the Soviet authorities 'a list of British, American and other Allied spies in Russia and their agents among the counter-revolutionaries'. After she was set free on parole, she continued to give the Cheka information about her own compatriots, those in Russia and those wanting to enter Russia. The report also stated that many American journalists were refused entry to Russia due to Marguerite's activities, and that 'some Americans who were put into jail in Moscow might like to know that Mrs Harrison had something to do with that also'.

From the outset, the report continued, there had been many objections to her appointment from the 'initiated quarters'. In some cases, she gave perfectly correct information to the Soviet authorities, while in others she gave 'deliberately false information led by personal malice'. The report concluded that the allegations of her mistreatment and ill health while in prison were, in fact, untrue. 'She was housed and fed more comfortably and better than any other prisoner in Moscow.'[3]

Marguerite was not to know of this report, and on a Saturday at the end of March 1923, a meeting was arranged for her to call on Colonel Naylor where she was able to discuss her experiences in Russia and her wish to go public. Naylor's notes of the meeting record that Marguerite stated that 'when she was arrested she was confronted with the evidence showing Mrs Harding's status and her own, and was asked to confirm or deny it. Being at that time in imminent danger of being shot, Mrs Harrison defiantly stated, "Yes, it is all true. You can do as you like".'[4]

Colonel Naylor wrote back to Churchill stating that, after considering all the facts, he thought it unwise for the MID to publish a statement that Marguerite was an American secret agent, and he warned Churchill to refrain from doing so as well. She was, however, permitted to make her own public statement and did so in April, disclosing that she had been working as an American Intelligence agent in Berlin when she first met Stan. She repeated her claim that Stan was an agent working for British Intelligence. Marguerite did not deny that whilst in Russia she provided information for the Soviets, but adamantly stood by her statements that she did not denounce Stan Harding. She maintained that the Russians knew all about the two women's previous activities from their own agents in Berlin.

* * *

Marguerite's statement was published in the Paris edition of the *New York Herald*. When Stan heard of it, she galvanised her supporters and the Parliamentary questions began appearing yet again on Ronald McNeill's desk. She had been active over the previous few months, continuing with her relentless mission to clear her name, and had gathered the support of fifty MPs. On March 12th 1923, they presented a resolution in Parliament urging His Majesty's Government to continue supporting her claim against Soviet Russia and the United States. A scribbled comment in the Foreign Office notes on the matter recorded that action had already been taken by McNeill, and that therefore there was no reason to reply. 'I notice that Lord R. Cecil, who, together with Sir Robert Burton-Chadwick and Mr T.P. O'Connor, was present at the interview with Mr McNeill,' the civil servant Robert Leepin wrote, 'has now given up the chase.'[5]

However, the Foreign Office should have realised by now that failing to answer Stan's letters and generally ignoring her would not make her go away, and indeed she continued to pressurise her Parliamentary supporters to pursue her case. George Middleton, Labour MP for Carlisle, submitted a Parliamentary question on the 23rd of March, asking whether McNeill had called the attention of the United States government to Stan's case. When McNeill answered in the negative, Middleton persisted, asking if he had reason to believe that the American government was protecting Mrs Harrison. McNeill stated that he had no reason to believe this and, when pressed further about Mrs Harrison's activities as a Soviet spy, wearily replied that he had no opinion one way or the other.

Now, Middleton alerted McNeill to Marguerite's renewed allegations in the *New York Herald*, and demanded to know when the Under Secretary of State was going to order the United States to retract this false statement. McNeill replied that he was not going to take any such action. A furious Middleton retorted: had the Under Secretary of State himself not given a categorical denial that Stan was not, and had never been, an employee of the British Secret Service? 'Certainly,' came McNeill's sheepish reply, 'both the Secretary of State and myself have repeatedly made that statement'. At which point Burton-Chadwick leapt into the fray, accusing McNeill of telling his constituents at the election that he was going to support Stan in every way, and was now failing to do so. McNeill made a final statement to the house that day: 'If one lady chooses to slander another that is not an international question.' But Stan thought otherwise, and the battle was far from over.

* * *

Meanwhile, despite the signing of the Anglo-Soviet Trade Agreement in March 1921, relations between the British and the Soviets had been steadily deteriorating. A secret memorandum entitled 'Soviet Policy, March 1921-December 1922' was circulated to the Cabinet. Evidence collected from British code-breakers proved that Russia continued to be involved in numerous anti-British activities: money was being sent to India and Afghanistan for anti-British propaganda work, anti-British newspapers in Persia were being subsidised and dissension sown between the tribes in the south. In addition, the Soviets had signed trade treaties with Turkey, and had offered them financial backing against Greece. There was evidence, too, that British banknotes were being forged in Russia and circulated in Constantinople and Odessa. Finally, it was understood that Russian funds were finding their way into the Communist Party of Great Britain and similar groups.

Lord Curzon was furious, believing his antipathy towards the Russians justified. In particular, he thought that Britain had 'loyally and scrupulously' observed the agreement, but Russia, right from the start, had consistently and flagrantly violated it. At the end of April 1923, Curzon secured backing from the Cabinet to send an ultimatum to Krasin: if Russia did not adhere to its terms, the trade agreement would be annulled. This became known as the 'Curzon Ultimatum', and in it he taunted the Russians by quoting intercepted cyphers verbatim. He also included the appalling treatment of British trawlers, referring to two incidents in which British ships were either scuppered or else impounded and the crews killed. The most recent incident a few weeks earlier had involved the trawler, *James Johnson*, which was impounded and its captain sentenced to forced labour. Tagged onto this list of grievances were Stan's claims for compensation for false imprisonment, plus another claim for compensation for the death of a British engineer who had been shot in January 1920 as a spy.

The Russians did not want to see the trade agreement annulled, and therefore Krasin sent a reply to Curzon on May 11th, agreeing to pay compensation to Stan, and to Mrs Davidson, the widow of the British engineer. He reminded Curzon that both incidents had occurred before the signing of the trade agreement, when foreign troops were still illegally fighting the Bolsheviks in Russia. Krasin also insisted, based on information provided by Marguerite Harrison, that Stan had been a British spy. Not wanting to miss a trick, he added that there were many more offences against Russians during this period than had been mentioned, one example being the case of the 26 Baku Commissars representing Soviet Russia who were arrested and exiled to India. According to Krasin, they never reached their destination, having been shot en route by the British.

It might be thought that Stan would be delighted to hear that she was finally to receive compensation from the Russians. Far from it. On learning of Krasin's comments, she dashed to the Foreign Office to deliver a letter demanding that His Majesty's Government reject Krasin's offer of compensation, since he was claiming that she had been justly imprisoned based on information provided by Marguerite Harrison. The following day, the 24th of May 1923, the Press Association printed a statement in the *Morning Post* on her behalf. In it, Stan stated that Lord Curzon had declared on more than one occasion that charges of espionage were baseless and yet, she claimed, 'by reiterating the false charge against me, the Soviet is accusing the British government of attempting to obtain money on false pretences'. Whether Stan was the originator of this sophistry, or if it was supplied to her, is unknown.

In May 1923, the British Prime Minister, Andrew Bonar Law, was forced to retire on grounds of ill health, and was replaced by Stanley Baldwin. The choice had been between Baldwin and Lord Curzon, but the latter was thought unsuitable due to his lack of domestic political experience and his aloof and 'superior' personality. This political setback would not have been taken lightly by Curzon. Among his enemies were many people in the government and the Foreign Office who did not share his hatred of the Russians, nor his wish to cease trading with them. Exports from the UK to Russia in 1922 had reached £4,716,998 and imports from Russia to the UK were worth £8,176,002 in the same period.[6] All of which helps explain a scribbled note on the memorandum about Stan's latest actions stating: 'but we need pay no attention to this.'[7]

Stan, knowing that Curzon was on her side, wrote to him in early June, thanking him for the steps he had taken on her behalf since 1921. She did, however, want to bring to his attention the fact that her case had been seriously aggravated by the distribution to the press of the libellous references in the Russian Note of the 23rd of May. She requested that he remedy this 'latest injury'.[8]

At this point, a further memo from Krasin arrived at the Foreign Office, reiterating his earlier offer to pay compensation to Stan and Mrs Davidson, and to refrain from hostile propaganda against British interests. He refused, however, to retract his earlier statement that Stan was a British spy. At 7.30 in the evening of June 12th, a distraught Stan, having just learnt that the Russians were repeating the charges against her, telephoned William Strang who dealt with Soviet affairs at the Foreign Office. Not having received the letter McNeill had sent her earlier that day, in which he had tried to reassure her that 'the lying accusation that you were engaged in espionage has been several times authoritatively denied by His Majesty's Government, and therefore do not worry yourself about what the Russians say',[9] she was anxious that the government issue a statement to the press that very evening, asserting her innocence. Strang, one of many Foreign Office employees infuriated with Stan's obsessive behaviour, scribbled a note to McNeill on an internal Foreign Office memorandum stating that Mrs Harding had 'formed the habit of calling on me daily. She will not be pleased with the terms of our latest note, but if she gets her £3,000 she should consider herself extremely fortunate'![10]

Predictably, Stan was not reassured by McNeill's letter, and her sense of injustice deepened. Never short of willing advocates to take up her cause, she turned next to 37-year-old Captain Reginald Berkeley, Liberal MP for Nottingham, who submitted yet more Parliamentary questions to the weary Under Secretary of State. Berkeley demanded that when His Majesty's Government formally replied to the latest Russian Note, compensation for Stan should be based on a withdrawal of allegations that she was a spy. McNeill replied that the British government had emphatically denied the Russian charges as being without foundation, but that it was not possible to force the Russians to agree. He felt that by paying compensation, the Russians were to some extent acknowledging her complaint. Berkeley then asked if he would be making a similar statement to the American correspondents, to which McNeill replied: 'I do not think I can take any steps which will give it greater publicity than an answer to a question in this House.'[11]

Stan was listening to this exchange in the gallery of the House of Commons. Still she was unsatisfied. She wrote to Esmond Ovey at the Foreign Office saying she was concerned that McNeill's answers in the House did not receive adequate publicity, as only *The Daily News*, *The Manchester Guardian* and *The Westminster Gazette* reported his reply. All of the other newspapers ran what she called the 'American lie' about her.[12]

* * *

London was an expensive city, and Stan was not a woman of means. It is unclear how she had supported herself since her return to England in January 1921, but as a cause célèbre she had made many influential friends, and it is likely that a few of them, such as Jessie Grosvenor, helped her financially. The Institute of Journalists and its members may also have assisted.

At the end of June 1923, George Springfield, President of the Institute of Journalists, wrote to McNeill asking if there were any way compensation to Stan from the Soviets could be hurried along. 'She's near breaking point!' he lamented, as indeed she was: mentally and physically as well as financially. But, although negotiations had begun behind the scenes, McNeill could not tell him when the payment would arrive. He added that he could not publicise her innocence any more than he already had, and it was now up to the press to do so.

The Russians had no intention of reneging on the payment, but they still used the Harding-Harrison feud to create a breach between the two countries, and Krasin deliberately repeated to the press the allegations behind Stan's arrest. George Middleton immediately challenged McNeill in the House to make a statement refuting Krasin's claim. By now utterly weary of Mrs Stan Harding, McNeill repeated what he had stated on so many previous occasions, that His Majesty's Government could not control what the Soviets said. And, his irritation evident, he added that he could not believe that these unfounded allegations were detrimental to Stan's well-being as they had been repeatedly denied by His Majesty's Government.

By the beginning of August 1923 there was still no sign of financial compensation for Stan, so Henry M. Richardson, representing the National Union of Journalists, wrote to Curzon on her behalf. 'My committee understand,' he explained, 'that Mrs Harding is in difficult circumstances financially, and this is due entirely to the physical and mental effects of her imprisonment and of her subsequent efforts to obtain redress.' What Richardson did not know was that on the 1st of August the Russian trade delegate, Jan Berzin, had sent a cheque for £13,000 to the Foreign Office, to cover compensation for Stan Harding and Mrs Davidson, and that their respective amounts would be forwarded to them within the next couple of weeks.

The first of Stan's battles had been successful. But money was not, of course, the only object of her quest. Still obsessed with revenge, she would now focus her attentions on the United States: Marguerite and the Americans must also be made to pay.

*Vladimir Lenin (centre, in dark coat) with Leon Trotsky (saluting)
at the celebrations on the second anniversary of the Bolshevik revolution, 1919*

Red Square, Moscow

(Left) *Soviet People's Commissar for Foreign Affairs, Georgy Chicherin; Soviet Diplomat-at-Large, Maxim Litvinov*

(Left) *Felix Dzerzhinsky, head of the dreaded Cheka (later the OGPU); Solomon Mogilevsky of the Soviet Foreign Intelligence Service and Moscow interrogator of Marguerite Harrison and Stan Harding*

(Left) *Merian C. Cooper in uniform as a volunteer in the Polish Kościuszko Squadron; Marguerite Harrison in Moscow*

Lubyanka, pre-revolution

Cells in the basement of Lubyanka

Butyrka Prison, Moscow

TELEGRAM

Riga,
Dated November 1, 1920,
Recd. November 2, 2:45 a.m.

S E C R E T
C O D E

Vilstaff,

Washington.

No. 110, November 1.

***   ***   ***

That "B" was imprisoned several days ago is stated
by Boni, who arrived at Reval from Moscow on Friday.

H O L L Y D A Y

(Top) *Telegram to the MID in Washington reporting Marguerite's probable arrest*

(middle left) *John Reed and Louise Bryant;*

(middle right) *People's Commissar for Social Welfare, Alexandra Kollontai;*

(left) *explorer and humanitarian, the Norwegian Fridtjof Nansen*

Emma Goldman and Alexander Berkman in court in New York where they were sentenced in July 1917 to two years' imprisonment for agitating against the military draft, after serving their sentences they were deported to Russia.

1923 Soviet cartoon depicting the Bolshevik response to Lord Curzon's demands

(Top left) *British Under Secretary of State, Cecil Harmsworth;*

(top right) *US Senator, Joseph France;*

(left) *Lord and Lady Curzon;*

(above) *Stan Harding as she appeared in the* Daily Mirror, *December 14th 1922*

(Left) Herbert Hoover, Head of the American Relief Administration (1917);
Starving Russian children during the famine of 1921-22

Russian women kneeling in gratitude for the ARA's efforts

Marguerite Harrison, circa 1924

*Transport mired on the steppes of Inner Mongolia during
Marguerite's 1,400-km trip from Peking to Chita*

(L to R) *Merian C. Cooper, Marguerite and Ernest Schoedsack in Ankara, Turkey, October 1923*

From left, at front) *Marguerite, Ernest Schoedsack and Merian C. Cooper, with their baggage during the migration of the Bakhtiari*

Marguerite sharing a meal in the Taurus Mountains of Turkey during her journey from Istanbul to southeastern Persia.

Marguerite (centre) *during the migration on the Zardeh Kuh (Yellow Mountain) which rises to nearly 15,000 feet*

(Top) *Devidasi troope;*

(middle) The philanthropists
*Dorothy and Leonard
Knight Elmhirst, with
Dartington Hall, Devon,
in the background;*

(left) *Kalakshetra Devidasis*

Chapter Twenty

The Bugbear of the Foreign Office

———∞∞———

In the summer of 1923, when Stan finally received her £3,000 compensation from Soviet Russia, Marguerite was living in Manhattan with her 21-year-old son, Tommy. True to form, Marguerite was restless. After returning to the States she lectured on her latest travels in the Far East and Russia, and had nearly finished the manuscript of her new book, *Red Bear or Yellow Dragon*, when her old friend 'Coop' – Merian C. Cooper – telephoned with the suggestion that they meet.

Since returning to the United States from Russia, Cooper had been writing autobiographical features for the *New York Times* under the by-line 'A Fortunate Soldier'. An evening spent catching up with him and Ernest Beaumont 'Shorty' Schoedsack, a six-foot-five-inch cameraman who had filmed infantry battles during the First World War – resulted in the idea that the three of them should make a travel film together. Marguerite found Cooper as 'stubborn as a mule, moody and quick-tempered', but she agreed to an expedition because they were kindred spirits, both 'somewhat at a loose end' and unable to readjust to normal life.

Unsure of whom or where they should film, Marguerite volunteered to speak to her friend Harry Griswold Dwight, a Middle East expert who had written several books on the region. Dwight suggested a film on either the nomadic Kurds of Anatolia (Asiatic Turkey) or the Bakhtiari people of Persia. The latter migrated seasonally with their flocks, camping in the winter months near the Persian Gulf and migrating in the hot weather to the higher plains of central Persia, in the process crossing six mountain ranges and the dangerous Karun River. Cooper and Marguerite decided on the Bakhtiari. It may have been no coincidence that the two American ex-spies and an experienced war correspondent picked a tribe on whose territory oil had recently been discovered.

Attempts to find oil in Persia in the late-nineteenth century had come to nothing, but a few years later, in 1901, a British solicitor, William D'Arcy, was successful in acquiring a 60-year concession to drill for oil, gas and bitumen. Assisted by the negotiating skills of John Preece of the Foreign Office, who knew the Bakhtiari chiefs personally, an agreement was signed giving the Bakhtiari 3% of all shares issued plus an annual payment for the provision of Bakhtiari tribesmen to guard drilling installations. In May 1908, oil was discovered and the following year the Anglo-Persian Oil Company was formed. The Americans, having been excluded from this agreement, were understandably frustrated. Significantly, it was this oil that would fuel British ships during WW1.

The two main groups of Bakhtiari, the Haft Lang and the Chahar Lang, were both extremely independent, seeing themselves as separate from wider Persian society. They did not need the British as much as the British needed them, so, guarding against the possibility of the Bakhtiari selling their stock to a higher bidder, the British craftily allowed the Bakhtiari chiefs to borrow large amounts of money from the Anglo-Persian Oil Company, using their stock as collateral.

Persia had experienced domestic unrest after the end of the First World War and during the subsequent collapse of the Ottoman Empire. As with Britain, Russia had had links with Persia since the early nineteenth century, and was particularly interested in her oil reserves. At the end of 1920, with Russian support, tribesmen marched on Tehran, and in February 1921, Brigadier General Reza Shah of the Persian Cossack Brigade staged a successful coup d'état, forcing the Shah of Persia, Ahmad Shah Qajar, and his weak government to resign. Qajar became a puppet ruler and Reza Shah was appointed Minister of War. They soon signed the Russo-Persian Treaty of Friendship and Soviet troops then left Persia with the proviso that if Soviet national security were threatened, they would invade Persia. Anxious to keep the Russians off Persian soil, the British backed Reza Shah's new government.

Reza Shah was keen to modernise the country. He renamed it Iran, constructed new roads, as well as the Trans-Iranian Railway and the University of Tehran, and banned women from wearing the veil or chador. Shah was adamant that his new Iran should not be aligned to any one foreign power. In 1922, Arthur Chester Millspaugh, a former adviser to the US State Department, was invited to reorganise the Finance Ministry. Millspaugh remained in Iran for five years, introducing a budget and tax system, and in the process being seen by many Iranians as the man who liberated them from British and Soviet influence. By October 1923, Reza Shah had seized full control of Iran, causing Ahmad Shah Qajar to flee to Europe. Two years later, Reza Shah declared himself the new Shah of Iran.

* * *

With the help of friends, Marguerite had raised $10,000 for the making of a travel documentary, and in September 1923 she, Cooper and

Schoedsack set off for the Middle East. Marguerite was dressed like any woman going to Europe on a cruise, with 'riding clothes, a rubber bath-tub, a plentiful supply of toilet necessities, and an evening dress'. She even had a permanent wave put in her hair. They must have looked an odd trio: the toweringly tall Schoedsack, always trying to mask his height; the smartly dressed and elegantly coiffed Marguerite; and Cooper, who looked like a pugilist: Marguerite described him as 'short, muscular and thick-set, with sparse sandy hair, a sharp pointed nose, eyes like blue china buttons, a pugnacious jaw and an aggressive man-ner'. She claimed he had no respect for women, seeing them as brainless creatures fit only to mind the home and bear children. 'He never thought of me as a woman at all and that was why we were able to get on together,' she reflected. But Marguerite's and Cooper's friendship was soon to be tested.

* * *

In the autumn of 1923, Britain was swept up in a general election, and Stan's fight for compensation from the United States became a cam-paign issue. In November, the Institute of Journalists and the National Union of Journalists appealed to all Parliamentary candidates to bring without delay Stan's demands to the notice of the government of the United States. The two organisations stated that, in their view, the American Government should be held responsible for the acts of its agent, whom it had never repudiated and whom it had continued to protect. The British Government, they suggested, should approach Washington directly over the matter. More than 600 cross-party affir-mative replies supported this pledge, including that from the leader of the Labour Party, Ramsay MacDonald.

The election was held on December 6th, and Stanley Baldwin's Con-servative Party netted 258 seats, resulting in a hung Parliament. The Labour Party won 191 seats; in a deal with the Liberals, Labour's Ram-say MacDonald became Prime Minister of a coalition government. Stan would now be forced to present and press her case to a new set of polit-ical leaders.

The illegitimate son of a Scottish farm servant, Ramsay MacDonald had first been elected in the general election of 1906 as MP for Leicester, rep-resenting the newly-formed Labour Party. He blotted his copybook with some of his followers due to his anti-war sentiments during the Great War, but after losing his Parliamentary seat he was re-elected in 1922, entering the House of Commons as leader of the Labour Party. When he became

Prime Minister, MacDonald did not appoint a Secretary of State to replace Lord Curzon, preferring to take on the role himself.

With the change of government, Stan's campaign was briefly in abeyance until she wrote to Prime Minister MacDonald in February 1924, reminding him of his pledge to support her in gaining compensation from the United States. She remained convinced that once he was aware that this American agent had also been in British employ, as she had been 'definitely informed', he would publish the truth and pursue her case for further compensation. The civil servants at the Foreign Office thought differently. Once again, Stan's plight drew only a scribbled note from a weary and unsympathetic civil servant. 'The idea of compensation from the United States government can only be described as fantastic,' the note on her Foreign Office file stated. 'I can only suppose that the recent notoriety has gone to her head.'[1]

Stan was by now a veteran at galvanising support from various quarters, and once again she went on the offensive. She cornered Dr Haden-Guest, who had met Marguerite in Russia on the River Volga trip organised for the British Labour delegation in May 1920, and asked him to speak on her behalf to Arthur Ponsonby, the new Under-Secretary of State for Foreign Affairs.

Stan's mental and physical condition evidently alarmed Haden-Guest as it had Cecil Harmsworth two years earlier. He obliged Stan by sending a letter to Ponsonby, reiterating her demands. He wrote, 'I also saw Mrs Harding in the lobby of the House several days ago. She is in a condition of very great excitement and I wish it were possible on medical grounds to do something to give her satisfaction.'[2] In Ponsonby's reply, he lamented that Stan's case is 'a very sad one, but I am afraid that it is quite impossible for us to do anything more for her'.[3] Ponsonby was certainly not going to approach the United States Government on the issue.[4] Meanwhile, Stan had also mobilised one of her earliest supporters, Harry Richardson, President of the NUJ, into writing to MacDonald on her behalf. He, too, was to receive a negative response.[5]

Stan continued to harass the civil servants in the Foreign Office. An internal Foreign Office memo dated March 27th 1924 stated that 'Mrs Stan Harding has been the bugbear of the Northern Department for some years. From the very first we were doubtful of the essential validity of her claim, since it appeared highly probable that she had brought the great majority of her troubles upon herself, and in 1921 it was decided not to take up the case.'[6] After her successful campaign involving prominent journalists and MPs, it continued, the Foreign Office had decided

to reconsider her case and had negotiated her compensation from Soviet Russia. 'So far from having contented Mrs Stan Harding,' the report
went on, 'this seems to have whetted her appetite.'[7] Her campaign rested
on two points: her reputation and compensation. On the first point the
previous Secretary of State, Ronald McNeill, made several statements
in the House of Commons clearing her name of any connection with
the British secret service. The question of compensation from the
United States was 'preposterous and fantastic', and the Foreign Office
steadfastly refused to make this clear to Stan. Tagged at the bottom of
this report were scribbled notes from Ponsonby noting that Stan and a
small party of MPs recently came to see him. He, too, found her on the
verge of a mental collapse: 'She is obviously ill and suffering from acute
persecution mania,' he wrote, warning that until a final refusal is sent to
her 'she will not leave us alone'.[8]

* * *

Marguerite, Cooper and Schoedsack arrived in Europe in the late summer of 1923. Travelling via Istanbul and Ankara, they crossed the Salt
Desert along a caravan trail, passing the Taurus Mountains to Syria and
then on to Baghdad in Iraq. Always on the lookout for a story, and able
to insinuate her way into the corridors of power, Marguerite interviewed
the new Turkish leader, Mustapha Kemal Pasha (Atatürk), as well as
turbaned Turkomans, whirling dervishes, and Kurdish nomads. In
Baghdad she met a fellow spy, the Englishwoman Gertrude Bell, the
noted Orientalist and author. 'I saw advancing toward me in the midst
of all this confusion a slender figure in a smart grey velvet frock which
looked as if it had just come from Paris.'[9] Marguerite was surprised when
she discovered that Bell was not the hard, masculine woman she had
imagined, and she formed an 'instant friendship' with her.

  But the three Americans had now been together for seven months,
and had not yet shot a single reel of film. Captain E.G. Peel from the
British Consulate, an authority on the tribesmen, introduced the trio to
the Bakhtiari princes who lived mostly in Tehran and in their remote
castles, meeting once a year to inspect their tribes. Peel took the travellers to Shushtar, an island city on the River Karun. A thriving metrop-
olis in the fourteenth century, it had become, as a consequence of
invasions and floods, a dilapidated, sun-baked town. Here they met
Rahim Khan, one of the Bakhtiari princes, who would introduce them
to the other ruling families. The young man spoke English with an
American accent, having been educated at the American College in

Beirut. Like the other Bakhtiari royals, he enjoyed an opulent lifestyle funded by tribal taxes and royalties from the Anglo-Persian Oil Company. Rahim, desperate to visit America, to see New York, Broadway and pretty girls, and to listen to jazz music, was extremely contemptuous of his backward tribesmen.

Rahim took the three Americans to meet the princes who would find them a tribe with whom they could travel. They learned that the 50,000 Bakhtiari and their half-million animals could cross the mountains by five different routes to reach the Persian Plateau. The easiest route was via a British-built road, but opting to travel in this way would not, they considered, make a very exciting movie. Having selected which route and tribe to join, they were invited by one of the princes on to his barge where he passed his opium pipe between them to seal the deal. Drawing a deep breath, Marguerite found that 'opium soothed my nerves and relaxed my muscles. It seemed the most natural thing in the world that I should be riding on a barge of goatskins down a mountain river'.

The three Americans were eventually taken under the wing of Haidar Khan for the migration. Beginning on April 16th, 1924, it was to be a testing journey during which Marguerite caught malaria and was bedridden for three days with a soaring temperature. When she was fit enough to travel again, she joined the tribe crossing the half-mile-wide Karun River on rafts made from inflated goats' stomachs. They then trekked with the barefooted Bakhtiari, who carried their children and possessions, accompanied by sheep and even donkeys, up the sheer, snow-covered rock face of the 15,000-foot-high Zardeh Kuh Mountain. On reaching the other side of the mountain, Marguerite saw a Promised Land with 'huge carpets of wild narcissi, beds of tulips that might have graced any garden, and clumps of mammoth black irises'.

Throughout the journey, the Bakhtiari would come to Marguerite for medical help, calling her Lady Doctor. It was only when she returned to the States that she discovered this was probably because a Glaswegian doctor, Elizabeth Ness MacBean Ross, had spent many years living with them, subsequently dying in Serbia in 1915 while working as a military surgeon.

Though ill-qualified, Marguerite did her best, giving out quinine for malaria, bathing suppurating sores caused by venereal disease with permanganate solution, and treating eye complaints with boracic acid. For stomach aches and intestinal troubles she offered castor oil and cathartic pills. The mother of a boy suffering from acute anaemia explained that he had swallowed a leech whilst swimming in the river. The creature had attached itself to his insides and was literally bleeding him to death. Marguerite made the boy drink warm salt water to vomit up the leech, after which he began to recover. One medical task she refused, however, was pulling teeth, although she gave iodine for toothache.

Marguerite was supposed to play a key role in the film, portraying a female explorer, weary of modern life, travelling to find her ancestors. The collaboration, however, ultimately soured her relationship with Cooper, whom she found as objectionable as the Bakhtiari. She wanted the film to portray the 'truth', and she preferred, she claimed, 'under-emphasis to over-emphasis', whereas Cooper, who directed the film, was looking for the dramatic. She also disagreed with Cooper's opinion of the Bakhtiari. He declared that the tribes lived 'in the way men and women ought to live: the women did all the work, every goddamned bit of it except during the migration … the men ate first, the boys second, followed by the horses, the dogs, and then the women.'[10] Marguerite did not find them commendable or interesting, but rather 'hard, treacherous, thieves, robbers without any cultural background, living under a remorseless feudal system, crassly material, and devoid of sentiment or spirituality'.

The migration had taken a gruelling 48 days and, when all the filming was completed, Marguerite, Cooper and Schoedsack travelled three days to reach the nearest town, Deh Kord. From Deh Kord they were collected by car and taken to Tehran, where Marguerite was able to interview Reza Shah, whom she found – rather like Cooper and the Bakhtiari – patronising and uninterested in talking to a woman.

The trio travelled onto Beirut, from whence Cooper and Schoedsack took the steamer to Marseilles then on to Paris to edit the film. Marguerite remained in the Middle East for a few more weeks, looking for interesting topics to write on. She travelled to Palestine – a land she predicted with some perspicuity 'would never cease to be a battleground of faiths and races and a permanent liability for Great Britain'. She also visited the international Bahai colony in Haifa and explored the streets of the new capital city, Tel Aviv.

The world's first travel documentary – *Grass: A Nation's Battle for Life* – would be the trip's legacy. This was Marguerite's last collaboration with Cooper, who was to sell the film to Paramount in January 1925. She was to see the film only once and was appalled by how it was edited and packaged, and by the crass subtitles, which in her opinion demeaned the seriousness of the migration.

This was to be Marguerite's last collaboration with Cooper, and their friendship had ended. Merian C. Cooper would go on to have a long and distinguished career in Hollywood as a director, studio executive and producer. In 1933, the film *King Kong*, based on one of Cooper's dreams, was released to great acclaim. Co-directed with Ernest Schoedsack, it was Merian who piloted the plane circling the Empire State Building at the end of the film.

Having re-enlisted in the Army Air Corps at the outbreak of WWII, at war's end Merian left as a brigadier general. During the course of his film career he would produce many Hollywood classics including *The Most Dangerous Game, She Wore a Yellow Ribbon, The Quiet Man* and *The Searchers*.

* * *

It was in July 1924 when Marguerite finally returned home and settled into an apartment in New York with her son. She had been away from America for an entire year, but never absent from the thoughts of Stan Harding.

Chapter Twenty-One

I am a Nuisance

Under Secretary of State for Foreign Affairs, Arthur Ponsonby, was finding aspects of his new job a trial. Much to his annoyance, Stan was regularly attending public sessions of Parliament. 'She has now taken up her permanent abode in the public lobby of the House of Commons,' he noted. 'I always avoid this lobby if I possibly can as there are a number of people there waiting to pounce on me.'[1] His opinion of Stan had not improved either: 'There is no doubt that she is partly out of her mind and will probably rapidly become worse.'[2]

Grasping the nettle, Ponsonby finally wrote to Stan, politely reminding her that the compensation she received from Soviet Russia was achieved by the 'unremitting efforts of His Majesty's Government' and that His Majesty's Government had done everything it could to inform the world that the charges against her were false and baseless. 'As regards to Mrs Harrison, I must point out that your controversy with this lady is a personal matter in which His Majesty's Government has no concern.'[3] Ponsonby then added that, after considering the facts, 'there can be no question of His Majesty's Government making any representations to the Government of the United States on your behalf.'[4] Stan scribbled off a reply that same day, pointing out somewhat ingenuously that she had no controversy with Mrs Harrison, but with those who employed and continued to protect her.

If the Prime Minister, Ponsonby, and Foreign Office staff thought that this letter would be the end of the Stan Harding campaign, and that the 'bugbear of the Northern Department' would go away, they were mistaken. On the 19th of June 1924, Stan attended Parliament and presented her case to a meeting of cross-party MPs. Beginning her speech by stating rather bluntly (albeit with some creditable self-knowledge), 'I am a nuisance,' she ended with, 'I know that you must feel that I am a nuisance.'[5]

Nevertheless, Stan made her case forcefully. 'Whether or not I have a legal claim against the United States Government,' she declared, 'I certainly have a moral claim.' In her eyes, America's support of the 'deliberate false denunciation of an innocent person' was on a lower ethical plane than what the Soviets had done to her. 'The Soviet has made some reparation for being the dupe of an American agent. Surely America, which, I am told, dominates the world by moral suasion, will do no less.'[6]

Whether or not they thought any success was likely, the MPs agreed to approach Prime Minister Ramsay MacDonald, requesting that he make a claim against the United States on Stan's behalf, or at the very least put the facts in front of the International Court of Justice in The Hague. The matter was then raised again in the Commons by a succession of MPs, starting with Innes Harold Stranger, MP for Newbury. MacDonald's reply was that His Majesty's Government was not going to approach the United States Government on her behalf on what was 'essentially a dispute with another lady'.[7]

Stan's previous employer, *The Daily News*, leapt to her defence by publishing a statement: 'If Mr MacDonald had been arrested in Russia and a false charge made against him by a man known to be a spy in the pay of the American Government... what would he think of the statesman who, knowing the facts and having given him the most definite assurance of sympathy and support, subsequently got up in his place and said that the matter was "essentially a personal dispute" between him and "another gentleman"?'[8]

A few days, later Ponsonby wrote in an Foreign Office internal memo: 'I'm sorry to say that since my letter to Mrs S. Harding turning her finally down, she has set to work by daily attendance in the House of Commons and succeeded in enlisting sympathy of over fifty members drawn from the three parties.'[9] They have formed a committee chaired by 'Courteous Charlie', Charles Bowerman, Labour MP for Deptford. This was the beginning, Ponsonby sighed, of yet another campaign.[10] It was not going to be safe for him in the lobby for some time yet.

At the end of July 1924, Charles Bowerman and a small contingent of MPs approached Ponsonby, asking for his assistance. They had recently requested at the American Embassy to meet the Ambassador Frank B. Kellogg to discuss Stan's allegations, only to be told by his staff that any meeting must be arranged formally through the Foreign Office. Ponsonby refused to write them a letter of introduction, claiming that this would be tantamount to taking up her case.

Early August saw a further onslaught of Parliamentary Questions. Changing emphasis, Richard Collingham Wallhead, Labour MP for Merthyr Tydfil, asked MacDonald if Marguerite Harrison had ever been in the employ of the British or if her reports were received by any British Government department or official. MacDonald answered in the negative to the first question and stated that 'no communication of any nature, so far as can be traced, has been received by any Government Department'.[11]

The lack of a definitive answer was never going to satisfy Stan and her allies. It did, however, ensure that if Ramsay MacDonald had such knowledge, he was not perjuring himself. Since 1919, British Secret Intelligence Services (SIS) had been placed under Foreign Office jurisdiction, and as MacDonald was then Secretary of State for Foreign Affairs, it might be assumed that he would have access to SIS information. However, the Foreign Office and SIS were never comfortable stablemates, and information was not always exchanged.

There is certainly evidence of cooperation between American and British secret services. Founded in 1909, Britain's Secret Service Bureau, as it was originally called, was split into two sections: MI5, a military section headed by Captain Vernon Kell, and MI1(c) (later to become MI6), a naval section headed by 'C' – Commander Mansfield Smith-Cumming. Personality clashes developed between these two very different men: Kell was an asthmatic linguist, modest and quiet, who enjoyed fly fishing, while Smith-Cumming was the monocled and be-medalled owner of a Rolls-Royce in which he sped through the streets of London. Their conflict resulted in Captain Kell taking on counter-espionage, with Commander Smith-Cumming in charge of foreign espionage.

Right up until 1919, when the Secret Services were restructured, the lines of responsibility between the two departments often overlapped, with neither section head wanting to be left in the dark. When America entered the war in 1917, it was MI5, however, that sent members of staff to its Washington and New York stations. They shared their 'American suspect index' of US citizens and German-Americans planning to visit Britain with Marguerite's boss, the Director of Military Intelligence, Marlborough Churchill.[12] US Intelligence officers were also known to have visited MI5 headquarters in London.[13]

These were not the only examples of cooperation between the American and British secret services. Before America joined the war in 1917, Smith-Cumming sent William Wiseman, a wounded Ypres veteran, to run the British Purchasing Commission in Washington. Much to the annoyance of Kell and his MI5 agents, however, Wiseman was also keeping a watch on German, Irish and Indian nationalist espionage activity. Both Wiseman and his deputy, another British officer, Norman Thwaites, had close links with Frank Polk of the State Department, who was in charge of the American Intelligence co-ordinating organisation

U-1, and 'Colonel' Edward House, Woodrow Wilson's personal adviser. Wiseman played a clever game in convincing House that he was relaying messages to him directly from the FO, whereas in reality nothing was passed on without Smith-Cumming's approval. Once the Americans joined the war, MI1(c) cooperated fully with all the United States' security services. 'Every one of them is in the habit of calling us up or visiting the office daily,' Wiseman said. 'They have access to the files under our supervision and we stand ready to give them all information in our possession. They, on the other hand, are equally ready to reciprocate, friendly cooperation makes the work extremely pleasant and, I venture to think, useful.'[14]

William Wiseman was so trusted by the White House that he jointly ran intelligence operations in Central and Eastern Europe with the Americans. In this capacity he recruited the British writer, Somerset Maugham, to travel to Russia in July 1917 on intelligence business. With the code name 'S' or 'Somerville' and $21,000 of American funding behind him, Maugham's brief was to support the Kerensky government and counter German pacifist propaganda intended to make Russia withdraw from the war. Smith-Cumming had instructed him to work independently of both embassies and to communicate directly with him. Maugham was to later claim that if he had arrived in Russia six months earlier, he might have succeeded in preventing the Bolshevik rise to power.

Smith-Cumming was always slightly wary of the special relationship with the Americans. When Wiseman asked Smith-Cumming for copies of MI1(c)'s political reports to pass on to Edward House, he categorically refused, claiming it was too dangerous. However, once Woodrow Wilson had left office, and the special relationship between Wiseman, House and the President ended, never again would any British representative enjoy so close a relationship with the White House.

Further evidence that Marguerite had provided information to the British in her role as a secret agent came in the form of a letter from Marlborough Churchill in September 1921 to the American Military Attaché in London. Churchill requested that Colonel Oscar Solbert approach the Foreign Office on 'the subject of closing Mrs Harding's mouth and preventing her from injuring Mrs Harrison any more, in view of the fact that Mrs Harrison has on occasion been of assistance to the British authorities.'[15] This correspondence does not, of course, prove that Ramsay MacDonald had seen copies of Marguerite's reports, as the records could easily have been destroyed later, either deliberately or accidentally.

There are many reasons why Prime Minister MacDonald might have turned a blind eye to any available evidence, one being the need to avoid further exacerbating an already strained Anglo-American relationship. The war had left Britain weakened industrially, commercially and financially, whilst it had strengthened the American economy. Britain was in debt to America and unable to repay the huge sum of $4.7 billion that she owed. And the Americas were extremely unhappy with Britain's oil-rich mandates and their monopoly of Commonwealth rubber supplies. Both nations were desperate to rebuild the world economy after the war, but each on its own terms. America looked for moderated reparations, balanced budgets, a reduction in armaments, private rather than governmental loans, equal access to markets and most importantly, a return to the gold standard, whereby nations held their own gold as a reserve for their currencies.

Britain, on the other hand, desperate to cling on to her Empire and trading monopolies, thought the best solution was a system where nations' gold reserves were deposited in reserve countries – mainly Britain and the United States – in return for IOUs. The reserve countries would link the whole system to gold by keeping their reserves in that currency – while Britain saw that the interest on the IOUs would help to repay her war debts. America worried that under this system there would be a scramble for the nominated reserve countries to acquire the most gold deposits, and that whoever controlled a nation's gold would have access to trade. In this event, Britain would have an automatic advantage, both with London being the pre-war financial capital of the world and with her considerable trade with her Dominions.

Now, some six years after the end of the 'Great War', geopolitical and economic rivalries between the Allies had resumed, but Stan's supporters were not, in spite of tensions in international relations, going to let the British Prime Minister off the hook. The MP Edmund Harvey infuriated the Foreign Office by repeating the question: was Marguerite Harrison ever employed by the British or had her reports been seen by the British government?

The Foreign Office was indignant: 'We cannot continually reopen the case every three weeks,' an internal memo stated, 'the case is closed and will not be re-opened.'[16] But MacDonald, forced to reply to the question in the House, explained on the 4th of August 1924 that it was impossible to take any steps relating to the assumption that Mrs Harrison was the secret agent of a friendly government. Asked if he had had this in mind when signing the election pledge to assist Stan in her compensation claims, he replied, 'We are all liable to get extra information. I did my best in the circumstances. I find it would be most improper to make the representation suggested.'[17]

The Daily News ran an article the following day questioning what action was available to a British subject if imprisoned by a friendly foreign power, when the Prime Minster refused to discuss the subject. 'Nobody asks him to do the impossible,' they stated, but 'if the American Government will not even hear the case – which seems to us incredible – there is nothing more to be said; but until it is stated, the onus rests on the British Government, and can be removed in one way only – by stating it.'[18]

* * *

Stan's temporary lodgings in one of the attic rooms above the Poetry Bookshop at 35 Devonshire Street (now Boswell Street), just off Theobalds Road, once housed poets such as T.E. Hulme and Wilfred Owen, and this proximity to literary greatness, if she knew of it, may have provided some inspiration for her new project. She now could support herself out of the compensation received from the Soviets and, although friends feared that her fragile physical and mental health would lead to a nervous breakdown, Stan had begun work on a memoir that would become an outlet for all her hatred and bitterness against anyone who she felt had wronged her.

Day after day, she worked on the manuscript. London in July 1924 was wet and cool. In the third week of the month, heavy thunderstorms struck the capital, with lightning, torrential rain and giant hailstones. More violent thunderstorms and torrential rains followed a week later, flooding streets and railway tracks.[19] Stan could not have enjoyed this unseasonably cool weather, since she suffered from chronic chest problems and once claimed that sunshine and warm temperatures were necessary to her happiness. Nor would she have been pleased that the newspapers in England were not full of her story. They were reporting on other matters, such as the Summer Olympics in Paris and the Inter-Allied London Conference. The London Conference aimed at implementing the Dawes Report and, as Ramsay MacDonald said in his opening address, 'bringing peace and security to Europe'.[20] Charles Gates Dawes and his committee had met earlier in the year to investigate the possibility of Germany paying her debts under the terms of the Treaty of Versailles by means of a $400 million loan from the United States.

Concurrent to her literary efforts, Stan's campaign continued. On July 8th, her supporting committee informed MacDonald that they would be sending a letter with the subject, 'Will America Do Justice? The Stan Harding Case', signed by over a hundred MPs, to every member of the United States Congress. Before taking this action, they asked for a definitive statement as to whether any of Marguerite's intelligence reports had been received by any government department or official. As no reply from the Foreign Office was received, the committee despatched their letter in August, accompanied by a statement outlining the facts and stating that Stan's case against Marguerite 'requires public investigation in America, not only in the interest of our country-woman, but also in the interest of justice.'[21] As a result, a few American newspapers, such as the *New York American*, quoted the appeal in full. However, it was not carried by other notable publications, such as the *New York Times* and *The Washington Post*. Their editors were more interested in reporting the Presidential campaign leading up to the November 1924 election.

The Stan Harding case was but one of the straws that broke the back of the Ramsay MacDonald premiership. The final blow was the publication of the leaked Zinoviev letter printed by the *Daily Mail*. A Soviet politician, Grigory Zinoviev, was alleged to have written a letter to the Communist Party of Great Britain urging armed insurrection and class war. Originating from the Secret Intelligence Service's (SIS) Riga station, the letter was handed to Sir Eyre Crowe at the Foreign Office, who in turn passed it on to MacDonald, recommending that he release the details to the press and send a formal letter of protest to the Soviets. When the Soviet representative, Christian Rakovsky, dismissed the letter as a 'gross forgery' and demanded proof of its source, none could be provided. Suspicions of a conspiracy between the right-wing press and the SIS against the labour government continued to persist, although there was no evidence to substantiate the claim. Whoever was behind the origins of the letter, MacDonald's fate was sealed and his government became a casualty of the affair. A new Conservative regime headed by Stanley Baldwin, the fifth government since Stan began her campaign, was sworn in on the 4th of November 1924. This was Baldwin's second term in office, and as Stan had not achieved her aims when he was last in post, she could not have been optimistic.

Following the installation of the new Conservative government, Henry Marriott Richardson and George Springfield, representing the National Union and Institute of Journalists, respectively, wrote to the new Foreign Secretary, Austen Chamberlain. Their letter began by complimenting the actions of His Majesty's Government which had thus far enabled Stan to receive compensation from Soviet Russia. However, they felt that this was totally inadequate as reparation for the 'physical and mental suffering which had permanently reduced her earning capacity was not from the quarter primarily responsible for the outrage.'[22] They urged the Foreign Office to take up the invitation from the American Embassy to make an official approach on the matter. The Foreign Office's reply was short and to the point: nothing would be gained by such action.

Stan's quest lapsed during the beginning of 1925, but the campaign resumed in March with a follow-up letter to Chamberlain from Richardson and Springfield. 'This is evidently the beginning of a new offensive,' the Foreign Office internal notes wearily recorded, and a reply was despatched stating that nothing could be added to Chamberlain's previous statement.

However on March 11th, Colonel Arthur Holbrook, founder of the *Southern Daily Mail* newspaper and Unionist MP for Basingstoke since 1906, submitted a Parliamentary Question, asking when the Secretary of State for Foreign Affairs was going to approach the American Embassy on Stan's behalf. Ronald McNeill, now back in post as the Under-Secretary of State, replied that there was nothing to add to the answer given by the previous Prime Minster to a similar question on July 21st 1924. Questioned as to whether there was a reason behind Foreign Office hostility towards making representations, McNeill replied that there was no hostility, merely that there was no case to make.

On the 16th of March 1925, Holbrook asked in the House if the Under-Secretary of State for Foreign Affairs would receive a deputation with evidence that Stan had been imprisoned as a result of false charges made by Marguerite Harrison. McNeill replied categorically that he would not see a deputation as 'it has been explained by three successive governments that the facts of the case do not warrant representations on the subject to the government of the United States'.[23] Immediately, Holbrook and a few friends sent a further letter to Chamberlain, informing him that, as a result of the letter that had been sent to every United States Congressman, a resolution of enquiry had been proposed in the US Senate. Holbrook therefore requested a statement from Chamberlain confirming whether or not any reports from Harrison had been received by the British Secret Service or any of its branches, or by any department or official of the British Government. William Strang from the Foreign Office replied stating that no further information had come to their attention to modify the answer given to Richard Wallhead's Parliamentary Question the previous summer.

Having failed to change the long-held positions of the British government, Stan's increasingly quixotic pursuit now pinned its hopes for success through pressure on and by the US Congress. But the governments of Britain and the USA were fully determined, in spite of the intense lobbying, to finally bury her case.

PART FOUR

1925-1967

Chapter Twenty-Two

The Underworld of State

Throughout the winter of 1924-25, Marguerite had covered her living costs by writing magazine articles and lecturing throughout the United States, but she was frustrated at still not being taken seriously as a journalist. Irritated at how she was repeatedly asked if she had fallen in love with a sheikh on her trip to Iran, she resented the assumption that a woman would always set aside professional obligations for romantic pursuits. Other female travellers had experienced similar patronising attitudes, and Marguerite joined with three like-minded women – Gertrude Shelby, Blair Niles and Gertrude Emerson Sen – to found the Society of Woman Geographers in early 1925. Excluded from the male-only Explorers Club of New York, woman were routinely overlooked for any legitimate geographical work sponsored by universities and museums; this new society would enable them to create their own legitimacy.

It was also during this period that she met Arthur Blake. English-born Blake, six feet tall, grey-haired and blue-eyed, lived in New York where he worked as an insurance broker. Marguerite described him as someone who was disillusioned and, like her, was seeking some sort of meaning in life. Because of this, 'it was only natural that we should have been drawn to each other,' she later remembered.

However, even after helping to found the Society of Woman Geographers and beginning a love affair with Blake, Marguerite remained unsettled. The intensity of her new relationship frightened her and so she sought an opportunity to escape, accepting an offer to represent the Near East Relief Society.

The Near East Relief Society had been set up in New York in 1915 by the American Ambassador to Turkey, Henry Morgenthau, in response to the Armenian genocide. Many of the Armenians, long treated as second-class citizens in the Ottoman Empire, had supported the Russians during the war. In April 1915, Mehmed Talaat Bey, Minister of the Interior, ordered all Armenians in the Ottoman Empire aged five years and upwards to be slaughtered. Children were burned alive, poisoned or drowned, and whole families dumped in the desert without food or water and left to die a slow and horrible death. When the genocide ended, over a million and a half Armenians had died.

With his round spectacles and goatee beard, Morgenthau looked more like a Bolshevik official than an American ambassador, but he was instrumental in alerting the American public to the atrocities committed against the Armenians. There is no doubt that the money donated by the general public for relief work saved thousands of lives. By 1921 the charity, with a budget of $70 million, was funding operations throughout the Middle East and Western Asia, helping displaced Armenians, Assyrians, Greeks, other minority groups. Marguerite was hired to report on the progress of the Society's relief efforts.

She set off alone for Paris in July 1925, travelling on to Constantinople to organise her visas and then to Ankara (Angora), the new Turkish capital, which she found much changed since her previous visit with Cooper and Schoedsack. Everywhere new buildings were springing up and the city was brilliantly lit by electric light. From Ankara she continued her journey, visiting displaced Turks from Thessaly and Macedonia who had been resettled in farms in Anatolia to grow tobacco, then on to Syria where 45,000 Armenian refugees, including thousands of orphans, were crammed into camps in Aleppo, Beirut and Damascus.

From Syria, Marguerite headed for Athens, visiting Thessaly and Macedonia to see the Anatolian Greeks resettled there. 'It was wild country, forbidding and hostile,' she wrote, 'and the colonists were housed in rows of cheap wooden cottages, all exactly alike, all distressingly ugly'. They were also growing tobacco and seemed to be as out of place in Greece as the Turkish refugees were in Anatolia. Furthermore, Marguerite worried that the market would be over-saturated with tobacco, causing yet more poverty.

Adding to the misery of the region, the Greeks had acquired a slice of territory from Bulgaria by terms of the Peace Treaty, and the farmers who had inhabited it had been driven across the border into Bulgaria where no provision had been made for them. Many, she noted, had starved to death.

During her travels, Marguerite wrote daily to Blake. 'Here in the near East, as in Europe,' she told him, 'I was continually confronted with the consequences of Wilson's idealistic and misguided policy'. She was referring here to Point Twelve of Wilson's Fourteen Points which called for the autonomous development of other nationalities within the Ottoman Empire. Marguerite, tired by witnessing all the suffering, and by the travelling, was at last ready to go home. She believed she had finally come to the realisation that not only did she miss Blake, but that she was now ready to settle down with him – and that meant marriage.

* * *

By early 1925, Britain had 1.4 million unemployed. Only Austria, Hungary and Danzig[1] remained tied to the British pound; Canada had accepted the American Gold Standard and Australia and South Africa were about to follow suit, thus giving America access to advantageous trading opportunities with Britain's dominions. On May 4th 1925, Winston Churchill, now Chancellor of the Exchequer in Baldwin's Conservative Government, reluctantly announced that Britain would adopt the American Gold Standard as the only alternative to economic isolation in Europe.

However, despite Britain's capitulation to American monetary hegemony, Stan's latest group of supporters were not prepared to give up the fight. They wanted a definite answer to the question of whether Harrison had supplied the British authorities with information. Another letter was despatched to Chamberlain on July 7th from the Labour MP for Lambeth North, Frank Briant, and fifteen other MPs: 'If this agent's reports were at no time received by the British Government, we fail to see why His Majesty's Government cannot categorically state this to Members of the House of Commons, as was done in another case.' Briant then added: 'The only conclusion that is possible to draw from the continued absence of such a statement is that it cannot be truthfully made.'[2]

Two weeks later, the Foreign Office replied, merely repeating the statement made in August 1924 by Ramsay MacDonald, confirming that 'this lady [Marguerite Harrison] was never in the employment of His Majesty's Government and that no communications from her of any nature have, so far as can be traced, or been received by any department of His Majesty's Government, and so far as is known, no such communications were ever made.'[3] This still did not answer their question so Richard Wallhead, MP for Merthyr, repeated the question in Parliament. McNeill replied sarcastically, 'As the Honourable Gentleman was informed by my predecessor on 4 August 1924, nothing can be traced.'[4]

Stan's supporters still refused to be swayed. They kept pushing for a definite statement that Marguerite's reports were not used by the British authorities, and wanted words like 'so far as can be traced' or 'so far as is known' to be replaced by a categorical yes or no. A further letter was sent to Chamberlain by Sir Robert Newman, Unionist MP for Exeter, and signed by seven others, repeating the question. The letter concluded with: 'We offer no apology of again approaching you in this subject, feeling sure that you will appreciate the importance of the question.'[5]

On 19th of August the Foreign Office sent its final reply: 'I cannot do no better than enclose in reply a copy of the letter which Mr Chamberlain caused to be sent on the 23rd of the last month to Mr Briant in answer to a similar enquiry. I think you will find that it contains the information for which you ask.' And that was the last communication from either party on the matter. Stan's three-year fight with the United States had ended. Her dreams of receiving compensation – and, more importantly, of exposing Marguerite's treachery – appeared to be over.

She had spent more than three years fighting for justice as she saw it, but with only partial success. Without any positive response to the letter sent to the American Congressmen, she knew in her heart that the battle was lost. Her swansong was the publication of her memoir, *The Underworld of State*.

'We have all heard vaguely of Secret Service and read a novel or so with a Secret Service hero or heroine, villain or adventuress,' the book began. 'But what do ordinary men and women know of this service whose funds are drawn from the taxpayer's pocket, but whose operations are never admitted to the public conscience? I, too, knew little about this underworld of State before my visit to Russia in 1920.' This sinister and mysterious underworld of State, she claimed, involved licensing the secret agent 'to do anything which seems expedient to his employer, by fair means or foul, by diplomacy – or otherwise.'

What followed is a 220-page account of her visit to Moscow, her imprisonment by the Bolsheviks, and her eventual liberation. Taking up a long final chapter with the staccato heading 'Evidence–Intimidation–Hush-Money–Indemnity' was the account of her long search for justice.

The publisher was George Allen & Unwin, whose offices were a block south of the British Museum. Stan could hardly have hoped for a better publisher. Stanley Unwin, who bought control of the firm in 1914, was a pacifist and nonconformist (he had gone to the School for Sons of Missionaries in Blackheath). His backlist included Marx, Shaw, Freud and John Ruskin, and recently he had published two works by Bertrand Russell, *Principles of Social Reconstruction* (1916) and *The Practice and Theory of Bolshevism* (1920). Unwin later had strong links with the Fabian Society and published many left-wing books, including titles by Leon Trotsky.

A photograph of Stan appears opposite the book's title page. It seems unlikely that the (uncredited) photo was up-to-date, since she was forty-one years old in 1925 and the picture reveals a considerably younger woman. Most likely taken in Florence immediately before the war, the black and white studio portrait shows her in a tight-fitting, dark, collarless blouse, with an iridescent silk sash fashionably arranged over her left shoulder. Her hair is short and swept back from her brow and behind her ears. Thin-lipped and unsmiling, she looks stern, regal and somewhat androgynous.

One of Unwin's other authors, Bertrand Russell, whom Stan had met in Reval on her way to Moscow in June 1920, agreed to write a preface. He observed that she had become a very different person following her Russian experience, changing from a naïve left-wing enthusiast to an embittered woman with a grudge against the governments of Russia, Britain and the United States.[6]

The journalist Frederic William Wile, a political analyst in Washington, DC previously on the staff of the Chicago *Daily News* and the London *Daily Mail*, sent a copy of the unpublished proofs of *The Underworld of State* to the ex-head of MID, Dennis Nolan, asking, 'Have we any interest in the book?'[7] How he had obtained the proofs is unclear, but Nolan, now Deputy Chief of Staff, sent them on to the new head of the MID, Colonel James Reeves. Reeves concluded that there was nothing in the book of any interest to the War Department, but commented that 'it is believed that it would be most undesirable to have this book published in the United States as it would only add fuel to an old controversy.'[8] *The Underworld of State* did not see the light of day in America.

Now that Stan's campaign had finally come to an end, a question mark hung-over her future. Having just turned 41, there was no one special in her life, her father was dead, her mother was in a nursing home, and she had no contact with her relatives in Canada. She was not on speaking terms with her brother whom she had been so close to as a child. Harold still worked for the Foreign Service in China and now regarded his sister, according to Bertrand Russell who had met him in China in 1920, as a tiresome person always getting into some mess or another. It is a verdict with which the Foreign Office no doubt would have agreed. But Russell recalled how shocked he had been to discover Harold's heartless indifference to his sister's experiences in Russia.[9]

After years of battles, Stan had decided that she finally needed to move on with her life. Deciding that Britain was too cold and too expensive as a permanent home, she may have considered returning to Italy where she had spent twelve happy years, or to Germany where she still had many friends. But the place which Stan's thoughts kept going back to was India. The plan to return there had been the ultimate reason for her travels to Germany in 1918 so she could secure her divorce and regain her British passport. Moreover, her choice of a new profession must have been, to those who knew her, somewhat of a surprise. She was going to become a dancer herself, and continue her research and writing on Indian temple dance.

Initially, she aimed to get a thorough training in Western dance in order better to understand the Indian approach. Approaching middle age and in poor health, Stan marched unannounced into Léonide Massine's studio in Chelsea and offered to show him some of the dance moves she had learnt in India. It is likely that she had seen Massine dance in either Florence or Rome when the Ballets Russes performed there in 1917, and she may well have met him while mixing with the bohemian world of her earlier years. Massine and Diaghilev lived in Florence briefly at the start of the war, developing ballet movements inspired by Renaissance paintings in the Uffizi.[10]

Massine was a brilliant dancer and choreographer. Following initial training with the Bolshoi Ballet, he had been enticed by Sergei Diaghilev to join his Ballets Russes company in 1915. The Ballets Russes were famous for using well-known composers and artists such as Stravinsky, Picasso and Jean Cocteau in their productions, and Massine himself had worked with Picasso on the ballet *Parade*, a creation imbued with Cubist and Futurist ideas. Stan took it for granted that the famous Diaghilev prodigy would be interested in her ideas about dance. Surprisingly, he invited her to attend some of his practise sessions.*

On the face of it, this was certainly an eccentric pursuit, especially for someone who, raised by the Plymouth Brethren, would not have danced so much as a waltz as a child. To become a dancer at the age of forty-one would have been difficult for anyone, and everyone who met Stan during these years commented on her frailty and ill health – the toll taken by her time in prison as well as, perhaps even more, through her fight for justice. It is difficult to believe that Massine, who had begun his training a young age at the Bolshoi Theatre in Moscow, could have given much encouragement to his middle-aged pupil, regardless of her enthusiasm.

In any case, she did not stay long in his studio, quickly moving on to her next teacher. He, too, was a man of the moment, Vicente Escudero, a Catalonian flamenco dancer based in Paris. With his dark, smouldering looks, Escudero was extremely controversial, refusing to conform to tra-

---

* Massine was to become renowned in 1948 for his role as the shoemaker and ballet master in the British film The Red Shoes.

dition. His critics claimed he could not clap in time to the beat, which was essential for a flamenco dancer, but this criticism did not bother Stan because Escudero incorporated the avant-garde Parisian scene into his work. She sought him out in Paris and persuaded him to let her study under him. And, like Massine, attracted by her persuasive personality, he agreed. Finally, having taken all that she thought she needed from Escudero, Stan attended a French school of acrobatics, no doubt learning movements such as spins, splits, back flips and knee-drops. Armed with this eclectic knowledge, she returned to India, arriving in Bombay in December 1927.

* * *

When Marguerite returned from her trip to the Near East in the autumn of 1925, she took an apartment at 70 West 55th Street in Manhattan, resumed her relationship with Blake, and continued writing articles and lecturing. In January 1926, she accepted Arthur Blake's proposal: the couple were married in New Orleans and settled in New York. The following September, they were issued visas to travel to Britain from whence they were to embark on an extended tour of southern Europe and Africa. Both were listed as British subjects. Blake, although a long-term resident of the United States, had maintained his British citizenship, while Marguerite was not required to renounce her American citizenship and British law of the time stated that 'the wife of a British subject shall be deemed to be a British subject'. That Marguerite became a British national by default would have appalled Stan, had she known.

From 1928 to 1935, Marguerite lectured, wrote articles and published two books: *Asia Reborn* (1928) and a translation from German of *The Dissolute Years: A Pageant of Stuart England by Eduard Stucken* (1935), as well as an essay included in the book *All True! The Record of Actual Adventures that have Happened to Ten Women of Today* (1931). She continued to travel, accompanied by her husband, for pleasure rather than work, and settled comfortably into married life, as she collated her memoirs.

* * *

Once back in India, Stan focussed her attention to the study of her latest passion – the Dasi Attam Temple Dance. However, not everyone shared her enthusiasm. A movement was growing there to ban the tradition. Until the eleventh century, the dancers, known as Devadasis, were girls who were 'married' to the temple before puberty and trained in dance to honour the gods. In those early days the dancers were chaste and devoted to their art, but as the tradition lost popularity over the centuries and the temples were ransacked by Muslims, many Devadasis were forced into prostitution and poverty. By 1920, very few dancers remained, and some critics considered the sexualised dances evil and dirty, regarding the performers as little more than prostitutes. Those in favour of abolition caused further hardship by diverting temple funds away from the Devadasis. Meanwhile, the reformists, led by a Tamil lawyer and activist, E. Krishna Iyer, campaigned actively to make the tradition more acceptable by renaming it Bharatanatyam, by which it is known today.

Stan had found a new cause. Appalled by those in favour of abolition or reform, she made it her new *raison d'être* to keep the original tradition alive. With her usual confidence and blinkered determination she induced members of the Viceroy's Executive Council, Secretaries and heads of government departments, as well as notables such as Sir Alexander Tottenham of the Indian Finance Department and Sir Frank Noyce from the Indian Department of Education, Health and Lands, to support her campaign. And, in between campaigning for the retention of temple dance, she combed the Tamil-speaking country for a dancer whom she could study for her own work and eventually record on film. Widening her search to the West coast, she searched in Travancore, Cochin and Malabar – where she eventually discovered a famous teacher, Karunakara Menon, whom she engaged to teach her the dance of Kathakali.

Stan was used to living cheaply, but after three years she had exhausted her savings of £3,500 (approximately £200,000 in 2018). If she were to continue her mission, she needed more funds. The proceeds from an article sold to an American magazine in 1931 bought her a third-class passage to England on a French ship carrying a detachment of soldiers of the French Foreign Legion. Galvanising support from sympathetic souls in England, she decided, was her last chance of securing funding for her project and cause.

* * *

On October 29th 1931, two women, one in her early forties, the other approaching fifty, sat in the front row in the hall of the Royal Geographical Society in South Kensington, awaiting a presentation on Indian temple dancing by Mrs. Stan Harding, a visitor from India. The two women, Phyllis Barron and Dorothy Larcher, from Painswick in Gloucestershire, lived and worked together, and were famous for their hand-blocked printed textiles. During their professional and personal partnership they had achieved commercial success, completing commissions for Coco Chanel, the Duke of Westminster, Girton College, Cambridge, and Westminster Abbey. They were an odd couple: Phyllis Barron was tall, large and mannish, with an exuberant personality and sense of humour, while the younger Larcher was quiet, serious and sad-looking. Dorothy Larcher, however, adored India, where she had spent seven years before returning to England and joining Barron in her studio in the early 1920s. Stan was not only to strike up a lasting friendship with the two ladies, but also, through them she was introduced to Dorothy Elmhirst from Dartington Hall in Devon.

The American-born Dorothy Payne Straight was a widow when she met Leonard Knight Elmhirst whilst he was fundraising for Cornell University. Elmhirst hailed from a family of landowners in Yorkshire and had studied at Cornell before working extensively in India as an agronomist. Dorothy, who had inherited large sums of money from both her father and her late husband, used her wealth for philanthropic causes, assisting charitable and educational organisations. After their marriage in 1925, the couple moved to England, bought Dartington Hall in Devon, and embarked on creating a rural educational and artistic retreat supporting the arts. When Barron and Larcher wrote to their friend Dorothy suggesting that she meet Stan, a letter was quickly despatched from Dartington inviting Stan for a weekend there.

When Stan received the invitation she immediately packed her slides and left her lodgings at Beaufort Street in Chelsea to share with her hosts her new enthusiasm for Indian temple dancing. By the time she left Dartington Hall a few days later, the Elmhirsts had agreed to finance her work in India. 'Last Monday I came up to town,' Stan wrote to Mrs Elmhirst, 'with a heart made very happy by your offer of help for my work.' An understatement indeed: the Elmhirsts had offered her £2,000 to record the disappearing art of Dasi Attam.[11]

Chapter Twenty-Three

Life's Ugly Gestures

Stan arrived back in Madras on January 29th 1932. She was 48 years old and – perhaps ominously – ripe for another adventure. On her return journey she had met a fellow explorer and ethnographer, the American film director Robert Flaherty. In 1922, Flaherty had made the acclaimed documentary *Nanook of the North* and he and Stan discussed her planned work on the Dasi Attam dancers. She wrote excitedly to the Elmhirsts exclaiming that 'the first thing that met my eye on landing was a small green parrot sacred to Siva Sakti. As a thank-you offering for my glad return to India, I redeemed him from his tiny cage at the cost of a few annas'. All did not end well with the little green bird, as he bit her and refused food. 'He could not fly with clipped wings so I had to give him away,' she lamented. It is not difficult to see in this episode a metaphor for the failure of Stan's various idealistic schemes – and per-haps an ill omen for the enterprise that followed.

Stan had written the Elmhirsts with her plans to buy a second-hand bus and drive to the west coast where she would find the troupes of dra-matic dancers who performed the Indian epics. The Chevrolet agent for Madras, Sir Alexander MacDougall, found her an old four-cylinder, seven-seater Chevrolet bus and had it reconditioned to include a seat on which she could sleep and a cubby hole to be used as a darkroom. The latter was not particularly successful due to the lack of air and sti-fling heat.

Stan set off on her travels and at the end of April wrote to the Elmhirsts that she had parked her bus under a large tree: 'It is as airy as a pandal and whenever I am tired I can sleep comfortably on the couchette seat.' Unfortunately, the bus frequently broke down. One day, she wrote, 'We pushed the bus a hundred yards or so more than once into a small patch of shade which promptly dwindled away under the vertical sun. I lay on top of all the photographic material I had with me and hoped that my body was a good non-conductor and also that the emulsion of my brain was not super-sensitive.'

Stan's frequent letters to the Elmhirsts noted that people in India were becoming more politicised as they sought independence from the British. There was plague in Mysore, dead rats littered the streets, and some villages in Belgaum district had been abandoned. Visiting temple after temple, she gathered information on the dancing girls, but encountered a certain amount of resistance: 'My search was complicated by the fact that at first everyone was inclined to suppose that I was some inspectress working in connection with the Immoral Traffic Act, or else a missionary out to kidnap children trained as dancers, intern them in a mission and teach them to make lace crochet.'

When not travelling around the country in her bus, Stan's headquarters was a crumbling, condemned bungalow in Tellicherry (Thalassery) on the Malabar Coast of Kerala. Under British rule, Tellicherry became a major commercial port to transport spices such as cardamom and pepper crushed from locally grown peppercorns and a fort was build to protect this trade. Tellicherry was also known as the city where cricket was first played and the Indian circus was born.

Stan's bungalow was no more trustworthy than her bus. 'The roof of one room fell in the other day and my boy [servant] and two kittens had a narrow escape,' she wrote in one of her rambling letters to the Elmhirsts. 'I am afraid I shall have to find something else and it will not be easy to find anything which suits me as well.' In October, she returned to the bungalow because the rains had come early and soaked the bus and its contents. Fortunately, the film she had taken of the dancers, stored in a tin box, had been preserved. Stan complained about having to patch up the leaks in her darkroom at the bungalow where the rats had nibbled the black, pasted paper which now let in water and light. And if only she could keep staff: she wrote in despair that they kept leaving.

In one letter Stan detailed her plan to buy four children to be trained as dancers. This way, she reasoned, she would be able to record the dances to keep the tradition alive. However, as was so often the case in Stan's complicated life, things did not run smoothly. Only two children reached her, while the other two were reported to be wandering in the countryside nearby. She set about rounding them up. 'I have caught one,' Stan wrote, adding that she had 'heard that the other is at Vellineszhy, not on the map, but said to be about thirty miles from here.' In the meantime, Stan reported, 'three of the four children have cut off their long hair; from my point of view, this is a great pity. They just couldn't bear to be out of the new Western fashion any longer.'

In November, Stan wrote to the Elmhirsts apologising for yet more delays in sending them evidence of her work. 'Now I have all four child dancers here,' she explained, 'but the best boy by far is completely lame for the moment. Another boy in play flung an areca nut stick at him and the spines of it became embedded in his leg and he got blood poisoning.' She reported that she was having him treated by a local doctor and was trying to find a replacement. She complained that when the children settled in their new home they quickly forgot the old traditions such as the need for reverence, devotion and service to the teacher. As a consequence, the teacher hired by Stan quit.

More problems bedevilled her. Just before Christmas, a letter arrived for the Elmhirsts, filled with yet more excuses. Stan was finding it difficult to process her film in the heat and needed to move to a cooler climate, twenty miles from Mysore at the foot of the hills. On the journey, she had stopped her bus in two or three places to take a few photographs. Excitedly, she wrote how she had 'always returned to the little bus intoxicated with the beauty of the forest and, incidentally, with both legs streaming blood from leeches'! Then, silence for the next four months.

It turned out that Stan was intoxicated by more than the beauty of the forest. She had begun using opium.[1] Delirious, she had been taken to a hospital in Calicut, Kerala, suffering from rheumatic fever and malignant malaria. Nor was she the only casualty. She had trained a young lad to be her darkroom assistant, but 'this poor fellow was taken ill ten days after me and has been on his back ever since with rheumatic fever', she eventually informed the Elmhirsts. 'His people absolutely refuse to let him be taken to hospital for proper treatment. It is doubtful whether he will recover.' Her letter rambled on with more excuses for failing to finish the filming: 'For the moment if I sit down I have hardly strength to get up without help.'

Letters continued arriving at Dartington Hall throughout 1933, explaining why she had not completed her work – the climate was not conducive to film processing, she was running out of money, the bus kept breaking down, she had to let her driver go, and so forth. In July, her letter was full of the sad news that the famous Devadasi dancer, Jirvaratnam, had died of smallpox after bathing in infected waters. Stan fell into a black mood, blaming her own months of illness for preventing her from recording Jirvaratnam's work before she died.

By 1934, the Elmhirsts had still not seen any results from their investment. Stan continued to write letters filled with excuses for failing to complete the work, at the same time asking for more money. Elmhirst agreed to send her a further £200. She wrote back excitedly informing him that an Indian film company was interested in acquiring the rights of her film on dance and had offered to pay her £1,000. Would Mr

Elmhirst give her permission to follow this up? Relieved that finally there was a sign of some progress in Stan's work, Leonard Elmhirst replied that he would look into the company for her and in the meantime, if she needed more money, to forward him details. An unwise offer, perhaps, in the circumstances.

It became clear that by this stage Stan had no idea what to do next. It may have been due to her continuous bad health, the after-effects of her sojourn in the Lubyanka, the years of obsessive hatred of Marguerite, or the opium to which she was becoming addicted, but whatever the reasons, her focus wandered. She wrote to the Elmhirsts that she was now thinking of writing a book that would concentrate on Indian dance gestures, as well as making a film. But her financial situation was again dire, so she sent Elmhirst an article and photographs for him to place in the American publication, *Asia Magazine*. So confident was she that they would be published that she asked the Elmhirsts if they would advance her the £40 fee. 'Is this possible?' she wrote. 'This would spell relief from the harassment of solitary money-worry which gets on one's nerve to an extent which makes work difficult'. Elmhirst put the £40 in her bank in anticipation that *Asia Magazine* would buy her article and explained that his 'own financial situation is not too easy at the present time and I do hope you will succeed in placing some of the film as you suggest in order to get re-established yourself'.

In June 1934, eighteen months after returning to India, Stan continued to write of the difficulties of getting sound on film and of the practicalities of sending film to England. When a letter from Richard J. Walsh, editor of *Asia Magazine*, arrived for Elmhirst regretting that they could not use Harding's article 'Gesture', Elmhirst began to have serious doubts about Stan and her abilities. 'Naturally I dislike to turn down something from a person in whom you are interested,' Walsh wrote, 'and particularly one to whom you had made a substantial cash advance. Yet our best judgement was that the article was quite inadequate and the pictures not up to our standard.' To support his letter he enclosed a comment by a member of his staff: 'The article has little background; no richness of texture; it is all too bald, too unadorned, too uninformed and she hardly touches on any of the richness of the subject.' Walsh hoped that Elmhirst's advance would be returned to him when Stan's film was completed. Elmhirst immediately wrote to Stan to tell her the news and gently tried to extricate himself from his commitment to her by explaining that he feared his own position was 'so tight this year that I cannot do more for the time being'. He insisted that, from time to time, she keep in touch.

Stan remained upbeat, replying that she had a slight touch of influenza as a result of a drenching rain followed by a high wind, but was planning to offer her articles to the London weeklies. She thanked him for sending money: 'The arrival of a letter from the bank informing me of the receipt of your forty pounds has relieved me from racking anxiety. The relief from all this anxiety is intense and I thank you wholeheartedly.'

For the next few months Stan battled with illness as she travelled around in her bus, attempting to record Indian dance traditions. She wrote to the Elmhirsts in December telling them of her delight that *Asia Magazine* would print her article on 'Shadow-Play'. Two months later, in February 1935, she reported that *Asia Magazine* had decided not to use her article after all. 'I am afraid Mr Walsh does not like my stuff very much,' she lamented, but 'it can't be helped!' She explained that she was now trying to make a living by illustrated journalism. 'It is, as you can imagine, not easy and 'Life' makes ugly gestures at me from time to time.' Nothing materialised with the Indian film company that been interested in her work a year before, but she informed the Elmhirsts that they had renewed their interest.

By the end of July, Stan was again desperate for money and had been writing post-dated cheques in order to survive. She wrote to the Elmhirsts to tell them she would probably have to sell some of her cameras to pay her debts. She was not going to sell the bus, though, as it provided the roof over her head, but she pondered on whether to exchange it for a half-ton lorry and to try to 'live for the time being by bringing teak down the ghats to the coast and peppercorns on the up-trip'. She still dreamed of writing a 'Dictionary of West Coast Gesture' and of making a film with sound of Indian dance.

The Elmhirsts heard very little from Stan during the closing months of 1935 into early 1936, but received an update from Dorothy Elmhirst's daughter, Beatrice, who had visited India in January 1936. 'A strange lady in the hotel with grey hair done in a pigtail and tied with black ribbon and a grey man's suit, grey flat straw hat and man's shoes, accosted me and came to tea and she turned out to be Mrs Stan Harding!' Beatrice thought she was rather pathetic and a 'queer-eccentric', but said that she possessed great sincerity. Assuming that Beatrice knew about her relationship with her parents, Stan related the full story of her arrival in India filled with 'wild enthusiasm, a sum of money, a camera and no idea at all of what to do or how to use anything'. She foolishly explained in great detail to her benefactor's daughter how she had used the wrong film, tried to develop it all herself, and had difficulties with the boys whom she was training specifically to be filmed. She recalled that her female lead dancer had tragically died, and that she had run out of money with the 'film half-finished and of absolutely no use'. Relaying this all back to her parents, Beatrice told them that Stan lived in her old car outside Bombay and that she also had rented a room in a very disreputable part of the town. 'It seemed to me a tragic example of someone with wonderful ideas and no knowledge of how to carry them out – everything seemed to have gone wrong with her and I was very sorry indeed.' She thought that if her parents were to continue supporting this eccentric Englishwoman, she should have an expert photographer to accompany her to retake all the films which she could direct. Beatrice finally recommended that before any decision was made, Stan's work must first be seen to decide if it was worth continuing. 'I should also see the films that Uday Shankar has taken of dancing all over India which are now in Paris being edited – there would be no sense duplicating.'

Meeting Beatrice was not as beneficial as Stan might have imagined since the young woman's allegiances lay with promoting Uday Shankar. Uday was an Indian classical dancer and choreographer with whom Beatrice had fallen in love in the summer of 1934 after he and his troupe performed at Dartington Hall. She had accompanied him back to India where they had started up the Shankar School of Dance in Almora with her parents' money. Unfortunately for Stan, it would be Uday, rather than she, who would put Indian classical dance on the world map.

In September, Stan sent the Elmhirsts photographs with no accompanying letter. An explanation followed shortly: 'A few weeks ago I had to go to hospital for a major operation, which has left me luckily as fit and genuinely tough as ever,' she told them. 'As there is always some risk of coming to an end during or after such an operation, I wrote a few letters and also addressed two or three envelopes of photographs to be posted by my boy if anything went wrong. The letters were not posted as this emergency did not arise. My boy however posted the photographs to you.'

Life was ever more difficult for Stan. She was subsisting on illustrated journalism, some railway publicity, and a small amount of commercial cinematography – until her camera broke down and had to be returned to the manufacturers for a complete overhaul. When it came back, her misfortunes continued: an Indian heatwave damaged the lenses. However, always on the lookout for opportunities, she met the Hungarian film director and producer, Zoltan Korda, who said that he would enquire on his return to London about the possibility of his team putting a soundtrack to her film. But this was an empty promise and nothing ever materialised. Stan, as so often, was living on hope and promises.

By October, Stan was again desperate for money. She wanted to return to England for a few weeks to look for work in Fleet Street as a correspondent on India, and to talk to more people about the film and its production. She explained her dire situation to the Elmhirsts: 'I sold out all that remained of my life interest in some property with the exception of enough to bring me in one rupee a day! That is enough to live very much in the style of a naked ascetic beside some fairly clean Indian river, without begging! But I am not yet living like that: I have not yet made the great renunciation – that of work! The fact is I get a great kick out of work and dread the boredom of bare life without it.' She managed to keep two boys who helped with the cleaning, cooking, washing and photography, but she could not afford to live in Bombay. 'There are intervals of indescribable squalor,' she lamented, 'when one runs completely out of vitamins and waits on the bus, marooned somewhere in the jungle for a cheque to come in for some article from somewhere.' However, despite these hardships, she insisted that she did not want to live in England. Memories of her days above the Poetry Bookshop no doubt loomed in her head. 'Below 75 F, there is no physical wellbeing for me whatever! This sunshine is largely what remains of the splendour of life and without it life would have no charm for me.'

The Elmhirsts sent Stan £100 to enable her to close her affairs and return to England. She arrived in London in June 1937, and lodged with her friend Louise Pullen in Chelsea. 'When are you coming to London?' she asked the Elmhirsts. In early August she penned a further letter to the Elmhirsts from their home at 42 Upper Brook Street in Mayfair, to which they had left her a key. 'I have been in your lovely flat for the last week. The flat certainly is a vantage ground from which to explore the newspaper and celluloid world.' In the meantime, she lunched with Michael Huxley of *The Geographical Magazine*, and met her old friend Frederick Voigt, with whom she had once dodged bullets in Germany, and who was now diplomatic correspondent of *The Manchester Guardian*. Huxley took some of her pictures to use in the magazine, but neither friend could offer her any permanent work. She then contacted British film-makers Basil Wright and John Grierson in an attempt to persuade them to back her: nothing came of it. However, she relished meeting old acquaintances and attended a party of American and other ex-Berlin and Moscow newspaper correspondents. For the first time in ages, Stan was positive about her future prospects. Carried away with enthusiasm, she reported to the Elmhirsts that Batsford had offered to publish her book with plenty of illustrations.

She was delighted also to meet up again with Beatrice, who had just returned from India. Beatrice advised Stan to send her unfinished film to the Rockefeller Center in New York to coincide with the International Exhibition of Dance being held there in December. And then, just as fortune seemed to smile on her, she was confronted by her old adversary, Marguerite Harrison, and the battle lines once again were drawn.

Chapter Twenty-Four

The Lonely Trench

In 1935, Marguerite's memoir, *There's Always Tomorrow: The Story of a Checkered Life*, was published in the United States. The following year the book came out in Britain under the title, *Born for Trouble*. In the book, Marguerite repeated her claim that Stan was a British Intelligence officer. It was some months before Stan saw a copy; when she did, her reaction was – predictably – one of rage. Still in London, she immediately contacted Elmhirst who agreed to appoint his lawyer, Fred Gwatkin, from McKenna & Co, to help her sue for libel.

'It is difficult to thank you both enough for your real, practical kindness,' Stan wrote to Elmhirst in the autumn of 1937, 'it relieves the strain of this unexpected worry immensely.' She also wrote that 'any damages he [Gwatkin] may get me must be the repayment of whatever expense you incur now on my behalf'. Gwatkin imagined he would be able to settle the case against Marguerite quickly but Stan had her own agenda. After ten years, her obsessive hatred of Marguerite was consuming her once again, and she was demanding an unreal sum in compensation. Elmhirst, not having experienced this side of Stan's personality before, was understandably taken aback, and contacted Bertrand Russell for his assistance in 'bringing a sense of proportion to Mrs Harding over the amount of compensation she is asking for'.

A letter was then forwarded to Stan then at a flat in Marble Arch from the solicitors representing Gollancz, Marguerite's British publishers. Victor Gollancz was an unlikely publisher for Marguerite, with her strident anti-Bolshevism. A supporter of Socialist and Communist movements, he published books dedicated to social justice (a philosophy that saw him sacked from his first job as a schoolteacher). Gollancz had commissioned George Orwell to write *The Road to Wigan Pier* about the working class in northern England, and the same year he published A.J. Cronin's *The Citadel*, about medical ethics in a Welsh mining village. He had just founded the New Left Book Club, with its catchy jackets and canny advertising – and he was widely recognised as the most innovative publisher in London.

Marguerite assured Victor Gollancz that she could substantiate her statements about Stan Harding, and insisted that he remain firm and fight the libel suit in the courts. Gollancz, however, thought differently. He requested a meeting with Stan to discuss options, claiming that when he had read the manuscript he had assumed in good faith that Marguerite's reminiscences were true. He was prepared to print an apology in an approved newspaper – for example, in the personal column of *The Times* – and no further copies of the book would be published, although it might be difficult to remove them from all libraries. Gollancz then proposed settling the affair with a small sum for damages.

Stan wanted more than a small sum for what she regarded as libel, and wrote to Elmhirst explaining why she was demanding £1,000, a considerable amount in compensation: she would be 'heart-sick' to lose the two houseboys who assisted her in her work. She explained that when she returned to India she would need £8 a week for living expenses, including a central heating allowance, 'if I am to avoid getting one bronchial cold after another.' Presumably this would be for times when she returned to Tellicherry. Even though temperatures in the city rarely get below 23˚C (73˚F), the rains fall between May and August, making anyone with a weak chest vulnerable to infections.

In reply, Elmhirst offered to provide her with £8 a week for two months so that she could settle her affairs and move to warmer climes: 'I am no longer in a position to do more than attempt to give you a start again, but I hope it will be a clear start without other anxieties creeping in.' Elmhirst also wrote to Gwatkin, explaining that in his absence the lawyer might find it necessary to persuade Mrs Harding to accept a reasonable figure: 'May I suggest that you call in both Henry Brailsford [the left-wing journalist] and Bertrand Russell if you need any assistance.' Brailsford had first met Stan in Berlin immediately after the 1918 Armistice and his memories of her were of an artist who drew delicate and spirited drawings of Chinese scenes, and was sympathetic to the Russian revolution.[1] He had also crossed paths with her in Reval in 1920 as part of the Labour delegation to Russia on their return journey to Britain.

Without acknowledging or thanking Elmhirst for his generous offer, Stan wrote back, furious that Marguerite's book would be available in libraries: 'A published apology without withdrawal of the book from libraries and booksellers would be far worse than useless for me,' she raged. 'It might of course help the sale and circulation of the book and put some money in the pockets of publisher and author..!!!' By the same post, Elmhirst received a letter from Gwatkin, predicting trouble: 'I think I am going to have some difficulty with Mrs Stan Harding over the nature of her claim.' She wanted a payment of £1,000 and no less.

Bertrand Russell was called in to assist negotiations. Recently divorced, the prolific author had married his third wife, Peter (Patricia Helen Spence), in 1936. With a new baby in the house and tired of travelling, he attempted to return to academia in 1937. Perhaps due to his outspoken nature, Cambridge and Princeton both turned Russell down, but Oxford offered him a lecture series on 'Words and Facts'. While undertaking these duties he took time out to meet with Stan. In November 1937, he wrote to Elmhirst reporting on his encounter: 'I did what I could to abate her claims, but she is not easy to deal with.' Stan's obsession with clearing her name and damaging Marguerite's reputation into the bargain was only increasing. 'If the case had to go into Court,' she told Elmhirst, 'nothing short of a conspiracy on the Dreyfus Case scale could make anything go wrong with it.' She insisted that she could count on other men and women of international standing to back her.

Victor Gollancz would have been aware of the Stan Harding saga that had dominated the British press in the first half of the 1920s, and had probably made a decision to try to wrap the case up as soon as possible. At the end of November the publishers agreed to pay Stan the sum of £1,000. But she wanted more: apologies to appear in a variety of newspapers and a statement to be read out in court. Gollancz responded by claiming that this was unreasonable and that it would have to go in front of a judge. He stated that this meant an inevitable a delay of months, with no guarantee she would receive the £1,000 in compensation.

Gwatkin was beside himself with frustration. 'When I saw Mr Brailsford, before I saw Mrs Harding, he warned me that Mrs Harding might be difficult to deal with in this respect.' Difficult was probably an understatement. 'I am sorry that you are being troubled in the matter,' Gwatkin wrote to Elmhirst, 'but I think you may be able to influence Mrs Harding, as probably she thinks that I am a member of the 'Underworld of State' to which she refers in her book and have some ulterior object in advising her in the way I have done.' Alarmed by developments, Elmhirst wrote to Russell, asking again for his help in trying to encourage Stan to take the money, as it might not be on the table for long. 'I agree with you,' he concluded. 'She is not an easy person to deal with.'

A few days later Elmhirst received Bertrand Russell's reply, in which he explained: 'I did my utmost to get her into a state of mind that would make an agreed settlement possible, but I don't know how far I succeeded.' However, he did think that Gollancz should apologise to Stan, in court, but without printing apologies in the newspapers. 'My own feeling,' Russell told Elmhirst, 'is that as Gollancz has published a libel which was long ago proved to be false, he has not a leg to stand on, and must agree to what is a bare minimum of justice.'

Henry Brailsford was likewise finding Stan increasingly tiresome. 'She is very trying and it won't be easy to influence her,' he wrote to Elmhirst. But he agreed with Russell that a statement in court was essential. He added that on one point he also agreed with Stan: the book must be withdrawn from libraries. Gwatkin, however, remained adamant that the case should not go to court. 'In view of Mrs Harding's state of mind,' he told Elmhirst, 'I was strongly of the opinion that it would be better to get the whole thing out of her head and finish with it, because the more I see her on this subject the more exacting she becomes.' After all, he added, there were only 1,400 published copies of Marguerite's book.

Gwatkin was wise to suggest that Stan accept the compensation and be done with it, as from his years of experience he could foresee a long and costly court battle. However, this advice simply incensed Stan further. Her next letter to Elmhirst stated how upset she was with his solicitor. She demanded that a 'double writ' be presented at court – a claim against the publisher and another against the author – insisting that she was prepared to withdraw the writ against the author if her demands were met. Gwatkin adamantly refused to take this action. He thought her demands were already being met, so that other than for malicious reasons there was no point in the second writ against Marguerite. Exasperated, he suggested that Stan should find another solicitor.

Stan responded by writing yet again to Elmhirst: 'If you are still here, please spare me another minute. I beg you not to let Mr Gwatkin persuade you that I am unreasonable (should he take this view). I consider that he unconsciously sees the case from the Foreign Office angle, which is not that of his client in many respects! I beg you to confirm to Mr Gwatkin that it was the taking of a double writ which I discussed with you.'

By now Elmhirst, having clearly lost both sympathy and patience with Stan, was doing his best to extricate himself from his one-time protégé, as so many of her supporters had done before. He forwarded to her address in Chelsea the balance of money that he had agreed to give her. Stan immediately wrote back thanking him: 'Yesterday I felt that a sort of trench warfare which might go on for a long time, had come about. If only I had a sight or sound of the enemy to cheer me in my lonely trench! In the meantime, thanks to you, my dug-out will continue to have full central heating – no small mercy.' She informed him that she was living on a 'floating overdraft which doesn't float very well…'

On the 9th of January 1938, Stan received a letter from Gwatkin blaming her for the delay of the settlement because of her threat of issuing a 'double writ'. Stan immediately wrote to Elmhirst lamenting how this was a 'fantastically unfair suggestion'. Three days later, Rubinstein, Nash & Co., representing Gollancz, sent a letter to Gwatkin with their terms: they agreed to make a statement in court, would spend up to £50 on apologies in newspapers, and offer the sum of £1,000 in compensation. Stan was advised to accept. These, after all, had been her original demands. But Stan, typically obstinate, dug her feet in and refused. An exasperated Gwatkin wrote to Elmhirst: 'I have been fighting with Mrs Harding for some time back about her demands. She insists on making statements about Marguerite. They may be very relevant as in a quarrel between Mrs Harding and Mrs Harrison, but they do not appear to be very relevant in an action against Gollancz, but the difficulty is to get Mrs Harding to see reason.' Gwatkin added: 'Mrs Harding has such an exaggerated view of her own importance on the value of her wording as compared with the wording of others in a statement of this kind, that I really doubt at times whether we will ever come to finality.'

In Gwatkin's professional opinion, the case was a straightforward one: an admission, an apology, and payment of damages. Stan, however, insisted on the apology being in her own words. 'I really don't know what anyone can do for the lady,' Gwatkin complained. 'Every time I get the thing going she comes back with this desire to hit at Mrs Harrison through Gollancz.'

Stan then decided to contact Gollancz directly. Once again losing patience, Gwatkin sent Stan a firm letter: 'Your attitude in these matters makes it impossible to carry on the negotiations in the normal manner. As I told you, if you would let me and the very experienced Counsel who has been consulted on your behalf, deal with these matters as such matters are dealt with in the ordinary way, the case could be settled with every satisfaction to yourself.' Gwatkin was not personally bothered that she was contacting Gollancz directly, but he insisted that she must withdraw the threat of a double writ. The publishers had gone out of their way to accommodate her and had not held her at arm's length as she suggested.

Elmhirst, too, had lost patience and at the end of January wrote Stan a stern letter outlining a few home truths: 'My chief anxiety is that you seem to me to run the risk of building as dreadful a prison for yourself as any you have experienced in the past, by turning the full blast of your suspicion and accusation upon the world and upon your good friends that was once turned upon you.' Elmhirst told her that when she talked of justice she actually meant revenge. 'I am not attempting to blame you for this in view of your past suffering,' he told her, 'but when I see the ease with which you impute evil motives to people who have the very best intentions towards you, and the way in which you are prepared to squander the precious moments of the rest of your life which were given to you for creative activity,' he questioned whether he should continue to back her under these circumstances. Stan was truly shocked on receiving Elmhirst's letter. Her self-awareness was so lacking that it had not occurred to her that anyone might think of her in this way. She quickly penned a reply insisting that she was not after revenge on her false accuser, 'but should like to deprive her lies of credit – once and for all.'

Like many of the Foreign Office staff who had dealt with Stan between 1921 and 1925, Gwatkin told Elmhirst that he simply could not understand what was in her mind, as she distrusted everyone: 'If she finds out that anyone has any official connections she thinks that they will automatically be dishonest with her by reason of such connection.' Gwatkin was furious that the barrister he was using to present Stan's case was distrusted by her: 'The fact Mr Valentine Holmes is also a junior Counsel to the Treasury makes her think that he would give the case away if he had it,' he wrote to Elmhirst. Gwatkin was so frustrated and at the end of his tether with his client, he confided in Elmhirst that it was difficult to deal with such a 'mentality'. The professional relationship between Stan and Gwatkin finally came to an end, in order that she could submit a 'double writ' to the court.

* * *

In June 1938, Stan was still in London and the case remained unsettled. Her old feelings of insecurity and persecution, never far from the surface when she felt under personal attack, received a further blow when she came across a copy of Mabel Dodge Luhan's book, *Intimate Memories*, in which she was mentioned unfavourably. And to whom did she write? Leonard Elmhirst. His heart must have sunk when he opened Stan's letter. 'To my amazement I found a chapter of defamatory rubbish,' she wrote. 'If what she [Dodge Luhan] writes had been merely untrue it would not have been so bad but it was such mawkish nonsense. I don't suppose you read books of that kind but just in case you come across it, I enclose my comments.'

Stan denied being part of Mabel's Florentine group and explained that her contacts with Mabel Dodge were so unimportant that 'I was surprised to find my Christian name indexed with cross-references to my husband's name.' Stan desperately wanted Elmhirst to know that although she had 'greatly appreciated the easy hospitality of her villa and the *va et vient* of amusing people, there was a discrepancy of style between us', Mabel preferring 'voluminous robes of velvet and gold lace and loosely tied turbans', whereas Stan was of a plain, ascetic inclination. She neither mentioned nor denied Mabel's implication that she was a lesbian nor did she indicate that she had been close enough to Mabel to write to her from China in 1912 and had signed it, 'with much love, always, dearest Mabel, your friend, Stan'.[2]

It is a measure of Leonard Elmhirst that, although thoroughly tired of Stan, he was to follow up her 'injustices' one last time. Marguerite's book had been reviewed by Robert Cantwell in New York's liberal magazine, *New Republic*, and extracts had been printed, in one of which Stan was mentioned. Stan indignantly informed Elmhirst of this fact and asked if he would approach the editor on her behalf. Elmhirst knew the editor, Bruce Bliven, and suggested to him that a published apology might appease Stan. Bliven's response was that he was 'terribly sorry that Robert Cantwell should have repeated, in complete innocence of course, the false statement about her from Mrs Harrison's book. He did not, as you may have noticed, mention Mrs Harding by name.' Nevertheless, Bliven assured Elmhirst that he would print a correction immediately: 'I am writing to Mrs Harding about it.' This of course did not appease Stan, even though, true to his word, Bliven printed a full statement of the situation between the two women.

Ready for another fight, Stan herself wrote to Bliven, requesting that her letter be printed verbatim. He, however, was reluctant to publish, explaining to Elmhirst that 'I am sure you will agree with me that Mrs Harding's letter that I enclosed is a bad piece of writing, and would do her a good deal of harm if printed. Under the circumstances, I am sure you would be doing her a service if you would try to persuade her not to insist on publication.' When Stan read this she reacted in fury, sending back an angry missive, demanding that her letter be printed word for word, and insisting: 'The only amends that you can make is to print this letter as it stands.'

Bliven found himself in the uncomfortable position of being caught between two warring women. Harding threatened libel if he did not publish her letter, while if he did so, 'Mrs Harrison would undoubtedly sue us for libel, with good reason,' he wrote to Elmhirst in despair. 'Neither Mrs Harding nor anyone else can possibly know whether Mrs Harrison informed against her in Moscow. The only evidence on this point is the word of the Moscow government which as we all know is absolutely worthless.' In the hope of appeasing Stan, Bliven sent her a copy of a sworn statement by John H. Clayton confirming that Marguerite had asked him to try and warn her not to come to Moscow.

Eventually, whether due to lack of money or an ultimatum from Elmhirst, Stan dropped her campaign against Marguerite, Gollancz and the *New Statesman.* As a result, in the autumn of 1938 she received a compensation package of £1,000 from Gollancz, her costs were covered, and she was promised an apology to be printed in the leading British newspapers. Everyone involved in her case no doubt heaved an immense sigh of relief when she announced that she wanted to return to India and continue recording her life's work.

* * *

In November 1938, Stan arrived back in India. She soon found work photographing 'Picturesque India' for the Indian Railways, although this source of income dried up the following year with the outbreak of the Second World War.

By 1940, having gone through most of her Gollancz settlement, she was once again short of funds so, smartly dressed in a spotless white blouse and frilly cravat, a navy blue jumper slung over her shoulders, navy slacks and shiny white gym shoes, she strode into the office of Josselyn Hennessy in New Delhi's Imperial Secretariat, handing him a letter of introduction from the late Sir John Murray Ewart, Director of Intelligence for the Government of India. Stan had met Ewart and his wife some years earlier when campaigning to retain temple funds for the Devadasis.

When war was declared, India was divided about her commitment to the Empire. For the past few decades, there had been many different movements throughout the country desiring the end of British rule. Britain had declared that India was at war with the Axis powers without Indian representatives being consulted and, feeling vulnerable to counter-espionage, the colonial government beefed up its own Intelligence resources.

Ewart had died prematurely at the age of 45, a few months before Stan entered Hennessy's office looking for work, but Ewart had allegedly suggested to her that she should undertake intelligence work for him, reporting on subversive gossip picked up in Bombay. She informed Hennessy that she had told Ewart that she would rather starve: 'To be good at spying, you have to be able to lie convincingly and readily on the spur of the moment,' Stan declared. 'Your pride of craftsmanship is in your ability to deceive people. Horrible! Horrible'.

Hennessy, confused as to what he could do for her, was particularly struck by the monocle attached to a black ribbon that hung around the neck of this eccentric Englishwoman. Stan, in her usual abrupt manner, asked him outright for a job – any job except spying. She then showed him some of her photographs taken for the Indian railways which Hennessy recalled as being so exquisite (evidently Stan was finally learning her trade) that he hired her on the spot to record India's war effort.

Hennessy described Stan, who was now 56 years old, as someone who talked incessantly, with one idea leading seamlessly on to another. She had to be ruthlessly cut short and brought back to the point: 'You chivvied out of her what you wanted to know,' he was later to say. He found her far too much of a perfectionist, always setting herself unrealistically high standards; unless she was continually reminded to stick to the schedule, he feared that nothing would ever be recorded. She was incapable of carrying out administrative tasks such as filling in official forms for her expenses, which 'caused her dismay and semi-paralysis, and wasted hours that could have been spent productively'. Over the seven years that they worked together, Hennessy was to find a way of directing her talents to get the best out of her and, perhaps surprisingly, grew extremely fond her. This episode came to an end in 1947, however, when war work ceased, and she was let go with a small retirement sum of £350.

Chapter Twenty-Five

Hope Thou Not Much, Fear Not at All

In the autumn of 1949, for the first time in twelve years, Stan returned to London. During the war she had lost contact with the Elmhirsts and had only recently discovered that Leonard had seen duty in India during the war – a posting he no doubt deliberately kept from Stan. If Elmhirst thought he had heard the last of her, however, he was mistaken, for she wrote from the Imperial Hotel in London's Russell Square asking to see him. Ignoring her first two letters, the third one implored his help: 'I beg you to help me to assemble and complete my work with all its photographs and its diagrams of great gesture in different schools of ancient Indian dance'.

Dartington Hall had become much better organised since its early days; funding no longer came out of Elmhirst's personal bank account, but grants had to be agreed by the governing body of the Elmhirst Trust. Considering that Elmhirst had never seen any evidence of Stan's work despite his previous backing, it is surprising that he even bothered to forward her request on to the Trust. On this occasion, however, her plea was turned down as being too vague and lacking any costings.

Notifying Stan of this decision, Elmhirst urged her to send him a detailed proposal. But, as usual, she procrastinated, eventually writing at the end of November, and made the usual excuses for not having completed her proposal. 'The object of the award,' she told Elmhirst, 'is not to finance publication, but to enable me at long last to sit down and handle the great amount of negative material exposed without the impossible complication of having to earn my living at the same time.'

On December 1st 1949, a long-winded résumé and a grant request from Stan arrived at Dartington Hall. She asked for 1,200 rupees a month so that she could devote twelve months to collating all her information. She planned to produce two illustrated books: the first volume would cover the two southern schools of ancient Indian classical dance, and the second volume the two northern schools.

By chance, Stan now came across Martin Russell, Bertrand Russell's nephew, in India. Russell had been stationed in Ceylon (Sri Lanka) in 1942 and had served at Lord Mountbatten's South-Asia Command Headquarters in Peradeniya. While there, he had met Lionel Wendt, founder of the '43 Group', a collection of Sinhalese artists. Russell had fallen in love with their unique style of painting and spent the rest of his life sponsoring their exhibitions and promoting their work. Like Hennessy, Russell was attracted by Stan's personality and became her latest supporter. He wrote to Elmhirst from the Bristol Hotel in Paris in December 1949, agreeing to help finance her project in the amount of £1,000 over two years if the Elmhirst Trust also backed her.

Provided that Martin Russell confirmed his intentions in writing and that they were assured that Stan had a publisher lined up, the trust agreed to offer Stan a grant of £1,200. From the Taj Mahal Hotel, Russell wrote that a Bombay publisher might be interested in producing her books. Fortuitously, on January 26th 1950, Stan received a letter from Morley Kennerley of the publishers Faber and Faber, who were impressed with the proposal she had sent to them. If her completed manuscript met with their approval, she was assured that they would take it on. Stan was delighted, and this offer was also enough for Elmhirst and the Foundation to approve her grant. 'Thank you with all my heart,' she scribbled to Elmhirst on the 16th of February: 'I am so happy – too happy to write you a proper letter of Thanks! Am off to do what can be done to get an immediate passage to India.' After so many bitter setbacks – many of them caused by her own flightiness and obstinacy – Stan finally looked ready to achieve her dream.

* * *

Stan returned to India, and with funding assured for two years, there should have been ample time to collate the material she had collected on Indian temple dancing during the past twenty-two years, and to put it together in manuscript form. She was 66 years old and her benefactors expected nothing less than a masterpiece. It was, after all, her life's work. However, Martin Russell, still in contact with Stan, wrote on the 26th of March to Leonard Elmhirst with a familiar story. Their protégé had predictably run out of money and had not yet completed the manuscript. In fact, now she was thinking of producing four volumes. Russell asked Elmhirst if Stan could have an extension and another grant of £1,200, as he was not in a position to help any further. He outlined the problems Stan was facing: setting herself excessively high standards, interruption of work by illness, troubles with her dancers, the need of a darkroom and assistant, and her house being burgled, resulting in loss of photographic equipment, notes and manuscript: the same excuses that Elmhirst had heard fifteen years earlier.

This was enough finally to end Stan's pipe dream. Leonard wrote back to Russell on May 12th 1952 regretting that the Elmhirst Trust was 'no longer in a position to make any further grants to Mrs Harding'. Over the years they had supplied her with enough money to produce two volumes of her work and while they understood her misfortune in being robbed, they were concerned that her pursuit of perfection would postpone indefinitely her completion of the two promised volumes. Predictably, Stan was never to complete her work – and this was the last time that Martin Russell had any contact with her.

In 1953, just before leaving India for good, Josselyn Hennessy wrote to Stan who was now approaching seventy, inviting her to stay as his guest at the Malabar Hotel on Willingdon Island overlooking Cochin Harbour. Thinking that Hennessy was going to offer her work, she cashed in her last £30 and travelled hundreds of miles with her film crew of three to see him. It was to be their last meeting, and indeed here we get our last glimpse of her – in the bar of a plush hotel overlooking waters criss-crossed by boats and fringed with coconut palms. Stan had become forgetful and 'could not remember in the afternoon what she had done in the morning,' Hennessy observed, adding that 'she could not keep our plans for the afternoon fixed in her head'. It was at that moment that he had to acknowledge the sad fact that she would never complete her books on Dasi Attam.

* * *

The exact date of Stan's death has never been established. After 1947, British deaths in India were voluntarily registered with the Foreign Office, who sent details to be recorded back in Britain. As Stan was never part of the Anglo community, her death was not officially noted. Recording a death in India is not compulsory, so it is likely that her death has slipped through any records.

What is known, however, is that she was alive in March 1957 when, at the age of 73, she wrote to Leonard Elmhirst's private secretary, Doris Crump. Then in 1962, Stephen Haweis pencilled a note in the margin of his diary recording that Stan had been found dead in her caravan in India, having destroyed every name and number by which she could be identified. He implied she had committed suicide, but if, as Hennessy had earlier realised, she was developing dementia, her death might well have been accidental.

Haweis added that her addiction to opium and its availability in India were the real reason she settled there.

Stephen Haweis had been Stan Harding's first true love and, to judge from his poems, he had always had a soft spot for her. When Hennessy once asked her about the men in her life, Stan had said: 'Please turn to the Gospel of St. John, chapter four, verse fifteen: the woman of Samaria who had five husbands, and one man who had no claim to that title. In the case which interests you, we find one husband and five who have no such claim.' She added, somewhat cryptically, that they included an artist of some charm, an artist of distinction who was also an author and the son of a world-famous man, an author of numerous non-fictional works, a distinguished ethnologist, and an engineer in charge of a large-scale construction work. Whoever these men were, none was around for her in her final years. It was a sad and lonely end to an extraordinary life.

* * *

Marguerite Harrison in her later years fared much better than Stan. In the 1920s she and Arthur had bought a small château in France's Loire Valley, and until the outbreak of the Second World War they divided their time between Europe and the United States. In no way had Marguerite's life been much disturbed by the distant rumblings of the international feud with Stan.

Arthur and Marguerite Blake relocated to Hollywood on the approach of war. In 1943, she joined USO Radio (United Service Organizations), a private, non-profit organisation which offered morale-boosting and recreational services to the US military. Arthur died in 1947, and Marguerite, then 68 years old, left California and moved back to Baltimore to be near her son and his family.

Widowed for the second time, she spent her remaining years based in Baltimore, while continuing to travel widely, visiting South America, Africa, Indonesia, Australia and, frequently, Europe. In her early eighties, as intrepid a border-crosser as ever, she even managed to talk her way past Checkpoint Charlie and enter East Berlin. When at home, she played bridge, experimented with gourmet cooking, tended her garden, embroidered, carved wood and continued to lecture.

Marguerite Harrison was regarded in America not as a spy but as an intrepid journalist who travelled to exotic locations. Her book *Asia Reborn* was on university book lists, and *Grass: A Nation's Battle for Life* was selected in 1997 by the Library of Congress as being 'culturally, historically and aesthetically significant', and is preserved in the United States National Film Registry. She is remembered in particular in Catonsville, Baltimore, where she founded the Children's Hospital in

1905, on land donated by her father. For this act of generosity, she received an award from the Children's Hospital Women's Board in 1961, and in 1975 a plaque was placed on the hospital wall in her honour.

During her lifetime, Marguerite became involved with three notable organisations: the Baltimore Chapter of the Colonial Dames of America (her mother's side of the family having arrived in America with William Penn); the Society of Woman Geographers (as a founder member in 1925); and as an honorary member of the organisation for women journalists – *Theta Sigma Phi*.

This remarkable woman, who had chain-smoked for most of her life, died following a series of strokes on July 16th 1967 at the age of 88. She had chosen to be cremated and her ashes were scattered by her son Tommy in the Atlantic Ocean off the coast of Maryland.

* * *

Stan Harding was also a remarkable woman. Although she did not have Marguerite's social advantages, inherited wealth, or doughtiness and resilience, Constance Harding, at the age of nineteen, found the courage to escape her strict Plymouth Brethren upbringing, and to run away to start a new life in Florence. This was an extraordinary act of bravery for a young woman in 1906 without any form of financial support, and her courage should not be underestimated.

Twice she travelled alone to war-torn Germany during a time when few foreigners, let alone single women, entered the country. Later she ventured – alone again – into Bolshevik Russia, ignoring the British Foreign Office warning to Britons that travel to Russia was unsafe. Courageous, definitely – but somewhat wilful and unwise, too, and not always able to see where her best interests lay.

There is no doubt that Stan's dynamic personality was both a help and a hindrance. She charmed people easily with her passion and intensity, manipulating them so that they were willing to befriend her and to support her causes. Politicians, journalists, artists and rich patrons rushed to assist her – until, exhausted by her obsessions, one-by-one they tried desperately to extricate themselves from her tangled web. Such was the pattern of her life, and it was a pattern that left her feeling lonely and betrayed, for reasons that she, lacking self-knowledge, was completely unable to comprehend.

Was Stan a British spy, as Marguerite unwaveringly claimed? There is, as the British Foreign Office repeatedly stated, no evidence to suggest that she worked in an official capacity for either MI5 or MI1(c), unlike

Marguerite who received a monthly salary from the MID, with the rank of Captain and the code name 'B'.

Baron de Cosson, founder in 1881 of the Kernoozer's Club, a society of collectors and historians of arms and armour, had suggested that Stan worked for the British as a counterspy. De Cosson had lived in Florence since 1905 and was a close friend of Edward Hutton's, who helped set up the British Institute in Florence in 1917. After a disagreement with the Irish poet, Herbert Trench, regarding whether the Institute should promote British propaganda rather than just British literature, Hutton, with much bad feeling, returned to England in 1918. In a letter to Hutton, Baron de Cosson described Stan as a viper who fixed her attentions on Trench, 'hanging on his words and drinking them in as though they were inspired by the Gods'. It was Trench who had suggested that she go and talk to the British Ambassador in Rome about being sent to Germany as a counterspy while retrieving documents of her divorce.[1] However, according to de Cosson, nothing came of it.[2] And there is no evidence to be found in the private papers of Sir Samuel Hoare, the man then responsible for running British Intelligence operations in Italy, that she had been hired in this capacity.[3]

Did Stan provide the British authorities with information on an informal basis? That is highly probable. It was not uncommon for upperclass British women to pick up useful bits of gossip at diplomatic gatherings, while women from the lower ranks of society were more likely to become unpaid informers and couriers. Married women also would sometimes act as couriers, carrying money and messages from the British Government to their husbands abroad, but this, too, was usually on an informal and unpaid basis.

For a number of years, Stan travelled widely and moved in a variety of social and professional circles. It would thus have been easy for her to gather bits of information to pass on to the British authorities. And there is evidence that she did just that – one occasion being her visit to General Neill Malcolm to report on her interview with Trebitsch-Lincoln in Berlin in April 1920. Malcolm, who was responsible for ensuring that the Germans adhered to the military restrictions under the terms of the Peace Treaty, would have been open to any information that came his way.

However, while his diary records Stan's visit, there is no mention of any payment. The fact that she was always short of money and lived frugally for most of her life indicates that what she may have received for information would have been mere pocket money.

Why then did Marguerite continually insist that Stan was a spy? Because, in their first days together, Stan probably boasted to her that she was. Perhaps Stan exaggerated her – probably fictional – undercover activities in order to impress the glamorous American with whom she may have been infatuated, and who may have been, however briefly, her lover. And if Stan's deeper feelings for Marguerite were spurned, it may perhaps explain her long and bitter vendetta against her one-time friend. But a spy who boasts that she is a spy blows her own cover and is no use to any secret service. It is, therefore, unlikely that Stan was a genuine spy on the payroll with a code name and cypher table. And Marguerite would have come to that conclusion and probably confirmed the matter with her superiors.

So did Marguerite use Stan for her own purposes? It would seem highly likely. The intelligent American, as evidenced by her writings, was a perceptive observer of human nature. She would have realised that Stan, if handled correctly, could provide her with details of the Socialist contacts that she had made through her friendship with the bisexual artist, Käthe Kollwitz. She could also play the part of Marguerite's 'fool spy'. A fool spy, according to British First World War agent Ferdinand Tuohy, 'was a man or a woman, either a convicted spy or more rarely a simpleton, who was deliberately engaged by an Intelligence Department in order that he or she might be caught by the enemy. The purpose of the fool-spy is to deceive the enemy's contra-espionage organisation in order to protect the real spies, the valuable ones.'[4]

From the day Stan made the decision to visit Russia, she was doomed to play the part of a pawn in the great game between nations. And so she became first MID's 'fool spy', then a weapon to be used both by Britain and Russia in the negotiations over the Anglo-Soviet Trade Agreement, and finally as a tool for politicians and journalists seeking to promote their own causes. It was excellent sport for everyone except Stan, who was never able completely to recover either physically or mentally from her Russian ordeal.

Stan Harding and Marguerite Harrison's adventures throw light on part of a small contingent of foreigners who were closely involved both in Germany immediately after the First World War and in the early days of Bolshevik Russia. Also, they were lone women operating in a treacherous, male-dominated system, in which their lives were often in great peril. The imperturbable and resilient Marguerite was eventually able to settle comfortably back into life in America, seemingly unaffected by her experiences. When asked what she thought of Stan's campaign against her she wrote: 'I have never ceased to regret the terrible misunderstanding between us, for I was genuinely fond of her. She was such a brilliant person and so lovable that it seemed a thousand pities that her whole life should have been embittered by her fancied wrongs.'

But, for Stan life had never been easy, nor would it ever be. Maybe she best summed up the philosophy that helped her survive when bidding farewell to her friend Josselyn Hennessy before he left India. Asked what she thought the marvel of her life to be, she replied after much thought: 'Hope thou not much, but then fear not at all.' Stan had, of course, hoped for much in her life, but these words were appropriate nonetheless. If she was too often disappointed in her hopes, she had certainly lived her life courageously.

Appendix

'For Stan Harding Krayl'
by Stephen Haweis
14 November 1963

Once in a Blue moon
when we two, within view
of Santa Maria Novella
Together in the afternoon
Forgetting even poverty
And there dull sound to plod
Blind but to one another
Reached up I own hands
claiming as right of property.
So nearly – if not quite –
Touching the aura of almighty God –
How seldom, how little,
another end too soon –
Once in a blue moon.

Yet was enough to be
age old in memory
wherein to hide
Love, I'll ... [illegible] for me -
Those hours were comforting,
Even transforming
As a wood-fire.
And, though we wandered far
with all I still compare
With thee who gave
All that you were, and are
now in some Sirius moon
or more remote star
Once in a blue moon!

Underneath the poem Haweis wrote:
'Those who are wise in spiritual things grieve neither for the dead, nor for
the living' – Gita. I hope devoutly that your good fortune will continue.

'Heaven'
by Stephen Haweis

Time and their gift of tears wash all over sorrows
away with a gilded sunset, like the end of a natural day
Shall we meet at some future time and smile together
because we wept when she, our dearest on earth, had just then
ended her day, and slept?
Do you remember, we shall say, how I thought that I
never could be happy without your dear embrace, and your kiss to
comfort me?
Yet, here we are both together again, as we always longed to be
you and I together – one self – till the end of Time maybe ...
And not because we have anything more than we had when we
dwelt on earth; but that we reached up and touched – god – and
have no more need of birth.

Stephen Haweis, unpublished poems (1962-66), Rare Book and Manuscript Library, Columbia University, New York

Acknowledgements

I would like to thank the following people and institutions for supporting me in my quest to write this fascinating tale of two women's adventures.

Without the cooperation and help from archivists in the following institutions, I would not have been able to find and use the interesting material available. These include the National Archives, Kew; the National Archives, College Park, Maryland; Columbia University, New York; the National Library of Congress, Washington, D.C.; the New York Public Library, New York; The Baltimore Public Library, Catonsville; St Antony's College, Oxford University; Nuffield College, Oxford University; The Bodleian Library, Oxford University; The British Library, London; University of Cambridge Library, Cambridge; and the Parliamentary Archives, London.

A special thank you goes to Alyson Price from the British Institute of Florence and to Eleonora Pancani from the Archivio Contemporaneo "Alessandro Bonsanti", Gabinetto G.P. Vieusseux, Florence, who were so helpful in passing on information about the Anglo-American community living in Florence before the First World War. Also to Yvonne Widger from High Cross House, Dartington Hall and the Dartington Hall Trust Archives for allowing me to read correspondence between Leonard and Dorothy Elmhirst and Mrs Stan Harding. And to Bryce Rumbles, librarian and archivist from Baltimore's public library, Catonsville, who spent several hours with me tracking down information and photos of Marguerite.

I would like to thank the following people who were also particularly helpful to me. Marsha Filion tracked down a German copy of Beate Bonus-Jeep's memoirs, *Sechzig Jahre Freundschaft mit Käthe Kollwitz*, from which Anne-Marie Asquith made translations for me. My sister-in-law, Cara Bradley, librarian at the University of Regina, ordered the books in Canada that I could not find in England. Helen Rappaport pointed me in the right direction with anything related to Russia and introduced me to Phil Tomaselli, who dug out some amazing information for me on Stan at the National Archives, Kew. Armyn Hennessy sent me the unpublished biography of Stan Harding written by his father, Josselyn Hennessy. Tomi Ahoranta, Research Officer at the National Archives of Finland, found information on Dr Thure Gustaf Grönlund, the doctor who examined Stan when she arrived in Finland in 1920. Sir Michael Holroyd gave me useful background information on Edward Gordon Craig's relationship with Stan Harding. Thank you also to Mrs Helen Roosevelt for giving permission to reprint the poems of Stephen Haweis. And also to Sandra Kiemele, Beryl

Haslam and the staff at the Dundas Museum Archives in Dundas, Ontario, for sharing with me their information on the Lesslies, Stan's maternal family. I am also grateful for their hospitality in Dundas.

A special thank you goes to the Bradshaw family: Stephen and Destine for putting me up on my various trips to Washington, D.C., to Ben for researching material I couldn't get in the UK, and to Andrew, for keeping me amused. My father, Bunny, was responsible for keeping my spirits up by cooking his amazing Sunday roasts, and my best friend, Sue Adams, patiently read my first draft before I dared show my agent Christopher Sinclair-Stevenson. Christopher, along with Tom Wallace in New York, have proved to be the kindest agents a novice writer like myself can have. They spent a considerable amount of time reading drafts and offering invaluable comments and advice which have contributed to the final version. I am indebted to you both.

And finally, to my husband, Ross King. Ross never stopped believing in me or my project. His ability to reassure and calm me kept me going on more than one occasion. It goes without saying that his love and continuous support made this book happen, and that is why this book is dedicated to him.

Permissions

Permission to publish unpublished poems of Stephen Haweis, housed in the Rare Book & Manuscript Library, Columbia University, New York has been given by Mrs John E. Roosevelt; permission to publish Edward Gordon Craig's black cutouts of Beauty, The Beast and Eve has been granted by UCLA Library Special Collections; permission to publish photograph of Lesslie family home granted by Dundas Museum and Archives, Dundas, Ontario; permission to publish photograph of Ingleside, Baltimore Public Library, Catonsville, Maryland; permission granted by The Dartington Hall Trust Archive to quote from the Elmhirst letters. Map by John Gilkes.

Dramatis Personae

PART ONE

Ames, Joseph Sweetman – Physics professor at Johns Hopkins University and Marguerite's stepfather-in-law

Barnes, James Strachey – friend of Stan's

Berenson, Bernard – Lithuanian-American author of art history and lived at Villa I Tatti

Black, Van Lear – Chairman of the Board, *The Baltimore Sun*

Bouvier, Colonel – American Intelligence Officer Berlin and Marguerite's contact (1918-1919)

Churchill, Brigadier-General Marlborough – head of Military Intelligence, War Department (1918-20)

Churchill, Winston – British Minister of Munitions (1917-19) and Secretary of State for War (1919-1921)

Craig, Edward Gordon – British artist and avant-garde theatre director

Delmer, Frederic Sefton – Australian professor and correspondent for *The Daily News*

Dodge, Mabel – American expatriate, 'freelance intellectual' and writer

Ebert, Friedrich – moderate Social Democrat, 1st Chancellor of the German Reich (1918-1919) and 1st President of German Reich (1919-1925)

Harding, Harold – British Consul in China and Stan Harding's brother

Harrison, Thomas Bullitt – Baltimore lawyer and husband of Marguerite

Haweis, Stephen – English painter, husband of Mina Loy

Hoare, Samuel – Head of SIS in Italy

Kent, Frank – Editor of *The Baltimore Sun*

Kollwitz, Käthe – German painter and sculptor

Krayl, Karl – German doctor married to Stan Harding

Lees, Dorothy Nevile – English writer and lover of Gordon Craig

Liebknecht, Karl – Spartacus League Leader (1914-1919)

Litvinov, Maxim – Roaming ambassador for Russian Socialist Republic

Loy, Mina – English artist and poet, wife of Haweis

Luxemburg, Rosa – Spartacus League Leader (1914-1919)

Martens, Ludwig C.C.K. – Soviet representative in the US (1919-21)

Minor, Robert – American Socialist cartoonist imprisoned in Germany 1919 for distributing Communist propaganda to troops

Nolan, General Dennis Edward – American Chief of Intelligence based in Trier, Germany

Noske, Gustav – German Defence Minister (1919-1920)

Reed, John – American journalist and Communist

Ritchie, Albert Cabell – Attorney General of Maryland and 49th Governor of Maryland, Marguerite's brother-in-law

Thorold, Algar Labouchere – Head of Britain's Propaganda Mission in Italy

Trench, Herbert – an Irish-born poet and vice-chairman of the Istituto Britannico

Van Deman, Colonel Ralph – ex-head of MID and attached to the peace delegation in Paris (1919)

Wilson, Woodrow – President of the United States, Democrat (1913-21)

Part Two

Aksyonov, Ivan Aleksandrovich (Axionov) – Former member of Tsarist secret police, employed by Cheka. Manager of the Haritonevsky Guest House

Allen, Clifford – British Trades Union Delegate to Russia May 1920 and member of the British Fabian Society and pacifist

Astor, Lady Nancy – Conservative MP (1919-1945)

Balabanova, Angelica – stand-in for Karl Radek (1919-1920)

Berkman, Alexander – Russian anarchist and leader of the Union of Russian Worker (URW)

Bryant, Louise – American journalist and wife of John Reed

Chicherin, Georgy – People's Commissar for Foreign Affairs (1918-1930)

Cooper, Merian C. – American pilot with the Kościuszko Squadron and film director

Curzon, Lord George – 1st Marquess Curzon of Kedleston, Foreign Secretary, Conservative, (1919-24)

Dzerzhinsky, Felix – Head of the Cheka (1917-1926)

Emmott, Lord Alfred – Presided over the Emmott Committee collecting information on Russia (1920-21)

Goldman, Emma – Russian anarchist and leader of the Union of Russian Worker (URW)

Haden-Guest, Leslie – British Trades Union Delegate to Russia May 1920 and medical doctor

Kamenev, Lev Borisovich – Chairman of the Moscow Soviet and member Anglo-Soviet trade delegation to Britain

Kapp, Wolfgang – Co-founder of the Fatherland Party and leader of the Kapp Putsch (March 1920)

Karlin, Anna – Russian doctor and Marguerite's translator

Kilmarnock, Victor Alexander Sereld Hay, 21st Earl of Erroll and 4th Baron – British Chargé d'Affaires in Berlin (1919-1920)

Kollontai, Alexandra – People's Commissar for Social Welfare

Krasin, Leonid – People's Commissar of Ways and Communications

Lenin, Vladimir [Vladimir Ilyich Ulyanov] – Head of Russian Socialist Republic (1917-1924)

Lloyd George, David – Conservative Prime Minister (1916-22)

Malcolm, General Neill – Chief of the British Military Mission in Berlin

McCullagh, Francis – Journalist and British Intelligence Officer with the Expeditionary Force in Siberia

Menzhinsky, Vyacheslav Rudolfovich – Head of Special Section of the Cheka

Mogilevsky, Solomon Grigorevich – Head of the Foreign Espionage Department of the Extraordinary Commission (Cheka) in Moscow

Nansen, Fridtjof – Norwegian polar explorer, neuroscientist, diplomat and League of Nations representative organising repatriation of prisoners from Russia

Paderewski, Ignacy Jan – First Prime Minister of Second Polish Republic (1919)

Radek, Karl – Organised German Communist movement (1918-1920) and Secretary of Extraordinary Committee (1920-1924)

Rosenberg, Mikail – Translator from the Western Section of the Commissariat of Foreign Affairs in Moscow

Russell, Bertrand – British Trades Union Delegate to Russia May 1920 and Cambridge University mathematician and Socialist philosopher

Sheridan, Clare – British sculptor, cousin of Winston Churchill who visited Moscow (October 1920)

Snowden, Ethel – British Trades Union Delegate to Russia May 1920, wife of Philip and leading campaigner for women's suffrage

Snowden, Philip – British Trades Union Delegate to Russia May 1920, pacifist, and former British Labour MP

Solbert, Major Oscar – American Military Attaché in London

Tallents, Stephen – British Consulate in Riga, Republic of Latvia

Trebitsch-Lincoln, Timothy – Wolfgang Kapp's press censor (March 1920)

Trotsky, Leon [Lev Bronstein] – People's Commissar for foreign Affairs (1917-1918) and People's Commissar for Army and Navy Affairs (1918-1925)

Tuohy, James – European editor of the New York World who commissioned Stan to go to Russia

Voigt, Frederick Augustus – Correspondent for *The Manchester Guardian*
Wells, H. G. – British writer visited Moscow (October 1920)

PART THREE

Baldwin, Stanley – Conservative Prime Minister (1923-29)
Bonar Law, Andrew – Conservative Prime Minister (1922-23)
Cecil, Lord Robert – Under-Secretary of State for Foreign Affairs, Conservative (1915-1919) and Lord Privy Seal (1923-1924)
Chamberlain, Austen – Foreign Secretary, Conservative, (1924-29)
Coolidge, Calvin – President of the United States, Republican (1923-29)
France, Joseph Irwin – Maryland Senator (1917-23)
Gollancz, Victor – Gollancz Publishing
Grosvenor, Jessie – widow an friend of Stan who accompanies her to American Embassy for questioning
Gukovsky, Isidor – Head of Soviet Mission in Reval (Tallinn), Estonia (1920)
Harding, Warren G – President of the USA, Republican (1921-23)
Harmsworth, Cecil – Under-Secretary of State for Foreign Affairs, Liberal (1919-22)
Hoover, Herbert Clark – Mining engineer and founder of commission for the Relief of Belgium and the American Relief Administration – food aid to Russia (1920-22)
Hoover, John Edgar – Special Assistant to the Attorney General
Hughes, Charles Evans – American Secretary of State, anti-relations with Soviet Russia.
McNeill, Ronald – Under-Secretary of State for Foreign Affairs, Conservative, (1922-24) (1924-25)
Perlman, Philip – Secretary of State for Maryland
Pilchau, Romuald Pilar von – Assistant section head, Foreign Espionage secant of GPU, Moscow
Ponsonby, Arthur – Under-Secretary of State for Foreign Affairs, Labour, (1924)
Poole, D.C. – State Department, Washington D.C
Richardson, Henry Marriott – President of the National Union of Journalists, UK
Schoedsack, Ernest Beaumont – First World War film cameraman
Springfield, George – President of the Institute of Journalists, London
Tikhon, Patriarch of Moscow – Head of the Russian Orthodox Church under house arrest in Moscow (1917-1924)

Part Four

Elmhirst, Dorothy and Leonard Knight – Philanthropists who owned Dartington Hall in Devon.

Escudero, Vicente – Catalonian flamenco dancer based in Paris

Ewart, Sir John Murray – Director of Intelligence for the Government of India

Gwatkin, Fred – The Elmhirsts' lawyer from McKenna & Co. Solicitors

Hennessy, Josselyn – New Delhi Imperial Secretariat

MacDonald, Ramsay – Labour Prime Minister (1924) Foreign Secretary (1924)

Massine, Léonide – Russian ballet dancer who once danced for the Ballets Russes

Russell, Martin – Artist and member of '43 Group' and nephew of Bertrand Russell

Glossary of Terms

ARA –   American Relief Administration
Cheka – Russian Extraordinary Commission for the Suppression of Counter Revolution
FBI –   Federal Bureau of Investigation
FO –   Foreign Office
HMG – His Majesty's Government
IPI –   Indian Political Intelligence
MID –   Military Intelligence Department (American)
M1i(c) – Secret Intelligence Service, First World War (British)
MI5 –   Security Service (British)
MI6 –   Secret Intelligence Service after First World War (British)
MP –   Member of Parliament
NA –   National Archives, Maryland, United States of America
NUJ –   National Union of Journalists
OGPU – Obyedinennoye Gosudarstvennoye Politicheskoye Upravleniye (Soviet Security and Intelligence service, 1923-34) Successor of the Cheka (Russian)
ONI –   Office of Naval Intelligence (American)
PCO –   Passport Officer
SIS –   Secret Intelligence Service (British)
TNA –   The National Archives, Kew, United Kingdom
WO –   War Office

Endnotes

PROLOGUE – Lubyanka, October 1920

1   For details of the incarceration in Lubyanka, see Stan Harding, *The Underworld of State* (London: George Allen & Unwin, 1925), pp. 79-129. All quotes from Stan Harding unless otherwise stated are taken from *The Underworld of State*.

PART ONE

CHAPTER 1 – Born for Trouble – pp. 13-23

1   All quotes from Marguerite Harrison unless otherwise stated are taken from *Marooned in Moscow: The Story of an American Woman Imprisoned in Russia* (London: Thornton Butterworth Limited, 1921), *Born for Trouble* (London: Victor Gollancz, 1936) or *There's Always Tomorrow: The Story of a Chequered Life* (New York: Farrar & Rinehart, 1935).
2   Catherine M. Griggs, Beyond Boundaries (Doctoral Dissertation, George Washington University, 1996), p. 72.
3   Harold A. Williams, *The Baltimore Sun 1837-1987* (Baltimore: Johns Hopkins University Press, 1987), p. 151.
4   Quoted in Griggs, *Beyond Boundaries*, p. 85.
5   Marguerite Harrison, 'The Story of a Woman who Worked a Week in a Shipyard', *The Baltimore Sun*, 8 May 1918.
6   Marguerite Harrison, 'The Record of the First Day's Work in a Shipyard', *The Baltimore Sun*, 9 May 1918.
7   Marguerite Harrison, 'Baltimore's Bohemia Imbued with True American Spirit', *The Baltimore Sun*, 18 June 1918.
8   File PF-39205, RG 165, War Department General Staff, MID, Box 607, NA. Letter from Harrison to Marlborough Churchill, 21 September 1918.
9   *Ibid.* Letter from Dr Ames to Marlborough Churchill.

CHAPTER 2 – Agent 'B' – 24-34

1   *Ibid.*, Letter from Captain Dick Slaughter to Marguerite Harrison, 2nd December 1918.
2   Karl Baedeker, *Northern Germany as far as the Bavarian and Austrian Frontiers: Handbook for Travellers* (Leipzig: K. Baedeker, 1913), p. 55.
3   *Ibid.*, p. 23.

4 Stewart Roddie, *Peace Patrol* (London: Christophers, 1932), p. 14.
5 Anthony Read, *The World on Fire* (London: Jonathan Cape, 2008), p. 41.
6 The Dada artist Richard Huelsenbeck, quoted in Seth Taylor, *Left-Wing Nietzscheans: The Politics of German Expressionism, 1910-1920* (Berlin: Walter de Gruyter & Co., 1990), p. 187.
7 Read, *The World on Fire*, p. 74.
8 Roddie, *Peace Patrol*, p. 11.
9 Ernest Tennant, *True Account* (London: Max Parrish & Co., 1957), p. 86.
10 Jay Winter and Jean-Louis Robert, *Capital Cities at War* (Cambridge: Cambridge University Press, 1997), p. 321.
11 Nancy Caldwell Sorel, *The Women who Wrote the War* (New York: Time Warner, 1999), p. 4.
12 *Beate Bonus-Jeep, Sechzig Jahre Freundschaft mit Käthe Kollwitz* (Berlin: Boppard, Karl Rauch Verlag, 1948), translated by Anne-Marie Asquith for the author.

CHAPTER 3 – The Beauty and the Beast – 35-47

1 'Landmarks of Toronto: The Lesslie Stores', *Evening Telegram*, 17 August 1889.
2 Stephen Haweis, Unpublished diaries 1961-63. (Rare books, Butler Library, Columbia University, New York).
3 Josselyn Hennessy, *One Man and Three Extraordinary Women* (unpublished c. 1954), p. 8.
4 *Ibid.*, p. 15.
5 Jill Aebi-Mytton, 'An Explanatory Study of the Mental Health of Former Members of the Exclusive Branch of the Plymouth Brethren', M.Sc. Counselling thesis, Goldsmiths College, 1993.
6 Dodge Luhan, *European Experiences, Vol. Two,* (New York: Harcourt, Brace and Co., 1935), p. 337.
7 *Your Dear Letter: Private Correspondence of Queen Victoria and the Crown Princess of Prussia, 1865–1871*, ed. Roger Fulford (London: Evans Bros., 1971), p. 248.
8 *Ibid.*, p. 177.
9 Frederick Hoffman, *Freudianism and the Literary Mind* (Baton Rouge: Louisiana State University Press, 1945), p 45.
10 Handwritten notes by Dorothy Nevile Lees on her copy of Mabel Dodge's, *European Experiences, Vol. 2*, p. 343. Copy held at the British Institute in Florence.
11 Quoted in Michael Holroyd, *A Strange Eventful History* (London: Vintage, 2009), p. 468.
12 James Strachey Barnes, *Half a Life* (London: Eyre & Spottiswoode, 1933), p. 182.
13 Hennessy, *One Man and Three Extraordinary Women*, p. 15.
14 *Ibid.*

15 Dodge Luhan, *European Experiences, Vol. 2*, p. 342.

16 Strachey Barnes, *Half a Life*, pp. 120, 182.

17 Letter to Miss Doris Crump, 3 March 1957, Elmhirst Estate, Dartington Hall.

18 Haweis, Unpublished diaries, 1961-63.

19 *Ibid.*

20 All quotes from Käthe Kollwitz unless otherwise stated are from *Beate Bonus-Jeep, Sechzig Jahre Freundschaft mit Käthe Kollwitz* (Berlin: Boppard, Karl Rauch Verlag, 1948), translated by Anne-Marie Asquith for the author.

21 Hennessy, *One Man and Three Extraordinary Women*, p. 19.

22 *Ibid.* p. 19.

23 *Ibid.* pp. 20-21.

24 Käthe Kollwitz, *The Diary and Letters of Käthe Kollwitz*, ed. Hans Kollwitz, trans. Richard and Clara Winston, (Chicago: Henry Regnery Company, 1955), p. 62.

25 *Ibid.*

26 *Ibid.*, p. 87.

27 Dodge Luhan, *European Experiences, Vol. 2*, p. 317.

28 *Ibid.* p. 338.

29 Mina Loy, *The Last Lunar Baedeker* (Charlotte: The Jargon Society, 1982), p. 57.

30 Stephen Haweis, Unpublished diaries 1961-63 (Columbia University, New York).

31 Dodge Luhan, *European Experiences, Vol. 2*, p. 343.

CHAPTER 4 – Mrs Harding, I Presume? – 48-56

1 P.D. Coates, *The China Consuls, British Consular Officers 1843-1943* (Hong Kong: Oxford University Press, 1988), pp. 440, 483.

2 *Ibid.*, p. 483.

3 Hennessy, *One Man and Three Extraordinary Women*, p. 23.

4 *Ibid.*, p. 24.

5 *Ibid.*, p. 25.

6 *Ibid.*

7 Mabel Dodge Luhan, *Movers and Shakers* (New Mexico: University of New Mexico Press, 1985) p. 434.

8 Hennessy, *One Man and Three Extraordinary Women*, p. 37.

9 Quoted in Eric Homberger, *John Reed* (Manchester: Manchester University Press, 1990), p. 29.

10 Walter Lippmann, 'Legendary John Reed', *The New Republic*, 26 Dec. 1914.

11 Dodge Luhan, *Movers and Shakers*, p. 219.

12 Quoted in Homberger, *John Reed*, p. 52.

13 Quoted in *Ibid.*, p. 53.

14 Quoted in Stanley G. Payne, *A History of Fascism, 1914-1945* (Madison: University of Wisconsin Press, 1995), p. 63.
15 Ernest Samuels and Jayne NewcomerSamuels, *Bernard Berenson: The Making of a Legend* (Belknap Press of Harvard University Press, 1987), p. 200.
16 Quoted in Spencer C. Tucker, ed., *Encyclopedia of World War I* (Santa Barbara: ABC-CLIO, Inc., 2005), p. 941.
17 *Minutes of Evidence* taken before the Committee appointed to collect information on Russia. TNA 371/6867 – 4N103, p. 194.
18 Brock Millman, *Pessimism and British War Policy*, 1916-1918 (London: Frank Cass, 2001), p. 64.
19 Tom Kington, 'Recruited by MI5: The Name's Mussolini: Benito Mussolini', *The Guardian*, 13 October 2009.
20 *Minutes of Evidence*, p. 194.
21 Quoted in Ralph H. Lutz, *The German Revolution, 1918-1919* (Cambridge: Cambridge University Press, 1967), p. 128.

CHAPTER 5 – The Conveyance of the Twain – 57-66

1 Count Harry Kessler, *The Diaries of a Cosmopolitan 1918-1937*, trans. Charles Kessler (London: Weidenfeld & Nicholson, 1999), p. 85.
2 *Ibid.*, p. 86.
3 *Ibid.*, p. 89.
4 Quoted in Anthony Read, *The World on Fire*, p. 104
5 Marguerite Harrison, 'Intimate Glimpses of Life in Post-war Germany', *The Baltimore Sun*, 14 September 1919.
6 Edwin L. James, 'Minor was Warned by Max Eastman', *The New York Times*, 12 July 1919, p. 2.

PART TWO

CHAPTER 6 – Agent 'B' Redux – 67-68

1 File PF-39205, RG 165, War Department General Staff, MID, Box 607, National Archives. Note from Davis to Churchill, 5 August 1919.
2 *Ibid.* Memo from MID, Washington, D.C. to Military Attaché, American Embassy, Paris, 22 October 1919.

CHAPTER 7 – An Unkindness of Ravens – 71-81

1 *Ibid.*
2 Joe Fineberg (1886-1957) was born in Poland and lived in Hackney, London.

He returned to Russia in July 1918 and became an interpreter for the Bolshevik Foreign Office.

3 Letter from Kalamatiano to Samuel Harper, quoted in Harry and Marjorie Mahoney, *American Prisoners of the Bolsheviks* (Bethesda: Academica Press 2001), p. 307.

4 Quoted in Sheila Fitzpatrick, *The Commissariat of Enlightenment*: *Soviet Organisation of Education and the Arts Under Lunacharsky* (Cambridge: Cambridge University Press, 1970), pp. 1-2.

5 James H. Billington, *Fire in the Minds of Men*: *Origins of the Revolutionary Faith* (New Brunswick, NJ: Transaction Books, 1999), p. 479.

6 Quoted in *ibid.*, p. 480.

7 Hector Boon, *Russia From the Inside* (New York World, 1921), pp. 26, 37.

8 Billington, *Fire in the Minds of Men*, p. 62.

9 Quoted in Emma Goldman, *My Disillusionment in Russia* (New York: Doubleday, Page & Co., 1923), p. 260.

10 Quoted in George Leggett, *The Cheka*: *Lenin's Political Police* (Oxford: Clarendon Press, 1981), p. 252.

11 *Ibid.*, p. 189.

12 Quoted in John S. Craig, *Peculiar Liaisons*: *In War, Espionage, and Terrorism in the Twentieth Century* (New York: Algora Publishing, 2005), p. 66.

13 Quoted in Orlando Figes, *A People's Tragedy*: *The Russian Revolution, 1891-1924* (London: Jonathan Cape, 1996), pp. 524-5.

CHAPTER 8 – Striding into Strife with a Gleam in Her Eye– 82-91

1 J.C. Segrue, *The Daily News*, 2 March 1920.

2 Quoted in Read, *The World on Fire*, p. 320.

3 Morgan Philips Price, *Despatches from the Weimar Republic* (London: Pluto Press, 1999), p. 72.

4 *Ibid.*

5 Mrs Stan Harding, *The Daily News*, 30 March 1920.

6 Hennessy, *One Man and Three Extraordinary Women*, p. 48

7 *The Daily News*, 6 April 1920, p. 1.

8 Hennessy, p. 49.

9 Georgi Konstantinovitch Popoff, *The Tcheka*: *The Red Inquisition* (London: A.M. Philpot Ltd, 1925), p. 68.

10 Goldman, *My Disillusionment in Russia*, p. 25.

11 Francis McCullagh, *A Prisoner of the Reds* (London: John Murray, 1921), p. 66.

12 *Ibid.*, p. 190.

13 *Ibid.*, p.317.

14 Patriarch Tikhon was born Vasily Ivanovich Bellavin and died 7 April 1925 and is buried in the Old Cathedral at Donskoy Monastery.

CHAPTER 9 – The Death Ship – 91-98

1 McCullagh, *Prisoner of the Reds*, p. 272.
2 Popoff, *The Tcheka*, p. 125.
3 File PF-39205, RG 165 (War Department General Staff) MID, Box 607, NA.
4 McCullagh was issued exit papers the following month along with other British, including Reverend North and his family. Dr Karlin spent a couple of weeks with Marguerite before offering her services to the Bolsheviks as a doctor.
5 File PF-39205, RG 165 (War Department General Staff), MID. Box 607, NA.Ciphers no. 74 and 75.
6 The Malcolm Diary (unpublished), St Antony's College, Oxford University.
7 Quoted in Ruth Fischer, *Stalin and German Communism: A Study in the Origins of the State Party* (Cambridge MA: Harvard University Press, 1948; 2nd edition, New Brunswick, NJ: Transaction Publishers, 1982), p. 122.
8 *The Daily News*, 3 May 1920
9 File PF-39205, RG 165 (War Department General Staff) MID, Box 607, NA.Memo from Colonel Solbert to MID, Washington D.C., dated 21 June 1920.

CHAPTER 10 – A Completely Crazy Plan – 99-106

1 Quoted in Patrick Wright, *Iron Curtain: From Stage to Cold War* (Oxford: Oxford University Press, 2007), p. 131
2 Goldman, *My Disillusionment in Russia*, p. 59.
3 Box 1 Had/1 – The Papers of Haden-Guest, Parliamentary Archives.
4 *Minutes of Evidence* – the Committee to Collect Information on Russia, p. 161.
5 *Ibid.*, p. 162.
6 *Ibid.*
7 *Ibid.*, pp. 170-1
8 *Ibid.*, pp. 167.
9 *Ibid.*
10 *Ibid.*
11 Ibid., p. 163-4.
12 *Ibid.*
13 *Ibid.*, pp. 174, 183.
14 *Ibid.*, p. 164.
15 *Ibid.*, p. 165.
16 *Ibid.*, p. 166.

17 *Ibid.*, p. 168.
18 *Ibid.*, p. 169.

Chapter 11 – The House of Suspicion – 107-114

1   Boon, *Russia From the Inside*, p. 33.
2   *Minutes of Evidence*, p. 170.
3   *Ibid.*
4   *Ibid.*, p. 171.
5   Boon, *Russia From the Inside*, pp. 38, 39, 40.
6   *Minutes of Evidence*, p. 172.
7   *Ibid.*
8   *Ibid.*, pp. 172-3.
9   *Ibid.*, p. 173.
10 *Ibid.*
11 *Ibid.*
12 *Ibid.*
13 See Tammy M. Proctor, *Female Intelligence: Women and Espionage in the First World War* (New York: New York University Press, 2003).
14 *Minutes of Evidence*, p. 174.
15 *Ibid.*, p. 176.
16 *Ibid.*, p. 177.
17 *Ibid.*, p. 183.
18 *Ibid.*, pp. 178-9.
19 *Ibid.*, p. 180.
20 *Ibid.*, pp. 182-3.
21 *Ibid.*, p. 186.
22 *Ibid.*, p. 193.
23 *Ibid.*, p. 192-3.
24 *Ibid.*, p. 188.

Chapter 12 – A Dust Heap of Lies – 115-122

1   *New York Times*, 25 September 1921.
2   *New York Times*, 17 September 1921.
3   File PF-39205, RG 165 (War Department General Staff) MID, Box 607, NA. Telegram dated 1 October 1920.
4   *Minutes of Evidence*, p. 189
5   *Ibid.*, p. 193.
6   *Ibid.*
7   *Ibid.*, p. 194.

8   *Ibid.*, p. 195.
9   *Ibid.*, p. 196.
10 *Ibid.*, p. 194.
11 *Ibid.*, p. 197.
12 *Ibid.*, p. 200.
13 Quoted in Harry Thayer Mahoney et al., *American Prisoners of the Bolsheviks: The Genesis of Modern American Intelligence* (Bethesda: Academica Press, 2001), p. 307.

CHAPTER 13 – Prisoner 3041 – 123-129

1   H.G. Wells, *Russia in the Shadows* (London: Hodder & Stoughton Ltd, 1920), p. 128
2   File PF-39205, RG 165 (War Department General Staff), MID, Box 607, NA. Memorandum dated April 27, 1920.
3   Popoff, *The Tcheka*, p. 80.
4   *New York Times*, 4 September 1921
5   Popoff, *The Tcheka*, p. 141.

CHAPTER 14 – Freedom – 130-137

1   TNA, FO 371/4425 (32 A) – 4N88.
2   TNA, FO 371/5427 (32 A) – 4N88.
3   TNA, FO 371/5426 (32 A) – 4N88.
4   Moscow Political Red Cross, 6 October 1920.
5   Dr Thure Gustaf Grönlund specialised in epidemiology and was the chief surgeon at Terijoli and Kellomäki quarantine centres between 1918 and 1922. Information supplied by the National Archives of Finland.
6   TNA, FO 511/5 (32 A) – 3W1620.
7   *Ibid.*
8   *New York Times*, 4 September 1921.
9   RG 165 (War Department General Staff), MID, Box 607, National Archives. Letter from Harold Carlson, dated 18 August, 1920.
10 *Ibid.*, Letter from Dr Ames to General Nolan, dated 3 January 1921

PART THREE

CHAPTER 15 – Probably Undesirable to Call Attention to Her – 141-149

1   *New York Times*, 6 May 1921.
2   *Minutes of Evidence*, pp. 161-203.

3   TNA, FO 371/6857 letter from Lord Emmott to Lord Curzon.

4   *Ibid*. Internal memo from Harry Crookshank.

5   Quoted in X.J. Eudin, *Soviet Russia and the West 1920-1927* (Stanford: Stanford University Press, 1957), p. 6.

6   TNA, FO 371/6913 internal memo from C. Howard Smith.

7   Quoted in Bertrand M. Patenaude, *The Big Show in Bololand* (Stanford: Stanford University Press, 2002).

8   Despite the harsh winter of March 1922, the ARA negotiated hundreds of railroad cars over collapsing railroads filled with grain for planting and it should not be forgotten that the ARA played an important role in the reconstruction of the Soviet railways.

CHAPTER 16 – America Will Protect its Agent – 150-158

1   14 July 1921, Parliamentary Question from Lord Robert Cecil to Under-Secretary of State.

2   TNA, FO 371/6913 Draft reply to Parliamentary question 14 July 1921.

3   *Ibid*., reply to supplementary Parliamentary question 16 July 1921.

4   Statistics provided by Secretary for Foreign Affairs, Ronald McNeill to the House, 7 December 1925. HC Deb 7 December Vol 189 cc50-1w.

5   *Ibid*., Internal memo dated 15 August 1921.

6   TNA, FO 371/6913 Letter from S. Harding to Cecil Harmsworth, 19 August 1921.

7   *Correspondence with the Russian Soviet Government respecting the Imprisonment of Mrs. Stan Harding in Russia. Russia No. 1*, 1922.

8   Quoted in John Lofton, *The Press as Guardian of the First Amendment*. p. xiii

9   RG 165 (War Department General Staff), MID, Box 607, NA.Letter from Brigadier-General Marlborough Churchill to Major Oscar N. Solbert, 22 September 1921.

10 TNA, FO 371/6913. Copy of telegram from Louise Bryant, Moscow, to Karl Wiegand, Berlin Staff correspondent of Hearst Newspapers, 6 January 1921.

11 *Ibid*.

12 Letter from Solbert to Marlborough Churchill, 9 November 1921. RG 165 (War Department General Staff), MID, Box 607, National Archives.

13 TNA, FO 371/6913 Letter dated 3 November 1921 from Mrs Stan Harding to Cecil Harmsworth.

14 N.J. Crowson, ed, *Fleet Street, Press Barons and Politics: The Journals of Collin Brooks, 1932-40* (Cambridge: Cambridge University Press), 1998, p. 43.

15 *Correspondence with the Russian Soviet Government respecting the Imprisonment of Mrs. Stan Harding in Russia*. Letter dated 2 December 1921 from Lord Curzon to Hodgson.

16 *Ibid.*
17 TNA, FO 371/8169. Internal memo dated 4 January 1922.
18 *Ibid.*, letter from Stan Harding to O. Harvey dated 3 January 192
19 *Ibid.*, internal memo, FO, dated 2 February 1922.
20 *Ibid.*, internal memo, FO, dated 25 February 1922.
21 *Ibid.*, Letter to Harding from Harmsworth 7 April 1922.
22 *New York Times*, 12 June, 1922
23 TNA, FO 371/8169. Letter from Patrick Roberts to Esmond Overy, 3 July 1922.
24 *Ibid.*, Letter from Sir Philip Lloyd-Greame to Cecil Harmsworth, 4 July 1922.
25 *Ibid.*, Internal memo from Esmond Overy discussing Davison's Parliamentary question, 12 July 1922.

Chapter 17 – The Bane of Our Lives – 159-168

1 Written by Reverend Amisted Welborn in *The Baltimore Sun*, 17 December 1922.
2 Marguerite Harrison, 'Cross Currents in Japan', *The Atlantic Monthly*, July 1923, p. 134.
3 File PF- 39205, RG 165 (War Dept General Staff) MID, Box 607, NA. Memo from Colonel Burnett, American Embassy, Tokyo to Stuart Heintzelman, MID, 13 August 1922.
4 TNA FO 371/5295 memo from British Embassy, Tokyo.
5 *Ibid.*
6 File PF-39205, RG 165 (War Dept General Staff) MID, Box 607, NA. Memo from Colonel Burnett, American Embassy, Tokyo to Stuart Heintzelman, MID, 13 August 1922.
7 Marguerite Harrison, *Red Bear or Yellow Dragon* (London: Brentano's, 1924), p. 10.
8 File PF-39205, RG 165 (War Dept General Staff) MID, Box 607, NA . Letter from Churchill to Colonel Burnett, and Majors Philoon and Faymonville, 25 May 1922.
9 *Ibid.*, 13 March 1922. Report on one of Harrison's lectures at Arlington Hall, Virginia. Says she was favourable to Russia and said the blockade against Russia was causing great hardship.
10 *Ibid.*, Memo from D.C. Poole to Phillips, 31 August 1922.
11 *Ibid.*, Memo to Lieut-Colonel Charles Burnett at the American Embassy in Tokyo from Colonel S. Heintzelman, G.2. 13 September 1922.
12 *Ibid.*, Memo from Schurman to Secretary of State, 4 September 1922.
13 Quoted in Harding, *The Underworld of State*, p. 213.
14 *Ibid.*, p.214.

15 TNA, FO 371/8169. Internal memo discussing Burton-Chadwick's Parliamentary question, 1 December 1922.
16 *Ibid.*, Minutes of meeting between Stan Harding's deputation and Ronald McNeill, 13 December 1922.
17 *Ibid.*

CHAPTER 18 – Back in the USSR – 169-176

1 Originally, Chita had been inhabited by Mongolic and Turkic tribes, but after the 1825 Decembrist Uprising against the assumption of the Russian throne by Nicholas I, many intellectuals were exiled to Chita. As a consequence, the city became quite prosperous and a key trading post in Siberia. The Japanese had occupied Chita since 1918; despite this, in April 1920, the Bolsheviks made the city the capital of the 'Far Eastern Republic' – purely a paper exercise as they did not have the resources to expel the Japanese. However, it had been agreed that at some stage in the near future, the city would be returned to Russia.
2 Harrison, *Red Bear or Yellow Dragon*, p. 244.
3 File PF-39205, RG 165 (War Dept General Staff) MID, Box 607, NA . Internal memo from Colonel Naylor, Director of MID dated 2 April 1923.
4 *Ibid.*, Letter from Dr Ames to Colonel Naylor, dated 22 December 1922. Reply to Dr Ames, dated 29 December 1922.

CHAPTER 19 – Very Definite Proof of Her Real Character – 177-184

1 *Ibid.*, 1 March 1923: Report of a conversation with Mrs E. Harrison, Embassy of USA in Berlin.
2 File PF-39205, RG 55 (War Dept General Staff) MID, Box 607, NA. Letter from Marlborough Churchill to Colonel William Naylor, 29 March 1923.
3 *Ibid.* Report titled: In Re: Mrs Harrison 29 March 1923.
4 *Ibid.*, Confidential memo from Colonel Naylor, MID, dated 2 April 1923.
5 TNA, FO 371/9363. Internal memo dated 13 March 1923.
6 *Ibid.*, Confidential Memo from Department of Overseas Trade to Secretary of State April 17, 1923.
7 *Ibid.*, Minutes of Internal Affairs (49) 1923.
8 *Ibid.*, Letter to Lord Curzon from Mrs Stan Harding, 9 June 1923.
9 *Ibid.*, Letter to Mrs Stan Harding from Robert McNeill, 12 June 1923.
10 *Ibid.*, internal FO memorandum recording telephone conversation between William Strang and Mrs Stan Harding.
11 Parliamentary questions submitted by Captain Berkeley, MP to the Under Secretary of State, 18 June 1923.
12 TNA, FO 371/9363. Letter to E. Ovey from Mrs Stan Harding, 29 June 1923.

Chapter 20 – The Bugbear of the Foreign Office – 185-192

1 TNA, FO 371/10493. Internal note dated 20 February 1924.
2 *Ibid.*, Letter from Dr Haden-Guest to Arthur Ponsonby dated 3 March 1924.
3 *Ibid.*, Letter from Arthur Ponsonby to Dr Haden-Guest dated 4 March 1924.
4 *Ibid.*, Letter from Arthur Ponsonby to Dr Haden-Guest dated 25 February 1924.
5 *Ibid.*, Letter from Ramsay MacDonald to H.M. Richardson dated 4 March 1924.
6 *Ibid.*, FO internal memo regarding Mrs Stan Harding's latest requests dated 27 March 1924.
7 *Ibid.*
8 *Ibid.*, notes added by Arthur Ponsonby, dated 31 March 1924.
9 Quoted in Bonnie Frederick and Susan H. McLeod, eds., *Women and the Journey: The Female Travel Experiences*, (Pullman: Washington State University Press, 1992), pp. 591-592.
10 Quoted in Griggs, *Beyond Boundaries*, p. 333.

Chapter 21 – I am a Nuisance – 193-201

1 TNA, FO 371/10493. Memo from Arthur Ponsonby to Mr Butler requesting a letter to be sent to Harding to inform her the case is closed, dated 9 May 1924.
2 *Ibid.*
3 *Ibid.*, Letter from Arthur Ponsonby to Mrs Stan Harding, 16 May 1924.
4 *Ibid.*
5 'Will America Do Justice? The Stan Harding Case.' Printed for the Institute of Journalists and the National Union of Journalists, 1924.
6 *Ibid.*
7 *Hansard*, 21 July 1924, Vol 176, cc 874-5
8 'Brazening it Out', *The Daily News*, 23 July 1924.
9 TNA, FO 371/10493 internal FO Memo written by Arthur Ponsonby, 23 July 1924.
10 *Ibid.*
11 TNA, FO 371/10493. Parliamentary Question from Wallhead to the Under Secretary of State, 4 August 1924.
12 Christopher Andrew, *The Defence of the Realm* (London: Allen Lane, 2009), p. 105.
13 *Ibid.*
14 Quoted in Christopher Andrew, *For the President's Eyes Only* (Glasgow: HarperCollins Publishers, 1995), pp.51-52.
15 File PF-39205, (War Dept General Staff) MID, Box 607, NA. Letter from

Brigadier-General Churchill to Major Oscar N. Solbert (Military Attaché, London), dated 22 September 1921.

16 TNA, FO 371/10493. internal FO Memo written by Arthur Ponsonby, 4 August 1924.

17 *Hansard*, 4 August 1924.

18 'A Strange Doctrine', *The Daily News*, 6 August 1924.

19 *The Times*, 24 and 30 July 1924.

20 *The Times*, 17 July 1924.

21 Harding, *The Underworld of State*, p. 235.

22 TNA, FO 371/10493. Letter from National Union of Journalists to Austen Chamberlain dated 21 November 1924.

23 *Ibid.*, Parliamentary Question 16 March 1925.

PART FOUR

CHAPTER 22 – The Underworld of State – 205-213

1 Danzig (Gdańsk in Poland) was between 1918-1939 granted the status as a Free City with its own constitution.

2 TNA, FO 371/10493. Letter from 16 MPs to Austen Chamberlain dated 7 July 1925.

3 *Ibid.*, Letter from FO to Briant, dated 23 July 1925.

4 *Ibid.*, Parliamentary Question from Wallhead to McNeill, dated 22 July 1925.

5 *Ibid.*, Letter from Newman to Chamberlain, dated 5 August 1925.

6 Letter from Bertrand Russell to Josselyn Hennessy, 21 September 1954, Bertrand Russell Archives, McMaster University, RA113.

7 File PF-39205, (War Dept General Staff) MID, Box 607, NA. Note from Frederick William Nile to Major-General D.E. Nolan, dated 24 October 1925.

8 *Ibid.*, Note from Colonel James H. Reeves to Nolan, dated 27 October 1925.

9 Bertrand Russell Archives, McMaster University, Ontario. Letters from Russell to Josselyn Hennessy dated 15 September 1954, 21 September 1954.

10 Leslie Norton, *Léonide Massine and the 20th Century Ballet* (Jefferson, NC: McFarland & Co, 2004), p. 11.

11 The following quotes from Stan Harding are from letters she wrote to the Elmhirsts between 1931 and 1950. Dartington Hall Archives, Devon.

CHAPTER 23 – Life's Ugly Gestures – 214-221

1 This allegation was made by Stephen Haweis in his unpublished notebooks, 1961-63, Special Collections, Columbia University, New York.

CHAPTER 24 – The Lonely Trench – 222-230

1 Open letter about the Stan Harding case from H. Brailsford to the *New Leader*, 11 May 1923.
2 Dodge Luhan, *Movers and Shakers*, pp. 433-435

CHAPTER 25 – Hope Thou Not Much, Fear Not at All – 231-238

1 Letter from Baron de Cosson to Edward Hutton dated 16 May 1919. The British Institute, Florence.
2 *Ibid.*, letter dated 26 April 1919.
3 Templewood Papers, Part III: File 1-43, British Mission, Italy 1916-18. Cambridge University Library.
4 Ferdinand Tuohy, *The Secret Corps: An Intelligence on all Fronts*, 1920 (London: John Murray, 1920)

Bibliography

Memoirs

Balabanoff, Angelica, *My Life as a Rebel* (London: Hamish Hamilton, 1938)

Barnes, James Strachey, *Half a Life* (London: Eyre & Spottiswoode, 1933)

Boon, Hector, 'Russia from the Inside' (*New York World*, 1921)

Bonus-Jeep, Beate, *Sechzig Jahre Freundschaft mit Käthe Kollwitz* (Berlin: Bop-pard, Karl Rauch Verlag, 1948)

Bruce Lockhart, R. H, *Memoirs of a British Agent* (London: Putman, 1932)

'C' [Merian C. Cooper], *Grass* (New York: G.P. Putman's Sons, 1925)

— *Things Men Die Fo*r (New York: G.P. Putnam's Sons, 1927)

Chamberlain, Austen, *Down the Years* (London: Cassell and Co.,1935)

Dodge Luhan, Mabel, *European Experiences, Vol. Two, Intimate Memories* (New York: Harcourt, Brace & Company, 1935)

— *Movers and Shakers* (New Mexico: University of New Mexico Press, 1985)

Goldman, Emma, *My Disillusionment in Russia* (New York: Doubleday, Page and Co., 1923)

Harding, Stan, *The Underworld of State* (London: George Allen & Unwin Ltd, 1925)

Harper, Samuel N., *The Russia I Believe in*: *The Memoirs of Samuel N. Harper 1902 to 1941* (Chicago: University of Chicago Press, 1943)

Harrison, Marguerite, *Marooned in Moscow*: *The Story of an American Woman Imprisoned in Russia* (London: Thornton Butterworth Limited, 1921)

— *Unfinished Tales from a Russian Prison* (New York: George H. Doran Company, 1923)

— *Red Bear or Yellow Dragon* (London: Brentano's Ltd, 1924)

— *There's Always Tomorrow*: *The Story of a Chequered Life* (New York: Farrar & Rinehart, 1935)

— *Born for Trouble*: *The Story of a Chequered Life* (London: Victor Gollancz Ltd, 1936)

Haweis, Stephen, Unpublished bound memoir. Rare Books, Butler Library, Columbia University, New York.

Kessler, Count Harry, *The Diaries of a Cosmopolitan 1918-1937*, translation Charles Kessler (London: Weidenfeld & Nicholson, 1999)

McCullagh, Francis, *A Prisoner of the Reds*: *The Story of a British Officer Captured in Siberia* (London: John Murray, 1921)

Popoff, Georgi Konstantinovitch, *The Tcheka: The Red Inquisition* (London: A.M. Philpot Ltd, 1925)

Rodd, James Rennell, *Social and Diplomatic Memories 1902-1919* (London: E. Arnold & Co., 1925)

Roddie, Stewart, *Peace Patrol* (London: Christophers, 1932)

Russell, Bertrand, *Uncertain Paths to Freedom*: *Russia and China, 1919-22* (Toronto: McMaster University, 2000)

Sheridan, Clare, *Mayfair to Moscow – Clare Sheridan's Diary* (New York: Boni and Liveright, 1921)

Snowden, Ethel, *Through Bolshevik Russia* (London: Cassell and Co., 1920)

Tennant, Ernest William Dalrymple, *True Account* (London: Max Parrish & Co Ltd, 1957)

ARCHIVES AND LIBRARY SOURCES

Archivio Contemporaneo 'Alessandro Bonsanti', Gabinetto G.P. Vieusseux, Firenze

The papers of Dorothy Nevile Lees and the papers of Edward Gordon Craig, Baltimore County Library, Catonsville Branch, Baltimore

The Bodleian Library, University of Oxford

The British Institute of Florence, Florence – Archives and Library

British Library, India Office, London – The Curzon Papers

The University of Cambridge Library. Department of Manuscripts – Templewood papers of Sir Samuel Hoare

Columbia University, New York – Rare Book and Manuscript Library, unpublished diaries of Stephen Haweis.

Dartington Hall Archives, Devon – Information on Stan Harding's relationship with Dorothy and Leonard Elmhirst

Dundas Museum, Ontario, Canada – Information on the Harding family

University of Maryland, Hornbake Library, College Park, Maryland

National Archives, Suitland, Maryland.

National Archives, Kew, Surrey – FO information on Mrs Stan Harding

New York Public Library – Press cuttings of Marguerite Harrison

Nuffield College, University of Oxford – The Emmott Papers

Parliamentary Archives, Westminster, London – The Papers of Lord Alfred Emmott; The Papers of Leslie Haden-Guest

Somerset Archives, Taunton, Somerset – Information on Stan Harding's paternal side of the family

St Antony's College, University of Oxford – The Malcolm Diary

War Department File: Record Group 165 (War Department General Staff) Military Intelligence Division – PF Files 1917-1919, Box 607, File no. 39205. Information on Marguerite Harrison

SECONDARY SOURCES

Adamson, Walter L., *Avant-Garde Florence*: *From Modernism to Fascism* (Massachusetts: Harvard University Press, 1993)

Andrew, Christopher, *The Defence of the Realm*: *The Authorised History of MI5* (London: Allen Lane, 2009)
— *For the President's Eyes Only* (Glasgow: HarperCollins Publishers, 1995)
— 'The British Secret Service and Anglo-Soviet Relations in the 1920s Part 1: From the Trade Negotiations to the Zinoviev Letter', The Historical Journal Vol. 20, No. 3, Sept 1977, pp. 673-706

Baritz, Loren, *The Culture of the Twenties* (New York: The Bobbs-Merrill Company, Inc., 1970)

Barry, John M., *The Great Influenza*: *The Story of the Deadliest Pandemic in History* (New York: Penguin Books, 2005)

Bredbenner, Candice Lewis, *A Nationality of her Own: Women, Marriage and the Law of Citizenship* (London: University of California Press, 1998)

Burke, Carolyn, *Becoming Modern*: *The Life of Mina Loy* (Berkeley: University of California Press, 1997)

Campbell, Katie, *Paradise of Exiles*: *The Anglo-American Gardens of Florence* (London: Frances Lincoln Limited Publishers, 2009)

Coates, P.D., *The China Consuls, British Consular Officers 1843-1943* (Hong Kong: Oxford University Press, 1988)

Costigliola, Frank C., 'Anglo-American Financial Rivalry in the 1920s', *The Journal of Economic History*, Vol. 37, No. 4, (Dec 1977) pp. 911-934

Davis, Jonathon, 'Left out in the Cold: British Labour Witnesses the Russian Revolution', Revolutionary Russia Vol.18, No.1, June 2005, pp. 71-87

Dearborn, Mary V., *Queen of Bohemia*: *The Life of Louise Bryant* (Boston: Houghton Mifflin Company, 1996)

Eudin, Xenia Joukoff, Harold H. Fisher in collaboration with Rosemary Brown Jones, *Soviet Russia and the West 1920-1927*: *A Documentary Survey* (Stanford: Stanford University Press, 1957)

Geoghegan, Sally Branch Ingram, 'The Political Career of Joseph I. France of Maryland, 1906-1921' (MA Thesis, Unversity of Maryland, 1955)

Griggs, Catherine, M., 'Beyond Boundaries: The Adventurous Life of Marguerite Harrison' (Doctoral Dissertation, George Washington University, 1996)

Hastings, Selina, *The Secret Lives of Somerset Maugham* (St Ives: John Murray, 2009)

Hennessy, Josselyn, 'One Man and Three Extraordinary Women' (unpublished manuscript, c. 1954), Dundas Museum, Ontario, Canada

Higley, Stephen Richard, *Privilege, Power, and Place: The Geography of the American Upper Class* (Maryland: Rowman & Littlefield Publishers Inc., 1995)

Holroyd, Michael, *A Strange Eventful History: The Dramatic Lives of Ellen Terry, Henry Irving and their Remarkable Families* (London: Vintage, 2009)

Homberger, Eric, *John Reed* (Manchester: Manchester University Press, 1990)

Hughes, Michael, *British Foreign Secretaries in an Uncertain World, 1919-1939* (Abingdon: Routledge, 2006)

Jeffery, Keith, *MI6: The History of the Secret Intelligence Service, 1909-1949* (London: Bloomsbury Publishing, 2010)

Jeffreys-Jones, Rhodri, 'W. Somerset Maugham: Anglo-American Agent in Revolutionary Russia', *American Quarterly*, Vol. 28, No 1, (Spring 1976) pp. 90-106

'K', 'Russia after Genoa and The Hague', *Foreign Affairs*, Vol. 1, No. 1, September 15, 1922, pp. 133-155

Kearns, Martha, *Käthe Kollwitz: Woman and Artist* (New York: The Feminist Press, 1976)

Knightley, Phillip, *The First Casualty: The War Correspondent as Hero, Pro pagandist, and Myth Maker from the Crimea to Vietnam* (London: André Deutsch, 1975)

Leggett, George, *The Cheka: Lenin's Political Police* (Oxford: Clarendon Press, 1981)

Linton, Keith and Alan, 'I Will Build My Church' 150 Years of Local Church Work in Bristol (Bristol: C. Hadler, 1983)

Lofton, John, *The Press as Guardian of the First Amendment* (Columbia: University of South Carolina Press, 1980)

Loy, Mina (ed. Roger L. Conover) *The Last Lunar Baedeker* (Charlotte: The Jargon Society, 1982)

Mahoney, Harry Thayer and Marjorie Locke Mahoney, *American Prisoners of the Bolsheviks; the Genesis of Modern American Intelligence* (Bethesda: Academica Press, 2001)

Mahoney, M.H., *Women in Espionage: A Biographical Dictionary* (Oxford: ABC-CLIO, 1993)

Maugham, W. Somerset, *Ashenden or The British Agent* (Surrey: William Heinemann Ltd., 1928)

Miller, Nathan, *Spying for America*: *The Hidden History of US Intelligence* (New York: Paragon House, 1989)

Nagel, Otto (trans. Stella Humphries), *Kathe Köllwitz* (London: Studio Vista Ltd., 1971)

Newman, L. M., *Edward Gordon Craig*: *Black Figures*: *105 reproductions with an unpublished essay* (Wellingborough: Christopher Skelton, 1989)

Olds, Elizabeth Fagg, *Women of the Four Winds* (Boston: Houghton Mifflin Company, 1999)

Patenaude, Bertrand M., *Herbert Hoover's Brush with Bolshevism* (Washington: Kennan Institute for Advanced Russian Studies, Occasional Paper 1992)

— *The Big Show in Bololand* (Stanford: Stanford University Press, 2002)

Patterson, Michelle Jane, 'Moscow Chekists During the Civil War, 1918-1921' (MA Thesis 1991, Simon Fraser University, British Columbia)

Price, Morgan Phillips, (Ed. Tania Rose) *Dispatches from the Weimar Republic* (London: Pluto Press, 1999)

Proctor, Tammy M., *Female Intelligence*: *Women and Espionage in the First World War* (New York: New York University Press, 2003)

Rappaport, Helen, *Ekaterinburg* (London: Hutchinson, 2008)

— *Conspirator*: *Lenin in Exile* (London: Hutchinson, 2009)

Read, Anthony, *The World on Fire*: *1919 and the Battle with Bolshevism* (London: Jonathan Cape, 2008)

Rugoff, Milton, *America's Gilded Age*: *Intimate Portraits from an Era of Extravagance and Change 1850-1890* (New York: Henry Holt and Company, 1989)

Sanders, M. Taylor, Taylor, Philip, *British Propaganda during the First World War 1914-18* (London: Macmillan Press Ltd, 1982)

Scott, J.D., Vickers: *A History* (London: Weidenfeld and Nicolson, 1962)

Seldes, George, *Lords of the Press* (New York: Julian Messner, Inc. 1938)

Seton-Watson, Christopher, 'British Propaganda in Italy 1914-1918', (extract from *Inghiterra e Italianel '900 Atti del Convegno di Bagni di Lucca*, October 1972) published by La Nuova Italia Editrice, Firenze, 1973

Shreiber, Maeera, Tuma, Keith (ed.), *Mina Loy*: *Woman and Poet* (Maine: The National Poetry Foundation, 1998)

Stibbe, Matthew, *British Civilian Internees in Germany*: *The Ruhleben Camp, 1914-18* (Manchester: Manchester University Press, 2008)

— 'Civilian Internment and Civilian Internees in Europe 1914-20', *Immigrants and Minorities*, Vol. 26, Issue 1 & 2, March 2008, pp. 49-81

Tuohy, Ferdinand, *The Secret Corps: A Tale of "Intelligence" on all Fronts* (London: John Murray, 1920)

Wasserstein, Bernard, *The Secret Lives of Trebitsch Lincoln* (New Haven: Yale University Press, 1988)

West, Nigel, *MI6 British Intelligence Service Operations 1909-45* (London: Weidenfeld and Nicolson, 1983)

Wight Wise, Marsha, *Catonsville: Images of America* (Charleston: Arcadia Publishing, 2005)

Winter, Jay & Jean-Louis Robert, *Capital Cities at War: Paris, London, Berlin 1914-1919* (Cambridge: Cambridge University Press, 1997)

Williams, Harold A., *The Baltimore Sun 1837-1987* (Baltimore: The Johns Hopkins University Press, 1987)

Index

Paterson, New Jersey, 51
Pavlovsk, 105
Peace Treaty (1919–), 61, 64, 84, 85, 160, 206, 236
Peel, E.G., 189
Peking (Beijing), 54, 162-164, 169
Penn, William, 14, 235
People's Army, 90
People's Naval Division, 59
Peradeniya, 231
Perlman, Philip, 136
Persia, 97, 156, 180, 185, 186
Persian Cossack Brigade, 186
Persian Gulf, 185
Persian Plateau, 190
Petit, Gabrielle, 22, 109, 110
Petrograd, 80, 91, 93, 94, 99, 101, 103, 104, 105, 107, 129-132, 136, 141
Pflugk-Hartung, Heinz von, 64, 65
Phillips, William, 163
Piazza degli Ottaviani, Florence, 41
Piazza Donatello, Florence, 36
Picasso, Pablo, 210
Piccadilly, London, 26, 154
Pilar von Pilchau, Adolf, 175
Pillai, Averdaiappa, 51
Piłsudski, Józef, 62, 97
Pinkerton Detective Agency, 94
Pinsent, Cecil, 37
Pisa, 44
Pitigliano, 44
Pitti Gallery, Florence, 40
Plymouth Brethren, 36, 38, 210, 235
Poetry Bookshop, London, 154, 198, 220
Poland, 21, 62, 64, 68, 71-74, 82, 83, 92, 97, 145, 149, 173, 178
Polish Army, 98
Polish Corridor, 62
Polish-Soviet War, 73, 144
Politburo, 79, 86
Polk, Frank, 22, 195
Ponsonby, Arthur, 188, 189, 193, 194
Ponte Vecchio, Florence, 41
Pontius, Albert W., 49
Poole, D.C., 162
Popoff, Georgi, 91, 126, 127
Populonia, 44
Posen (part of Germany), 62
Potsdamer Platz, Berlin, 26

Pound, Ezra, 154
Practice and Theory of Bolshevism, The, 208
Pravda, 122, 146
Preece, John, 185
Pre-Raphaelites, 45
Press Association, 181
Price, Morgan Philips, 83
Princeton University, 224
Principles of Social Reconstruction, 208
Propaganda Mission, 53
Protestantism, 62
Prussia, 28, 55, 62, 64, 82
Prussian State Library, 26
Pudd'nhead Wilson, 53
Pullen, Louise, 220
Punch, 15

Qing dynasty, 49, 164
Quakerism, 14
Quiet Man, The (film), 192

Radcliffe College, 16
Radek, Karl, 78, 79, 89
Rakovsky, Christian, 199
Rapallo, 52, 158
Red Army, 67, 75, 84, 97, 101
Red Bear or Yellow Dragon, 185
Red Cross, 25, 64, 72, 73, 85, 88, 98, 123, 127, 130, 132, 133, 136
Red Guard, 30
Red Shoes, The (film), 210
Red Square, Moscow, 108
Red Terror, 97
Reed, John, 51, 52, 115, 123, 124, 153, 167
Reeves, James, 209
Reichswehr, 85, 86
Reilly, Sidney, 121
Renaissance, 38, 40, 210
Republicanism, 26, 27, 28, 82, 85, 145
Reval *see* Tallinn
Revolutionary Tribunal, 127
Richardson, Henry Marriott, 145, 164, 184, 188, 199, 200
Riga, 78, 115, 126, 130, 146, 148, 149, 177, 199
Right Social Revolutionaries, 129
Ritchie, Albert Cabell, 19, 20, 22, 23, 135, 136
River Ganges, 10

First published in the U.K. by

Ashgrove Publishing

an imprint of:

Hollydata Publishers Ltd
27 John Street
London
WC1N 2BX

ISBN 978 185398 191 3

Book design by Brad Thompson

Front cover design by Paul Bagshawe and Tom Gilchrist

Printed and bound in the U.K.